DATE DUE

DE 1 o'00			
No 1 '09			
AC 7 08			
APR			

DEMCO 38-296

Direct Marketing Rules of Thumb

Direct Marketing Rules of Thumb

1,000 Practical and Profitable
Ideas to Help You
Improve Response,
Save Money, and
Increase Efficiency
in Your Direct Program

Nat G. Bodian

McGraw-Hill, Inc.

New York   San Francisco   Washington, D.C.   Auckland   Bogotá
Caracas   Lisbon   London   Madrid   Mexico City   Milan
Montreal   New Delhi   San Juan   Singapore
Sydney   Tokyo   Toronto

on Data

practical and profitable
noney, and increase
. Bodian.

Includes bibliographical references and index.
ISBN 0-07-006340-0 (acid-free paper)
1. Direct marketing.   2. Telemarketing.   3. Advertising,
Direct-mail.   I. Title.
HF5415.126.B63   1995
658.8'4—dc20   94-23635
                                                                  CIP

  2 3 4 5 6 7 8 9 0   DOC/DOC   9 0 0 9 8 7

ISBN 0-07-006340-0

*The sponsoring editor for this book was Betsy N. Brown, the editing supervisor
was Frances Koblin, and the production supervisor was Suzanne W. B.
Rapcavage. It was set in Palatino by McGraw-Hill's Professional Book Group
composition unit.*

Printed and bound by R. R. Donnelley & Sons Company.

McGraw-Hill books are available at special quantity discounts to use as
premiums and sales promotions, or for use in corporate training programs. For more information, please write to the Director of Special
Sales, McGraw-Hill, Inc., 11 West 19th Street, New York, NY 10011. Or
contact your local bookstore.

This book is printed on recycled, acid-free paper containing a
minimum of 50% recycled de-inked fiber.

Contents

Part 2. Card Packs: A Comprehensive Understanding

Part 3. The Art and Science of Mailing List Usage

Part 4. List Brokers, Compilers, and Managers

Part 5. Telemarketing

Part 6. Printing, Production, and Letter Shop Procedures

Part 7. Mail-Order Space Advertising Techniques

Expanded Contents

6. Circular Preparation Techniques: Brochures and Fliers   33

7. Mail-Order Catalogs: Preparation and Selling Techniques   36

8. Sale Catalogs and Reduced-Price Offers   42

9. Envelopes: Guidelines for Selection and Use   45

10. Writing Envelope Teaser Copy

11. Headline Writing: Formulas and Effective Techniques

12. Copywriting: Guidelines and Techniques   55

20. Response Patterns in Direct Mail Promotion   88

21. Postage and Mail Delivery Guidelines   92

22. Budgeting Tips for Direct Mail   98

23. Credit and Collection Tips   101

Part 3. The Art and Science of Mailing List Usage

29. Mailing Lists: Approaches and Techniques   131

30. Rental Lists: Practices and Procedures   **136**

Part 4. List Brokers, Compilers, and Managers

41. List Brokers: When and How to Use them   183

Part 5. Telemarketing

Part 7. Mail-Order Space Advertising Techniques

Preface

Direct Marketing Rules of Thumb is a book of ideas, techniques, short cuts, and practical hints reflecting long years of experience by the author and scores of other practitioners. Its aims are (1) to spark your creative powers, (2) to channel your direct marketing efforts along successful lines, (3) to give you a vast amount of knowledge you can quickly absorb and immediately apply, and (4) to help you avoid numerous pitfalls encountered in direct marketing.

This quick reference incorporates an abundance of solutions to direct marketing problems, and it offers examples, research findings, and cautionary advice on hundreds of direct marketing procedures. *Direct Marketing Rules of Thumb* stands ready to serve you whether you are a beginner or a well-grounded professional.

Many of these practical ideas and "rules of thumb" were drawn from my career in business, industry, and publishing that began in 1948. These decades as a mail marketer involved inestimable experimentation and innovation, and the exchange of ideas with other mail marketing professionals. My experience covers the period of time during which the fledgling direct mail industry emerged from hand addressing and metal-plate addressing, linked itself to the emerging computer age, and became the thriving and successful giant it is today.

I have been a collector of "useful ideas" throughout my direct marketing career. It follows that many of the practical ideas among the more than 1000 assembled on these pages are bits of direct marketing intelligence accumulated and cataloged over a number of years. Some

have seen exposure in the texts of nine other marketing-related books I
have written since 1980 and in scores of articles appearing in periodicals and newsletters under my byline. The overall intent here is to provide the reader with as many practical and helpful insights in as many
areas of direct marketing as possible.

The techniques and approaches presented here have been influenced
by examination of various new, recent, and classic works on direct
marketing, starting with the post-World War II era and continuing
through the end of 1994—practically the entire life span of modern
direct marketing. In many of the entries, where a "rule" has been
influenced by one particular work in the literature of direct marketing,
I have cited the original source, so the reader can refer to it for additional information.

It is my hope that in your handling of this idea resource you will
elect to browse through it, as in a library of ideas, and to make your
own discoveries, marking off guidelines and useful procedures that
you can adapt immediately or set aside for future use.

If, however, you plan to use *Direct Marketing Rules of Thumb* to satisfy an immediate need for special information, the most helpful place
for you to start, aside from the contents, is the comprehensive key-
word index, which will instantly guide you to the information. In
addition, the key-word index includes hundreds of cross-references to
other entries or sections that offer related ideas and information.

Direct Marketing Rules of Thumb is divided into seven parts. Part 1
deals with the preparation, utilization, and evaluation of direct mailing.
It covers formats, offers, sales letters, brochures, mailing envelopes,
response devices, return envelopes, reply cards, offers, guarantees,
headline writing, copywriting, testimonials and endorsements, postage
guidelines, timing and seasonality factors, budgeting, as well as credit
and collections. Individual chapters are devoted to mail-order catalogs,
reduced-price offers, fund-raising, and international direct mail.

Part 2 gives in-depth coverage to one of the fastest-growing and
least-understood areas of mail marketing—the card pack. This revolu-
tionary, relatively new, and surprisingly efficient and economical
direct-response format is being widely adopted by direct marketers,
both domestically and internationally. Part 2 is a veritable four-chap-
ter textbook on card pack marketing practices and procedures based
on the author's pioneering experience in this medium.

The twelve chapters in Part 3 are devoted to the art and science of
mailing lists, the essential key to success in every direct marketing
effort. Individual chapters cover the various types of mailing lists,
how best to understand and use each to the best advantage, and how

each works in comparison with the others. As mailing lists are the principal area in which direct marketing errors are made and money wasted, the valuable guidelines in Part 3 can help save you thousands of dollars. There is a full chapter in Part 3 on testing—not only of mailing lists, but also of direct mail variables.

Part 4 gives a comprehensive understanding of what mailing list brokers and mailing list managers do, how to find them, how to work with them, and when to use each. There are also helpful tips on how to select the best ones for your particular needs from the different types in each category.

Part 5 deals with telemarketing—a highly effective medium that has grown from $56 billion in 1983 to more than $300 billion in 1992. Three information-packed chapters show you how to get started and how to find suitable help. They offer tips on script preparation, tell you who your best prospects are, and show you where to find the names of people to call. A fourth chapter in Part 5, devoted to inbound telemarketing, tells how to use the 800 number as an invaluable tool of marketing.

Part 6 is loaded with unique and practical ideas for printing, production, and mailing shop services that will save you time and money. The chapter on printing shows you how to find a good printer and work with him, how to get the highest quality of work at the lowest possible prices, how to get quotes, prepare printing dummies, compare estimates, cancel orders, and settle claims. The chapter on paper covers selection, usage, and buying economies. The chapter on ink covers use and psychological preferences. The chapter on type provides useful information on selection, legibility, readability, placement, capitalization, and spacing.

Part 7 is a veritable treasury of imaginative and useful ideas on mail-order space advertising. In four chapters, it covers the basics, shows you how to get started with a minimum investment, provides guidelines for ad placement and positioning, explains when to use or not use coupons, their design and placement, and concludes with a chapter on how best to use the 800 number in ads, how to set it in type, and how to correctly position it to maximize response.

It would be difficult to acknowledge the scores of individuals whose knowledge and experience are represented in these pages. However, I do want to recognize the knowledge and innumerable insights gained from various members of the Professional Publishers Marketing Group (PPMG), a mail marketing organization on whose steering committee I served for eight years.

I would like to acknowledge the special help of Stanley Getz, editor at Standard Rate and Data Service, for late-breaking information on

SRDS publications; also Frank Hudetz, CEO, and Liz Queally-Osborne at Solar Press for their help on evolving developments and forthcoming changes in card pack marketing practice and production technology. Also to the Ethics and Consumer Affairs staff of the Direct Marketing Association in Washington, to Les Bodian in Washington for his research on government regulations, to Peter Miliziano of the U.S. Postal Service for helpful postal information, to the reference staff of the Cranford Public Library, to Catherine Rogers at Prentice-Hall, and Dee Dee De Bartlo at John Wiley & Sons. And last, but not least, I also want to thank my editor at McGraw-Hill, Betsy Brown, for her patience, encouragement, and support while I inundated her with late-breaking material during this book's final preparation stages.

As presently offered, *Direct Marketing Rules of Thumb* is intended to complement three of my earlier related reference guides: *NTC's Dictionary of Direct Mail and Mailing List Terminology and Techniques*, *The Publisher's Direct Mail Handbook*, and *Beyond Lead Generation: Merchandising Through Card Packs* (with Robert Luedtke).

I hope you find *Direct Marketing Rules of Thumb* a useful and dependable everyday desk reference and companion, whether you are active in direct marketing or are just planning to enter this fascinating and challenging activity.

Nat G. Bodian

PART 1

Overview of Direct Mail

1

General Guidelines

Direct mail is the least expensive, most
effective, and most direct way to tell your
story to all the people on your prospect list
                          —VICTOR O. SCHWAB
      How to Write a Good Advertisement, 1962

1:01   Direct Marketing: Basis, Size, and Market

The spectacular growth of direct marketing reflects its greatest virtue: It's the most cost-effective way to sell anything to anyone. U.S. direct marketing revenue is currently at $350 billion, according to the U.S. Postal Service publication *Focus* (Sept. 1993) and involves 5 percent of the U.S. workforce. More than half of U.S. households make at least one purchase each year through a direct marketing effort.

1:02   Distinguishing Characteristics of Direct Marketing

In *The Portable MBA in Marketing* (1992), Alexander Hiam and Charles Schewe distinguish direct marketing from general advertising by the following three characteristics: (1) a definite offer is made, (2) all the information necessary to make a decision is provided, and (3) a response mechanism is given.

1:03   The 40-40-20 Rule for Success in Direct Marketing

The 40-40-20 rule was developed by direct marketing maven Ed Mayer many years ago. It divides direct marketing success into three segments as follows: 40 percent to using the right mailing list; 40 percent to who the mailer is and what he has to offer; 20 percent for everything else—postage rate, format, paper, stock, color, copy, graphics, etc.

1:04   Cost Criteria for Direct Marketing Success

As a rule, direct marketers use two major criteria for evaluating the success of a direct marketing effort: (1) cost per inquiry and (2) cost per order. Some direct marketers in book publishing include a third criterion—the "echo effect," i.e., the indirect or spillover sales produced by a direct marketing effort that shows up in ways other than by direct response and can sometimes be measured and evaluated.

1:05   Steps in Direct Marketing Efforts

Most direct marketing efforts involve either one or two steps. A one-step or single-shot effort tries to pull in an order immediately. A two-step effort first elicits an inquiry, usually for additional information, from which an order may subsequently be generated. Occasionally, some direct marketing efforts require three steps—the first of the three being to obtain prospect names.

1:06   Basic Cost Elements in Direct Mail

The cost per thousand, or CPM, to put a promotion in the mail involves these four basic elements: (1) printing and envelope costs; (2) mailing list rental, and merge/purge if applicable; (3) letter shop costs; (4) postage.

1:07   Attributes of Direct Mail

Seven attributes of direct mail can be identified: (1) advertiser can select own circulation; (2) advertiser can control own timing; (3) mailing can take any size, color, or shape; (4) mailing has a flexible unit cost; (5) with mailing there is less competition for the reader's attention; (6) mailing is more confidential; (7) mailing is self-testing. (Adapted from "Direct Mail Advertising" by Ed Mayer, *Harvard Business Review*, July 1951.)

1:08   Offer Identification in Direct Mail Packages

When doing a multiple-piece mailing, it is a good idea to check that each enclosure identifies the offer and includes sufficient information for an ordering decision even if separated from the other enclosures in the same mailing.

1:09   Location of Price in a Mail Offer

Make it a firm rule that the price always appear in the main enclosure(s) of a mail offer—not just on the order form. Failure to do so may dilute the value of the entire offering.

1:10   Locating Address in Multipiece Offer

It is a good idea to have your address on every component of a direct mail promotion. Sometimes, after the initial recipient has mailed in the order card, pass-along readers may also want to order.

1:11   Rule for Locating Phone Number Near Price

If you accept telephone orders, it is a good idea to display the telephone ordering number prominently on every page of the offer that includes a priced offering. This will be even more effective if the number is an 800 toll-free number.

1:12   Give Mailing Hurried and Breathless Look

"Direct mail that must bring immediate orders should look a bit hurried and breathless and have some of the time pressure of a newspaper." So advised Paul Bringe, a direct mail consultant, in the September 1979 U.S. Postal Service bulletin. He pointed out that a highly polished or too carefully structured sales package gives the impression that someone struggled long hours to get an order, and this is likely to arouse suspicions.

1:13   Time Rule in Evaluating Campaign Result

A direct mail campaign designed to generate leads or sales inquiries takes much longer to evaluate than an order-generating campaign. The reason: Resulting sales from leads or inquiries evolve over a period of time.

1:14 Mail-Order Acceptance Rule

The acceptance rate on trial offers is about 85 percent. The rate can be higher with better offers, lower with poorer ones. If product returns are unusually high, your offer may be promising more than the product delivers, or the product may not appear to be worth the selling price.

1:15 Retention of Mailing Piece Versus Publication Ad

As a rule, a mailed offer is more likely to be retained for future reference than an identical presentation in a magazine advertisement. Reason: It requires no additional effort to separate (clip and retain) and it is accompanied by an order envelope or response form, making for easier retention and future response.

1:16 Adding Fresh Look to Customer Mailings

If you mail to your customer list on a cyclical basis—say three or four times a year—as a rule, it's best to vary the offer from one time to the next so that each mailing has a "fresh" look.

1:17 Replacing Duds in Follow-up Mailings

When a multiproduct offer is to be repeated after a test, it is best to replace those items that didn't sell well in the earlier mailing test. This not only gives other products a chance for exposure, but also freshens up the offer.

1:18 Direct Mail Versus Space Advertising

As a rule, direct mail advertising is most effective when you have a substantial message and you want the full attention of the reader. In contrast, advertising messages in newspapers and magazines are designed to compete with everything else in that publication.

1:19 Ongoing Source of Direct Mail Ideas

You can often get good ideas from the direct mail efforts of other mailers. If you want a good ongoing source of direct mail ideas, make purchases from one or more competitors or from leading direct mailers and study the mailings you subsequently receive from them as a "valued customer."

1:20 When to Consider Using a Direct Mail Consultant

Particularly in your early mail marketing efforts, it may be worthwhile to engage a direct mail consultant with experience in your product area to evaluate your own plans or help develop your program. A direct mail consultant can save you money, help you avoid mistakes, and suggest fresh approaches based on what has worked or not worked with similar clients.

1:21 FTC 30-Day Delivery Rule

If you're new to mail order, it is important that you acquaint yourself with the Federal Trade Commission's "30-Day Delivery Rule." For a copy, write to: Federal Trade Commission Enforcement Division, B.C.P., Washington, DC 20580. Your local consumer protection office may also have special requirements for mail orders shipped in your local area. (*See also 3:31.*)

1:22 Sales Tax Collection Rule for Direct Mail

As a rule, a mailer is not required to collect sales tax for sales made to states where the mailer has no physical presence—office, warehouse, resident salesperson, or the like.

1:23 What the Law Says About Shipping Without Consent

If you mail merchandise without the prior expressed request or consent of the individual mailed to, as a rule, you will have no claim for its return. The law says the item may be treated as a gift by the recipient.

1:24 Getting a Mail-Order Education for $20

A good way to learn about mail order, says one expert, is to respond to mail-order ads that offer information. Buy a hundred 20-cent postcards for this purpose, key the cards, and study the response for each. You can learn about response, timing, format, pricing, and various other aspects of mail order. You will be amazed, the expert adds, at how much duplication you will find in the replies.

1:25 Erosion Rule for Subscription Sales

When a mail-order product is sold serially by subscription, and each subscription element is billed separately, the subscription base will shrink by cancellation with each succeeding shipment. The greater the time lapse between shipments, the higher the rate of shrinkage.

1:26 Sweepstakes Cautionary Rule

A sweepstakes promotion should not be attempted without checking to ensure that it complies with all federal, state, and local regulations. Since laws vary from one state to another, it is best to retain an independent judging organization to assist you in arranging and handling the promotion.

2
Formats

The perfect mailing piece contains a combination of credibility, clear, crisp, succinct copy that is easy to read and understand, is repeated more than once so that the message gets across, contains a definite offer, and makes it easy for the buyer to respond.

—RON TEPPER
Secrets of a Mail Order Guru, 1988

2:01 Basic Direct Marketing Formats

Most direct mail fits into one of three basic formats: (1) the *classic package*—a letter, circular, and an order or reply form (and any other enclosures including card packs) in a single envelope or wrapper; (2) the *self-mailer*, which is any direct mail piece that can be mailed without an envelope; (3) the *catalog*—a booklet, usually stitched, offering multiple products to a customer or prospect.

2:02 Format Selection Based on Name Recognition

As a rule, a mailing package works best in fields or to lists where the mailer is not known to recipients. When the mailer is known to recipients, a less formal mailing format, a self-mailer, will work just as well.

2:03 Direct Mail Package Reading Pattern

Recipients of a direct mail package, as a rule, go to the letter first, then to the flier, and then to the order form or response device. Card packs yield the fastest response of any format because the advertisement is also the response device.

2:04 Successful Business Mailing Format

The self-mailer format works well for business mailings because it is easier to pass along to a decision maker than a multipiece package.

2:05 Qualities of Self-Mailer Format

Use the low-cost self-mailer format when you have an inexpensive design with quickly recognizable content and need a built-in device to achieve a return response through the mail.

2:06 News Value of Self-Mailer Format

As a rule, says Peter Hodges, a highly regarded direct marketing consultant, a self-mailer format suggests something of immediate news value. In effect, the format says, Hey, look at me!

2:07 Most Efficient Direct Marketing Format

For many types of business and professional offers, the card pack offers the greatest ease of response of any direct marketing format. Card pack recipients need only fill in name and address and drop the card, usually postpaid, into the mail.

2:08 Catalog or Card Pack: How Each Works in Business

"A catalog format," says business cataloger Robert Luedtke in *Beyond Lead Generation: Merchandising Through Card Packs*, 1986, "is leafed through, stacks neatly, fits into standard files, and is retained or thrown away as a whole. The card pack, by contrast, is disjointed, broken up, impossible to file, and scanned quickly with only cards of interest retained. And those retained are usually mailed quickly, producing most of the sales within a small number of weeks."

2:09 Cautionary Note on Trying New Formats

As a rule, when a direct mail format is working well, it should not be changed without a test mailing against the new format being considered.

2:10 Lesson From Mailer's Repeat Use of Same Format

When a major mailer uses the same format over a long period, as a rule, it indicates that this format has stood up well against other formats in tests and continues to draw the best responses.

2:11 How to Choose Between Using a Brochure or Catalog

As a rule, use a brochure when you want to describe a single product in great detail. Use a catalog when you want to cover many products in less detail.

2:12 The Whys and Wherefores of Using Broadside Format

When you have an important offer to a business or professional audience and you want your mailing to dominate the day's mail, as a rule, you can accomplish this by using a broadside format. This single-message-on-a-large-sheet type of offer when opened is likely to cover any other mail received at the same time, and will also command attention by virtue of its size.

2:13 How to Choose Between Using Booklet or Broadside

When you have a lengthy story to tell and you want to tell it in a simple, prestigious way, use a booklet format. When you want "smash" impact and standout emphasis, go to a broadside format. The large surface of a broadside permits a boldness of expression and a sense of size unattainable with other formats.

2:14 Converting Package to Self-Mailer

A package mailing can be converted to a self-mailer without losing its personalized effect by placing the letter near the mailing face or front cover of the self-mailer. Such letters are best kept to one page in length, or two at the most.

2:15   Converting Advertisement to Mailer

When you have a highly effective Time-magazine-size space ad, as a rule, you can convert it into a low-cost mailer by adding an order form at the bottom and reprinting the ad on legal-size paper.

2:16   Formats With Longest and Shortest "Shelf Life"

As a rule, a catalog will be retained much longer than most other direct mail formats. The card pack has the shortest life, with most cards being discarded upon receipt.

2:17   Best Format for Mailings Requiring Prepayment

As a rule, if you're looking for prepayment, use a package format with reply envelope enclosed.

2:18   Formats for Multiple and Single Offers

As a rule, a comprehensive package with multiple product offerings has a higher success rate than one that offers a single product. By contrast, a self-mailer works best with a single-product offer.

2:19   Content and Guidelines for "Lift Letters"

The "lift letter" is that small personal note you often find in a direct mail package that assures you of the worthiness of the offer or gives a final reminder. As a rule, such lift letters should be very short and from someone in higher authority than the signer of the sales letter.

2:20   Statement Insert Advantage Over Co-Op Mailing

A statement-insert program will, as a rule, be more effective than a co-op mailing effort. Here's why: The co-op mailing, consisting of varying offers from different advertisers in a single envelope, usually goes to a compiled list from an unknown sponsor. The statement insert, by contrast, accompanies a bill or statement sent by a business to supposedly satisfied customers and carries the implied endorsement of the business doing the mailing.

2:21 Advantages of Package Insert Over Statement Insert

Statement inserts are advertising enclosures sent to business customers as accompaniments to a bill or statement. Package inserts go out with the shipment of a product to a customer. As a rule, a package insert tends to elicit a more favorable response than a statement insert. Theoretically, the recipient of a package is in a better mood than one receiving an invoice or statement by itself.

2:22 Package Insert Versus Mailing to Same List

A package insert program, in which the participant is charged per thousand inserts to be included in another company's mailing, can sometimes be a viable alternative to a mailing effort to the same list. Typically, the cost of an insert program is less than rental cost of the same list and, while package-insert yield may be lower, the economy of an insert program may place the cost per order on par with one generated through a mailing effort.

2:23 Format Selection Essentials

As a rule, selection of a direct mail format should be guided by these two considerations: (1) appropriateness for its intended audience; (2) size sufficient to allow all the copy and illustrations necessary to deliver the message or meet the objectives.

2:24 Most Effective Format for Mailings to Professionals

For mailings to professional audiences, where minimal copy is required to induce a sales response, a self-mailer is usually the most cost-effective format.

2:25 Influence of Format in Mailings to Libraries

As a rule, librarians are not influenced by mailing format. Their primary interest is in the message.

2:26 Format Approach Favored by Law Librarians

As a rule, law librarians favor single-sheet offers. They consider cover letters of little importance.

2:27   Sources of Co-Op Mailings and Package Insert Programs

Cooperative or co-op mailings and package insert programs fall into two classifications—business and consumer. Separate, detailed listings of co-op mailings and package insert programs, arranged into these two groupings may be found in the SRDS publication *Card Deck Advertising Source,* which prior to March 1994 was known as *Card Deck Rates and Data.* The SRDS listings include such requirements as minimum and maximum size of insert, and minimum order, as well as descriptions of principal mail content and audience, and mailing frequency.

3
Offers

*An "offer" is what your prospect gets when
they respond to your ad or mailing, combined
with what they have to do to get it.*
                                    —ROBERT W. BLY
        Business to Business Direct Marketing, 1991

3:01   The Offer—View of Award-Winning Writer

"The offer in direct marketing," says Ed McLean, an award-winning
direct mail writer, "is the content and manner of the presentation you
make to your reader as to price and terms, quantity or length of service, premium for immediate action or payment with order, and trial
period or guarantee." (In *The Basics of Copy,* 1977)

3:02   Strongest Ingredients of Successful Offers

The two most powerful ingredients in successful mail offers are
money-back guarantees and free trial offers. They work because each
eliminates all fears of risk on the part of the respondent.

3:03   Most Powerful Word in Direct Marketing Offer

"The single most powerful word in the vocabulary of direct marketing
offers is 'Free,'" says Ed Nash, head of one of the top direct marketing
agencies. "It is frequently used in two-step offers where the free offer is
a first step toward getting an interested prospect's name and address

for a later solicitation. It's also used to upgrade catalog orders." (In *Direct Marketing*, 1986)

3:04 Various Types of Free Offers in Direct Marketing

Free Book...Free Booklet...Free Catalog...Free Estimate...Free Discount Coupons...Free Fact Kit...Free Issue...Free Copy of___...Free Gift...Free Gift Certificate...Free___Guide...Free Information...Free Introductory Offer...Free Introductory Offer Discount...Free Issue...Free Sample...Free Subscription...Free Trial Examination...Free Trial Subscription

3:05 30 Basic Offers in Direct Marketing

In his classic *Successful Direct Marketing Methods*, 1994, Bob Stone suggests there are 30 basic offers in direct marketing that can be used singly or in various combinations. He cites among them: long-term acceptance based on a sample, a Yes-No involvement offer, a time offer, contests, discounts, a charter offer, a guaranteed buyback, optional terms.

3:06 Offer Classifications

Jim Kobs, a highly regarded direct mail authority, outlines 99 successful offers in *Profitable Direct Marketing*, 1992. All of them fall into these twelve offer classifications: (1) basic offers, (2) free gift offers, (3) other types of free offers, (4) discount offers, (5) sale offers, (6) sample offers, (7) time-limit offers, (8) guarantee offers, (9) build-up-the-sale offers, (10) sweepstake offers, (11) club and continuity offers, (12) specialized offers [a catchall for offers that do not fit into the other classifications].

3:07 Free Gift or Discount: Which Is Best

As a rule, a consumer offer of an attractive free gift will have greater appeal than a discount of the same value.

3:08 When Free Trial Offer Is Substitute for Guarantee

As a rule, a mail offer can succeed with a free trial offer as a substitute for a money-back guarantee, since it eliminates the burden of risk. However, if prepayment is an option, a money-back guarantee should be included.

3:09   Free Gift Offers as Response Stimulators

As a rule, a free gift or premium will stimulate response to a mail offer. The most popular type is one that offers a gift incentive just for examining the product. The other kind is one that must be returned if the product is not purchased.

3:10   Way to Enhance Appeal of Free Gift Offer

If your direct mail offer includes a free gift, as a rule, making the gift offer a separate enclosure along with the flier or brochure usually will make it more effective.

3:11   Headline as the Offer

As a rule, the headline is the offer. If the offer is appealing enough in the headline, the reader will proceed to the first paragraph to learn how he or she can benefit from it.

3:12   Objective of the Offer

The offer encourages the reader to seek a worthwhile benefit by taking immediate action.

3:13   Offer Appeals That Work Best

Money-saving offers, as a rule, work best with consumers or individuals likely to enjoy a personal benefit. In business offers, saving money is not a strong primary appeal.

3:14   The Good and Bad of Premium Offers

An offer of a premium will sharply increase response. However, as a rule, as the response rate goes up, the response quality goes down. You pay for the increased response with more bad debt and larger merchandise returns.

3:15   Guidelines for Price-Appeal Offers

As a rule, price-appeal offers do best when they fall below a price break. Some examples: $9.95 instead of $10, $19.95 instead of $20, $29.95 instead of $30, etc. On prestige-related offers, however, Ed

Nash, a highly regarded marketing authority, advises using rounded figures. Nash cautions: Decide what's appropriate for your business and stick to it.

3:16   Time Limit With Offer Speeds Buying Decision

"By placing a time limit on the offer," says Andrew Svenson, "you can lend urgency to a sales message and overcome a prospect's natural inertia. Asking for the order by a specific date helps the prospect face the buying decision immediately while the benefit-filled sales presentation is still fresh." (In *DMA Fact Book*, 1983)

3:17   Mailing Guideline for Dated Special Offers

As a rule, never mail a dated special offer that has a very short cutoff date. There is always the risk that because of printing or mailing delays—or slow postal delivery—the dated offer could be delivered with insufficient time for a response, or even after the offer has expired.

3:18   The Good and the Bad of Sweepstakes Offers

A good sweepstakes," says Walter Weintz, a direct marketing pioneer, "will as a rule increase the pull of any mailing by at least 25 percent— more likely 50 percent, or even 100 percent....The big drawback is the legal obligation: you have to distribute all prizes...even if you abort the effort after a test. (In *The Solid Gold Mailbox*, 1987)

3:19   Cautionary Note on Sweepstakes Offers

As a rule, you should obtain legal advice before attempting a sweepstakes-type offer. There are complex legal ramifications concerning such offers, as well as varying laws concerning such offers in individual states.

3:20   Price-Range Guideline for Direct Mail Offers

As a rule, pricing for any mail offer should be in a range that is common or deemed reasonable for the type of product offered. Offers priced beyond what the market deems reasonable rarely succeed.

3:21 When High Return Rate Matches High Response

When a direct mail offer produces a high rate of response, followed by a high rate of merchandise returns, the high return rate can be attributed either to the copy promising more than the product actually offers or to the product not offering sufficient value for the asking price.

3:22 List Quality Versus Offer Quality

A weak offer to a well-targeted list will produce a better response rate than an excellent offer to a poorly targeted list.

3:23 Direct Mail Approach to High-Priced Offers

As a rule, mail-order offers of high-priced products or services work best when preceded by a simple inquiry-producing advertisement or mailing. As sales inquiries are generated, qualified prospects can then be approached either with more elaborate mail offers or by telephone or by a combination of both.

3:24 Winning Offer for High-Priced Reference Works

For high-priced reference works, as a rule, the most effective direct mail offer is a special prepublication price. This can be 10 to 15 percent off the established list price for orders received before the official publication date.

3:25 Offers for Magazine Circulation Promotions

As a rule, the most successful magazine circulation offer is one offering a free trial subscription for a given number of issues. At the end of the trial period, the prospect who does not wish to subscribe just writes "Cancel" on the bill and is free of further obligation. About three out of every five magazine promotions rely on this type of offer.

3:26 Offer Approach for Libraries

As a rule, librarians are most receptive to mail offers that include a generous library discount or those that have a limited-time special price.

3:27 Tying Response to Commitment

In direct mail offers, the less the respondent's commitment to buy, the easier to get the order. A free examination generally draws the highest response. Adding a credit card payment option slows down the response. Requiring payment by credit card alone slows response even more. Requiring cash payment in advance is slowest of all.

3:28 Bad Dept Ratios in Free Exam Offers

In business and professional free examination offers, there will always be a certain percentage of recipients who neither pay nor return the shipment. One study by a publisher of professional and reference books indicated that bad debt varied greatly from one group or profession to another. Best payers: chemists. Worst payers: small business entrepreneurs.

3:29 Fastest Medium for Offer Testing

Compared with direct mail, telemarketing is the most effective medium for testing an offer, says Dr. Gary S. Goodman, a telemarketing consultant. It yields data immediately. (In *Reach Out and Sell Someone*, 1983)

3:30 Inexpensive Large-Scale Offer Pretesting

As a rule, you can pretest a mail offer to a large audience at relatively low cost with a one-card participation in a cooperative card pack mailing to a related market. If the single-card offer in the card pack indicates sufficient interest, you can later schedule a larger solo promotion to a like or more targeted audience, as card responses indicate.

3:31 FTC's Revised 30-Day Delivery Rule on Merchandise Offers

On offers requiring prepayment, it is a good idea to study the changes in the FTC's 30-day delivery rule (Mail Order Merchandise Rule) that became effective early in 1994. Basically, under the rule, you should not solicit orders you do not expect to ship within 30 days of receipt of order, or within the time stated in the offer. The original rule applied only to mail orders. As amended in 1994, the law now includes phone and fax orders. The amended FTC rule has new guidelines on marketer's obligations and customer's rights on delayed delivery orders.

3:32   FTC Interpretation of When 30-Day Delivery Period Starts

Under the FTC's 30-day delivery rule, as revised in March 1994, a mail-order company must ship merchandise within 30 days of receiving payment and a completed order form. As a rule, the FTC recognizes the order as valid on the date the order is received with a check, or on the date when the credit card slip is deposited with the direct marketer's bank.

3:33   Caption Copy Rule for Illustrations

As a rule, when an illustration reinforces an offer, the illustration caption copy should be about the offer—not about the illustration.

3:34   Product-in-Use Rule for Offer Illustrations

As a rule, an illustration in an offer showing a product in actual use will make twice the impression as one showing the product as inactive merchandise.

4
Sales Letters: Approaches, Preparation, Evaluation

As the letter is one of the least costly segments of a direct mail package, you should not skimp on it...How many pages?—As many as are needed to tell the story.
> —EDWARD L. NASH
> *Direct Marketing: Strategy, Planning, Production, 1986*

4:01   Sales Letter: Prime Ingredient in Mail Selling

The sales letter is the most widely used format in mail-order selling. The letter may be used by itself or in combination with folders, brochures and order forms, as well as other types of envelope enclosures.

4:02   Personal Approach in Sales Letters

As a rule, most people prefer to deal with other people—not with companies. Consequently, your sales letter should aim to be as personal as possible...conversational...intimate...and specific.

4:03 Composition Formula for Successful Letter

A successful sales letter is easy to read, has short paragraphs, is broken up by underlined words and phrases, and has no complex or hard-to-understand words and phrases.

4:04 Giving Letters Personalized Look

As a rule, a sales letter looks more personal if it has a dateline, a salutation, short indented paragraphs, a complimentary close and signature, and a postscript.

4:05 Salutations for Nonpersonalized Letters

A sales letter requiring a salutation, if not personalized, should best be addressed to an occupational or professional title, such as *Dear Professional*, or *Dear Doctor*. If to a nonspecialized audience, it is always best to go with *Dear Reader*.

4:06 Rule for Dating Letters

When you are dating a sales letter, use an exact date. For first-class this is usually the mailing date. For a third-class mailing, use month and year only.

4:07 Salutation Rule for Business Letters

When you use a salutation in nonpersonalized letters to high-level business professionals, the best salutation is *Dear Reader*. It directly targets the individual holding the letter and asks the recipient to read it.

4:08 Substitute for Letter Date

When it is not convenient to put a date on a letter in a third-class mailing, as a rule, you can give the semblance of a date by putting a day of the week in the place where the date would normally appear.

4:09 Omitting the Salutation

"Although many direct-mail specialists still use salutations," says Herman Holtz, "the modern idea is that a salutation is not a necessity for salesletters, especially when that salutation could have to be 'Dear Friend,' or some similarly obvious insincerity." (In *The Direct Marketer's Workbook*, 1986)

4:10   Letter Contents as Enhancement Vehicle for Flier

As a rule, a sales letter is most effective when it enhances the accompanying flier and has a message that is not a duplicate of what is said on the flier.

4:11   Lead-Off Sentence in Sales Letters

As a rule, your sales letter will be more effective if the lead-off sentence is reasonably short and promises a benefit.

4:12   Rule for Positioning Offer in a Sales Letter

If you state the offer in the opening paragraph of a sales letter and again in the postscript, you will have gotten your message across even if the reader does not proceed beyond the letter's opening.

4:13   Improving Chances for Getting Letter Read

Your sales letter will have a better chance of getting read if you come to the point quickly. As a rule, never start a letter with an irrelevant story or anecdote no matter how interesting it may be.

4:14   Paragraph Indentations and Spacing

As a rule, indented paragraphs with double spacing between them make for a more attractive and readable sales letter.

4:15   Paragraph Length

As a rule, you can improve the readability of a sales letter by varying the lengths of the paragraphs. Following a very long paragraph with a very short one can lend emphasis to the longer paragraph.

4:16   Popular Letter Technique for Key-Point Emphasis

One of the most widely used techniques for directing a reader's attention to key points in a sales letter is to underline them.

4:17 Rule for Underlining Letter's Key Points

As a rule, use underlining sparingly and only for a few key points in intermittent paragraphs. When overdone, too many underlines tend to weaken the overall effect of the sales letter.

4:18 Rule for Emphasizing Important Letter Material

"The best way to emphasize important material in a sales letter," says Harry B. Walsh of Ogilvy & Mather, Inc., "is to paragraph it and indent it on both sides. But don't overdo indenting or you will lose its effect." (In [Barton] *Handbook of Advertising Management*, 1970)

4:19 Use of Connectors in Sales Letter Copy

As a rule, you can give a sales letter a sense of movement by using transitional sentences or phrases at the ends or beginnings of paragraphs. Some popular examples: Better yet...So that is why...And in addition...More important than that....

4:20 Reading Continuity Rule for Two-Page Letters

If you want continuity in readership of a two-page sales letter, make it a rule to end the first page in the middle of a sentence and add "over, please..." in the lower right-hand corner.

4:21 Length of Sales Letter

As a rule, you should keep your letter as short as possible if its aim is to generate business leads. On the other hand, if the letter offers a consumer product, it should be as long as necessary to get the complete message across.

4:22 Letter Length for Professional Book Offers

As a rule, a free examination offer for a professional or scholarly book need not be longer than a page. The author's credentials and the book's contents usually do most of the selling.

4:23 Success Rate of Multipage Versus Single-Page Letter

As a rule, a lengthy letter will pull twice as many responses as a one-page letter, provided it has something important to say, and says it skillfully.

4:24 Should You Use One or Two Sheets of Paper for a Two-Page Letter?

As a rule, a two-page letter using two sheets of paper will do far better than a letter printed on both sides of a single sheet of paper.

4:25 The Odd-Page-Length Rule for Sales Letters

When long sales letters are printed on both sides of the paper, a three- or five-page letter will pull better than a two-, four-, or six-page letter. The Reason: The letter ending—the part you want your readers to act on, will fall on a right-hand page where it is more likely to be seen and read.

4:26 Multipage Letter Continuity Indicators

As a rule, multipage sales letters should include continuity instructions. Letters printed on two sides usually favor: (*over, please*) on each page. Letters on multiple sheets of paper often use: (*Please turn page*) on all pages.

4:27 Letterhead Recognition Value Rule

If your letterhead has little or no recognition value, as a rule, your mailing offer may be more successful if you omit the letterhead from the first page of your sales letter and replace it with a strong benefit-oriented headline. Run the letterhead at the bottom of the letter or at the end of the last page.

4:28 Sales Letter Last Paragraph Rule

The last paragraph of any sales letter should tell readers why they should act now and not delay the response the letter calls for.

4:29   Letter Signature Authority

As a rule, a signature-bearing sales letter is more effective than an unsigned one. By the same token, the higher the authority of the signer, the more credible the letter.

4:30   Letter Signature Safety Rule

It is a good idea to have the executive signature on a sales letter written by someone other than the actual person to avoid any possibility of its fraudulent use.

4:31   Postscript Content Rule

The postscript is one of the most-read parts of a sales letter and, therefore, should always contain an important message—usually the principal benefit of making the purchase.

4:32   Postscript Length Rule

A sales letter postscript of three lines or less will be more effective than a longer one.

4:33   Best Signature Ink Color for Sales Letters

As a rule, a blue ink signature in a sales letter will produce a better response than one printed in the same black ink as the letter.

4:34   Paper Color for Sales Letters

As a rule, a sales letter looks more businesslike and attracts more attention when it is on white paper—which is why most sales letters are printed on white paper.

4:35   Best Typefaces for Sales Letters

As a rule, sales letters with typewriter-style typefaces are more effective than sans serif typefaces. A ragged right style has been shown to be more effective than a justified right margin.

4:36 Making Claims Believable

As a rule, claims in a sales letter that are not supported by proof will not be believed.

4:37 Attaching a Coupon to a Sales Letter

As a rule, if your sales letter requires a coupon response and you want to avoid adding a coupon to the mailing, you can make the lower inch or two of a short letter a tear-off coupon by adding a dashed line where you want the coupon to begin. If the letter requires the full page, use an 8½- by 13-inch sheet of paper.

4:38 Incorporating Sales Letter Into Self-Mailer

You can incorporate a sales letter into a multipanel self-mailer by (1) placing it on the mailing face or front cover; (2) placing a simulated letter, with a letterhead, typewriter-style typeface, a salutation, and a signature, within a border.

4:39 Using Involvement Devices to Increase Response

As a rule, a sales letter that incorporates a device which gets the reader more involved in the sales message will enjoy an increased response as a result of that device. These devices can be anything that asks the reader to take some physical action in addition to reading the message and sending in the order form. Involvement devices may include check boxes, checks, coins, coupons, quizzes, rub-offs, stamps, stickers, sweepstakes, tokens, and Yes-No questions.

4:40 Eye-Flow Pattern for Personalized Sales Letter

As a rule, the common pattern of eye flow for a personalized sales letter is from recipient's name and address to salutation to end of letter—first to signature and then to postscript, if any. The person tends to skip the body of the letter and scan highlighted words only.

5
Fund-Raising and Charity Appeals

The secret of direct mail fund raising is the ability to portray a fund-raising program in a truthful but unique way that captures the imagination of specific groups of supporters.
—C. F. MCCARTY AND JAMES G. ALDIGE III
In (Nash) The Direct Marketing Handbook,
1984

5:01 Key Element in Direct Marketing Fund-Raising

In direct marketing, the key element is the offer—what the prospect gets by responding. By contrast, in fund-raising, the offer is not the key element—the appeal is.

5:02 Ingredients of Good Fund-Raising Letter

A good fund-raising letter outlines specifics on why the funds are needed and what is being done with the money raised.

5:03 Basic Content of Fund-Raising Letters

As a rule, fund-raising letters usually deal with heartrending descriptions of the individuals being helped before making an appeal to the reader in later paragraphs.

5:04 Positioning of Emotional Impact in Fund-Raising Letters

Most of the emotional impact in a fund-raising letter must be in its opening paragraph. If it doesn't involve the reader instantly, the balance of the letter will not be read.

5:05 Guilt Factor in Fund-Raising Appeals

Most people feel guilty when throwing away charity appeals. "To turn that guilt into action," says Jim Kobs (in *Profitable Direct Marketing,* 1992), "you must paint a grim picture of what things will be like [for the beneficiaries of the charity] without the funds to protect them."

5:06 Testimonials in Fund-Raising Appeals

As a rule, testimonials from beneficiaries of a charity or persons carrying out the work of the charity will add credibility and strength to any fund-raising direct mail appeal.

5:07 Impact of Letterhead in Charity Appeals

In charity appeals, the impact of the letterhead and the names of the committee members have a powerful influence on response. However, committee members' names should not overwhelm the letter.

5:08 Use of Prestigious Name in Charity Appeals

As a rule, use local names for local charity appeals. Use national names for national charity appeals. The more prestigious the name, the more prominent should be its appearance in a committee listing on the letterhead.

5:09　Building Credibility in Fund-Raising Letters

As a rule, a fund-raising letter signed by a prominent person other than an official of the fund-raising organization will have far more credibility. It implies the endorsement and support of the letter's signer for the fund-raising effort.

5:10　Reply-Envelope Message in Charity Appeals

As a rule, the return envelope with a fund-raising letter mailing should carry a powerful appeal message as a final effort to tap the recipient's generosity.

5:11　Role of a Postscript in Fund-Raising Letters

As a rule, the postscript in a fund-raising letter should make one last try to get the "meat" of the appeal across to the reader. Here is a classic handwritten postscript used by the National Jewish Hospital in Denver to add a closing "bang" to its appeal: "During the minute it took you to read this letter, a total of eight people died somewhere of tuberculosis and forty-three were infected."

5:12　When Not to Use Reply Envelope in Charity Appeal

When you are sending a highly personalized letter to a charity's known large contributor, as a rule, it is not necessary to include a return envelope.

5:13　Ink and Paper Importance in Charity Appeals

Tests have shown that a fund-raising appeal printed in two colors of ink with cheaper paper will often produce a better response than the identical appeal printed with four colors of ink on high-quality paper.

5:14　Fund-Raising Follow-Up as Part of Program

A fund-raising effort should not end with the receipt of a contribution. As the contributor may be expected to continue giving to future appeals, an acknowledgment letter should be part of the program.

5:15   Mail Frequency in Fund-Raising

In fund-raising, the greater the frequency of contact with the names on the solicitation list, the greater the potential for contributions. As a rule, not all the mailings should solicit funds. Some should be informational, designed to improve the relationship between the fund raiser and the donor.

5:16   Mailing Patterns in Fund-Raising Promotions

As a rule, a list of known contributors to a charity can usually be solicited several times a year. Over time, as a recognized contribution pattern is established, donor lists can be segmented by contribution frequency and mailed accordingly to eliminate unproductive efforts.

5:17   Mail-Order Buyers as Fund-Raising Prospects

As a rule, people known to be highly responsive to direct mail offers are also good prospects for fund-raising appeals.

5:18   Return Envelopes in Fund-Raising Appeals

As a rule, fund-raising appeals do not require postage-paid return envelopes. The majority of contributors consider the postage as doing a little extra to help the cause, and they do not mind putting on the postage stamp.

6

Circular Preparation Techniques: Brochures and Fliers

The brochure is designed to illustrate the product and its benefits and to demonstrate its value in relation to the prospect.
—CHRISTIAN BRANN
Cost-Effective Direct Marketisng, 1984

6:01 Components of an Effective Brochure

An effective brochure in a mail package elaborates in an impersonal way on the accompanying sales letter, lists benefits in detail, provides illustrations and technical details, provides comparison and proofs, offers testimonials from satisfied customers, and gives details of the guarantees offered. In effect, it provides all the information necessary for the recipient to reach a buying decision.

6:02 How Brochure Function Differs From Sales Letter

As a rule, the brochure in a mail package has a different function from the sales letter. The letter aims to be read from start to finish and makes the promise, develops the argument, and urges the action. The brochure is intended to be scanned rather than read in its entirety. It illustrates and amplifies on the offer's benefits and aims to demonstrate its value to the prospect. It provides all the supporting evidence for claims made in the sales letter. And, by its design, the brochure may try to convey a quality look to the offer that would not be possible with the sales letter by itself.

6:03   Should You Call It a *Flier* or a *Brochure?*

As a rule, if your mailing package contains a small, inexpensively produced advertising piece on a single sheet of paper, refer to it as a flier (or flyer) or leaflet. If the advertising piece is more elaborately prepared, and with more attention given to its design, call it a brochure.

6:04   When to Choose a Brochure Over a Flier

As a rule, you should use a brochure rather than a flier when you have a high-priced or luxury item, or a colorful product of sufficient price to merit clear, colorful, detailed illustrations, or when a wealth of information is essential to help the recipient reach a buying decision and mail in an order. Unlike a flier, a brochure can be designed to reflect the high quality of the offer.

6:05   When to Choose a Flier Over a Brochure

As a rule, a flier will suffice for a simple offer, one that does not require illustrations and is reasonably low priced. It is also used when the intention is to generate a sales lead rather than a direct order.

6:06   One Expert's View on Brochures

"There have been some split-run tests of 'brochure' versus 'no brochure' where 'no brochure' was the winner," says master marketer Ed Nash. "However, I have never seen a successful mailing which left out the letter." (In *Direct Marketing: Strategy, Planning, Execution,* 1986)

6:07   Where Brochure Can Be Counterproductive

As a rule, overdoing an enclosure in a mailing package can be counterproductive. Simplicity should prevail in charity appeals where an elaborate brochure may lead to the impression that solicited funds are being used for fancy promotions. Lead-generating enclosures should also not aim at giving too much information lest they deter a prospect from responding.

6:08   Fliers and Brochures in Direct Mail Packages

The rule for a direct mail package is that it contain all the elements of a direct mail effort. A package may omit a flier or brochure and still be a "package," although some direct mail guides define a package as always including a brochure.

6:09   Rule for Size of Flier or Enclosure in Mail Package

When a flier or brochure supports a letter in a direct mail package, the supporting enclosure—whatever its nature—should always be in a different size and, preferably, a different color or paper stock from the accompanying letter for maximum impact.

6:10   Cost Rule for Flier or Brochure

The brochure portion is the most expensive element in a direct mail package to prepare and produce. However, when a single-sheet flier is used, letter-preparation cost and special paper may make the letter easily exceed the flier cost.

6:11   Illustrations in Brochures

As a rule, using photographs instead of drawings in a brochure will increase both readership and response.

6:12   Illustration Content

As a rule, a brochure illustration of a product offer will be far more effective if it is shown with a person using the product.

6:13   Illustration Purpose

When you are selecting brochure illustrations, you must answer two questions: (1) Is the illustration related to the offer? (2) Does it help get the selling message across?

7

Mail-Order Catalogs: Preparation and Selling Techniques

People like catalogs. Most don't even think of them as advertising mail. A catalog is considered something special and catalog shopping is a favorite pastime for many consumers.

—JIM KOBS
Profitable Direct Marketing, 1992

7:01 Most Economical Catalog Size

As a rule, the most economical catalog size is a 16-page signature with an 8½- by 11-inch page size.

7:02 Most Economical Catalog Planning

You can save money on printed catalogs if you use a self-cover, lightweight paper, and standard paper that is readily available at the printer.

7:03 Most Economical Way to Buy Catalog Paper

As a rule, if you're planning a catalog on standard paper stock, it is likely to be as economical to draw from the printer's paper inventory as to buy from a paper house and run the risk of having too much or too little.

7:04 Economical Way to Increase Catalog Pages and Bulk

When your catalog is small, you can get more pages and more bulk to your catalog by going to a 5½- by 8½-inch size.

7:05 Mail-Order Catalog Efficiency

The most efficient mail-order catalog is one printed from one or more complete signatures. If your catalog lacks sufficient material to fill a signature, use the blank pages as convertible self-mailer order forms and envelopes, or to offer reduced-price closeout items that are in surplus inventory.

7:06 Rule for Getting Best Catalog Printing Price

Never plan a catalog printing without confirming in advance that it is compatible with the equipment on which it will be printed. Conversely, if you plan a nonstandard format, using a printer with the right equipment can save up to 50 percent of the printing cost.

7:07 Prime Catalog Selling Pages

As a rule, the prime selling pages in a consumer catalog are the front cover, inside front cover, and center-spread. If you must include a mailer's message or letter, move it to the inside back cover or use only a fractional portion of the inside front cover.

7:08 Way to Maximize Catalog Sales

As a rule, the best way to maximize catalog sales is by remailing with either a changed cover or by replacing the outer pages to give the catalog a completely different look.

7:09   Mail-Order Catalog Content Rule

The majority of buyers from mail-order catalogs do so because the item cannot readily be obtained elsewhere. This suggests that catalog content should strive to stress the new, the different, and the unusual, as well as the ease and convenience of shopping by mail.

7:10   Testimonials for Consumer Catalogs

Catalog copy for consumer products should, as a rule, include proofs or testimonials on the product's durability or performance capability.

7:11   Mail-Order Catalog Relationship Rule

When the various items in a mail-order catalog are closely related, there is a greater tendency to purchase more than one item.

7:12   Vehicle for Increasing Catalog Orders

Here are two effective ways of converting single-item catalog sales into multiple sales: (1) Set a reasonably high (but not unfair) shipping and handling charge for an order (regardless of the number of items ordered). (2) Set a reasonably high (but not unfair) shipping and handling charge for the first item ordered and only a trifle more for two or more items.

7:13   Credit Card Use in Catalog Sales

Nearly all successful mail-order catalogs emphasize payment by credit card.

7:14   Postage Requirement on Catalog Return Envelopes

Most mail-order catalogs include a return envelope that requires the responder pay the postage.

7:15   Increasing Response With 800 Number

As a rule, including an 800 number ordering option in a mail-order catalog will increase response by about 20 percent.

7:16 Increasing Catalog Pass-Along

When you send a catalog to an academic or institutional address, where it may have appeal to more than one person, as a rule, you can substantially increase the catalog's sales potential by including or cover-imprinting a routing slip or instruction asking the recipient to pass the catalog along to other associates or departments after any selections have been made.

7:17 Way to Speed Up Catalog Response

Response from a catalog format tends to be slower than from other direct mail formats, although dollar amount of catalog-generated orders may be larger. To speed response from a catalog, include a cut-off date and indicate prominently that prices will be honored only up to the expiration date.

7:18 One Way to Boost Consumer Catalog Orders

As a rule, response from a consumer catalog can be increased by up to 100 percent by including a separate dated certificate or coupon that offers a cash credit for any prepaid order received by a certain cutoff date.

7:19 Improving Catalog "Mileage"

If you issue catalogs periodically, you can get extra benefits out of your catalogs by including them with outgoing shipments.

7:20 Mail-Order Catalog Repeat Buying Patterns

As a rule, about one third of all first-time mail-order catalog buyers will buy again. Another third are likely buying prospects if encouraged by special promotions.

7:21 Catalog Profitability Evaluation

As a rule, catalog sales results are evaluated in two principal ways: (1) overall dollar sales are compared with cost of catalog, (2) a prorated charge for each entry in the catalog is established and a comparison of dollar sales per item is made with that charge. With the latter method, a nonprofitable catalog item can be eliminated and replaced in subsequent mailings.

7:22   Requirements for Producing a Catalog

"Producing a catalog," says Fred Hahn, "permits, but does not require, copious creative flair, combined with meticulous mastery of mountains of minutiae, expertise in half a dozen technical specializations, financial acumen, and management skills." (In *Do-It-Yourself Advertising*, 1993)

7:23   Enhancing Value of Catalog Gift Incentives

If you offer a free gift as a catalog-ordering incentive, as a rule, you can enhance the value of the "free gift" as well as its appeal by including the gift in the catalog at its suggested retail value.

7:24   Catalogs Are Big Business

If you're thinking about becoming a cataloger, be aware that catalogs are big business and face a lot of competition. Catalogs make up more than a third of all third-class mail (source: USPS publication *Focus*, September 1993), and 85 percent of all bound printed matter mailed fourth class is catalogs. As of January 1994, the Direct Marketing Association began testing private delivery of catalogs in 12 markets across the United States.

7:25   Best Time to Start Mail-Order Catalog

"You're not ready to publish your own mail-order catalog," says L. Wilbur Perry, "until you have at least 10,000 customers." (In *Money in Your Mailbox*, 1985)

7:26   Sales Pattern for Neiman Marcus Christmas Catalog

Christmas catalogs, as a rule, have a six-week life span. A unique exception is the famous Neiman Marcus Christmas catalog. It boasts a five-month life span, and a strange sales pattern. The approximately three million catalogs of this upscale Texas retailer go out in early September. Orders begin almost at once, peak for the first time in mid-October, trail off for a month, and begin to surge again until a final mid-December peak. However, orders continue to flow in through the end of January. From the second week of November, Neiman Marcus will ship 100,000 catalog orders a week. During this period, the inbound telemarketing staff will handle more than 20,000 calls a day.

7:27   Catalog Order Form Format That Works Best

The catalog order form format favored by many successful mail-order catalogers is one which uses a combination order form/envelope that is bound into the middle of the catalog. As a rule, this order form/envelope format will produce better results than an order form printed on a page of the catalog.

7:28   Special Benefit of Using Catalog Overwrap

As a rule, you can target the same catalog to different audiences by adding a specially prepared four-page outer cover over the outside of your catalog and affixing your special-audience letter or other special-audience message or offer on this overwrap.

7:29   Catalog Introductory Page Advantages

As a rule, advises Jim Kobs (in *Profitable Direct Marketing*, 1992), "It is often a good idea in business catalogs to open each section or department with a separate introductory page. It provides a visual break and lets customers know they are moving from one merchandise category to another."

7:30   Cataloger Tries Two-Step Distribution Program

Pategonia, a Ventura, California, mail-order cataloger, "went out on a limb" in spring 1993 by introducing a new two-step catalog distribution program for prospects. Beginning in 1993, only customers and space advertising responders would get catalogs. Prospects would be sent a postcard asking if they wanted a catalog. Pategonia, which had been averaging $24 million in catalog sales, believes the new procedure will cut its more than half a million normal catalog distribution by 200,000 copies, reducing production and postage costs. The company's officials indicate they believe it will take two to three years to see if this two-step catalog distribution is effective. (From *DM News*, September 20, 1993)

7:31   First Mail-Order Cataloger and Catalog

Mail-order catalogers credit Aaron Montgomery Ward as being the father of the mail-order catalog. Shortly after establishing the nation's first mail-order house in Chicago in 1872, Ward mailed his first "catalog"—a single-sheet price list without illustrations, measuring 8 inches by 12 inches.

8
Sale Catalogs and Reduced-Price Offers

The bargain appeal dates back to time immemorial. It worked yesterday. It works today. It will work tomorrow. It is the most frequently used of all sales appeals.
—JOHN CAPLES
How to Make Your Advertising Make Money,
1983

8:01 Why Sale Offerings Work Well in Direct Mail

Some people buy only when a product is on sale. Consequently, a sale offering will usually work better than many other types of offers. When making a sale offer, be sure to give it a legitimate-sounding reason like Annual Pre-Inventory Clearance...Tenth Anniversary Sale...etc. Avoid such trite sale names as Giant Sale! or Whale of a Sale!

8:02 Expiration Date Helps in Sale Catalog

As a rule, a sale catalog is much more responsive when it includes an expiration date. So says Abbot Friedland, a Princeton, New Jersey, mail marketing professional.

8:03 Sale Offering Time Allowance for Expiration

As a rule, a sale offering will be most responsive when the mailing is made at least 90 days prior to the expiration date.

8:04 Way to Extend Life of Sale Offerings

A sale offering can have a double life if, shortly before the expiration date, the original offering is remailed to the same audience with an overprint on the offering cover stating: "Sale extended 30 days."

8:05 Sale Offering Mixing

As a rule, sale offerings are more successful when they are *not* mixed with regular-price offers.

8:06 Sale Offering Order Form Rule

A sale offering should have its own identifiable order form and a cut-off date. It should clearly state that sale terms apply only when accompanied by that special sale order form.

8:07 Pricing Multiproduct Sale Offers

When you make a multiproduct sale offer, as a rule, response is much better when you show both list and sale prices than when you show the list price only with the amount of discount.

8:08 Sale Offer Essentials for Library Mailings

As a rule, any reduced-price offer to libraries should include list price, discount, net price, and offer expiration date.

8:09 Way to Increase Sale Catalog Order Value

As a rule, you can often increase order value from a sale catalog by offering a discount on orders over a certain level, such as 5 percent on orders for $100 or more. Some mailers use a double discount, adding an additional discount for a second, higher level of purchasing, such as 5 percent over $100, 10 percent over $250.

8:10   Sale Offer Prepayment Rule

When a sale offer requires prepayment, it is a good idea to exclude businesses, institutions, and libraries from the prepayment requirement when they submit a purchase order.

8:11   Honoring Orders After Expiration Date

As a rule, it is good business to honor orders received for a sale offer up to 30 days after the announced expiration date, provided they are received on the sale order form.

8:12   FTC Regulations on Reduced-Price Offers

If the article you offer in a reduced-price sale was not offered at the former higher price for a reasonably substantial period of time in the normal course of business, the reduced price will be in violation of Federal Trade Commission regulations against deceptive pricing.

8:13   Original-Price Wording in Reduced-Price Offers

As a rule, when a reduced-price offer is made, the original price is usually set forth in the copy and described by such adjectives as *regularly*, *formerly*, *originally*, or *previously*.

8:14   Sale Offering Profitability

As a rule, a sale offering that generates a minimum of three times its cost should be considered successful.

9

Envelopes: Guidelines for Selection and Use

The envelope is to a mailing what the top half of a page is to an advertisement.
—WALTER WEINTZ
The Solid Gold Mailbox, 1987

9:01 Favorite Envelope Sizes in Direct Mail

As a rule, most direct mail packages use one of three standard envelope sizes: $4\frac{1}{8}$ by $9\frac{1}{2}$ inches (No. 10), 6 by 9 inches (No. $6\frac{1}{2}$), or 9 by 12 inches (either a No. $9\frac{1}{2}$ booklet envelope or a No. $10\frac{1}{2}$ catalog envelope).

9:02 Envelope Importance in Mail Package

As a rule, the envelope is the most important element in any mailing package. According to master mail-marketer Walter Weintz, "The creation of the mailing should start with the envelope." (In *The Solid Gold Mailbox*, 1987)

9:03 Envelope Color for Business Mailings

Envelopes have a higher chance of being delivered to a business address when the envelope paper color is one commonly used in business, with white being the most common.

9:04 Best Envelope for Addresses on Labels

If you plan to mail using addresses on labels, as a rule, the labels are less likely to identify themselves as advertising when affixed to standard white wove envelopes than on fancy paper stock.

9:05 Most Successful Look for an Envelope

As a rule, the most successful envelope is one that has no label or window, is typed or computer addressed, and has a personalized look.

9:06 Best Envelope Look for Business Mailings

Envelopes that look like advertising have a high risk of being discarded when sent to business addresses. A delivery study of business mail indicated more than half of all business mail is screened by secretaries who pass along to executives only mail that has a business look to it.

9:07 Envelope Corner Card Rule

A mailing with the mailer's name and address printed on the outside will outperform one recognizable as advertising but that does not identify the mailer.

9:08 Return Address Positioning Rule

You greatly reduce the chances for getting undeliverable mail back if you print the return address on the envelope back flap instead of on the face of the envelope.

9:09 Eye-Flow Pattern for Envelope Copy

As a rule, the common pattern of eye flow by the recipient of a sealed envelope is first to the recipient's name and address, then to teaser copy adjacent to the address, then to the corner card return address, and last to the postage corner of the envelope.

9:10 Envelope Name Recognition Rule

An envelope with a printed company name and address in the corner card will do better when the name is known to the recipient than when it is not.

9:11 Influence of Envelope Quality on Response

For most mailings, as a rule, response will not vary whether you use a standard-format envelope or a custom-made envelope.

9:12 Timing of Envelope Order in Relation to Package

When special envelopes are planned for a particular mail campaign, as a rule, it's best to order the envelopes before any other elements of the package, since their manufacture will require the longest lead time.

9:13 Value of Teaser Copy on Oversized Envelopes

As a rule, a mailing in an oversized envelope is more likely to be opened and read if it has teaser copy on the outside.

9:14 Value of Die-Cut Address Window in Large Envelopes

As a rule, a large-size envelope with a die-cut opening for the mailing address will have a higher opening rate than a similar-size envelope bearing a Cheshire label on the outside.

9:15 Sizing Rule for Envelopes With Windows

If you allow $\frac{1}{4}$ inch of space between address and window, the entire address will always be visible, even if the inside insert bearing the address slides around.

9:16 Envelope Imprint That Improves Response

If you plan to send a promotion by first-class mail, as a rule, imprinting the words *First-Class Mail* on the envelope will improve response.

9:17 Envelope Cost Reduction Guideline

If you plan to mail on a cyclical basis with the same type of envelope, you can reduce your envelope costs by ordering your estimated yearly requirements from an envelope manufacturer in a single order and requesting split or periodic shipments of portions of the order as needed.

9:18   Low-Cost Envelope Color Test

As a rule, you can color-test an envelope face at very little cost by using a light tint screen of the ink color used for the envelope's printed matter.

9:19   Envelope Size: Way to Change Look of Mailing

As a rule, you can change the look of a mailing without actually changing the mailing by going to a different envelope size.

10
Writing Envelope Teaser Copy

Teaser copy on an envelope sets the stage for the sales message, creates a mental picture, and makes your prospect drool receptively.
—DIRECT MARKETING ASSOCIATION
Envelopes: Their Use and Power in Direct Advertising, Research Report, 1956

10:01 Envelope as Headline of Direct Mail

"The outer envelope," says Ed Nash in *Direct Marketing*, 1986, "is the headline of direct mail." Make it a rule to devote as much time and effort to your envelope teaser copy as you would to a good headline for a letter or advertisement.

10:02 Purpose of Envelope Teaser Copy

The sole purpose of envelope teaser copy, as a rule, is to get the recipient to open the envelope. Anything beyond that is likely to be counterproductive.

10:03   Envelope Teaser Copy Rule

Unless you can come up with compelling teaser copy, the envelope
will do better with no copy.

10:04   Teaser Copy Promise Must Be Observed

"Whatever the promise on the envelope, live up to it in the envelope...if it says Free Gift, make that the first item of business. Keep the
envelope promise." So says Herschell Gordon Lewis in *More Than You
Ever Wanted to Know About Mail Order Advertising*, 1983.

10:05   Teaser Copy for Customer Mailings

As a rule, envelope teaser copy is not necessary on mailings to established customers. The corner card name identification is sufficient to
get the envelope opened.

10:06   Using Reverse Psychology to Get Envelope
Opened

A good way to get an envelope opened is to omit both corner card and
teaser copy. This way, the recipient has no way of determining the
envelope's content without opening the envelope.

10:07   Placement Position for Teaser Copy

As a rule, the ideal location for envelope teaser copy is in the lower
left-hand corner of the envelope. Some promotional mailings that have
a window at the left corner, use the right corner of the envelope for the
teaser.

10:08   Envelope Teaser Readership

Teaser copy on an envelope, as a rule, is the second thing a recipient
reads after first viewing the recipient's name and address.

10:09   Targeting Envelope Teaser Copy

As a rule, teaser copy on the outside of an envelope will be more effective if it is targeted to the specific interests of its intended market than
if it is of a general nature.

10:10   Envelope Teaser Copy: General Approaches

Most mailers rely on teaser copy to get the recipient to open the envelope. When envelope copy describes its contents, as do some newsletter promotions, it's called *informational copy*. Professional and educational book marketers sometimes omit envelope teaser copy to give envelopes a more personal look.

10:11   Envelope Teaser Copy in Business-to-Business Mail

"As a rule," says Brian Christian Turley, a respected direct mail copy pro, "go slow with [envelope] teasers in business-to-business mail and reserve teasers for consumer efforts....When they're 'right on' they can be wonderfully effective in getting your mail opened, but quite often teasers wave a red flag...saying 'This is advertising!'" (In *DM News*, February 28, 1994)

10:12   Envelope Teaser Copy Placement Guideline

If you use envelope teaser copy, it is a good idea to ensure that it appears above the bottom line of the mailing address. The reason: It might interfere with the U.S. Postal Service optical character reading equipment used for mail sorting.

10:13   Interesting Envelope Alternative to Teaser Copy

As a rule, there's another way to arouse curiosity on an envelope other than teaser copy. It's an interesting postmark. Check the U.S. Postal Manual. You'll find scores of towns with names you can tie to almost any kind of promotion. Some examples: Santa Claus, IN; Valentine, AZ; Miracle, KY; Bread Loaf, VT; Cucumber, WV; Truth or Consequences, NM; and Bird in Hand, PA.

11
Headline Writing: Formulas and Effective Techniques

A good headline motivates prospects to continue reading...starting the process of persuasion that leads to a direct response.
—SY LEVY
In (Nash) The Direct Marketing Handbook,
1984

11:01 Headline Readership Rule

About five times as many people will read a headline as read the body copy.

11:02 Headline Writing Rule

You'll find writing a headline much easier after you've written the body copy. More often than not, the headline words may already appear in the copy you've already written.

11:03 Adding Vitality and Excitement With Words

As a rule, you can give a headline more vitality and excitement with words than by adding an exclamation point.

11:04   Headline Punctuation Rule

A good headline should not require punctuation unless it asks a direct question. A study of 106 moneymaking headlines, reported in John Caples' *How to Make Your Advertising Make Money,* 1983, showed only eleven with punctuation, eight of which were direct questions. In *The Copywriter's Handbook,* 1985, by this author, only four of over 300 headline examples shown included any punctuation, and not one at the end of the headline.

11:05   Headline Message Rule

The best place to tell readers about a major benefit and what you want them to do is in the headline.

11:06   Headline as Answer to Envelope Teaser

As a rule, the letter headline must answer the envelope teaser and lead the reader into the letter.

11:07   Shortest Headline Viewing in Direct Marketing

The shortest attention span for a headline in any direct marketing format is in the card pack. As a rule, a card pack recipient flips through 50 to 100 cards in a minute or less. If the headline doesn't grab in that fleeting instant, the card is wasted.

11:08   Way to Increase Headline Readability

As a rule, your headline will gain greater readability if it is stated in terms of the reader's interest and promises a benefit or reward. Example: Increase Your Word Power.

11:09   Established Headline Attention Getters

As a rule, you can make a headline more effective if you include any of these established attention getters: *Here, Now, New, Announcing, Introducing, You, Save, Learn, Gain, Discover.*

11:10   Rule for Using Pronouns in Headlines

A pronoun in a headline should be in the second person (you) if you want it to stop readers. Headlines in the first person (I) or in the third person (he/she) are not as effective.

11:11   Negative Words in Headlines

As a rule, a headline containing a negative is ineffective.

11:12   Contribution of Meaningless Headline

As a rule, a meaningless headline will serve the same function in a mail promotion or advertisement as no headline at all.

11:13   Headline Not for Selling

As a rule, the selling message should be in the copy, not in the headline.

11:14   Tailoring Headline to Its Market

As a rule, the same headline will not work equally well for all markets. It is sometimes useful to reshape a headline so that it will have special appeal for a particular market. For example, an engineering reference headline that says "Update Your Knowledge in_____" to engineers, would do much better if, when addressed to librarians, it said "The Most Complete Reference Resource in_____."

11:15   Combining Headlines With Subheads

Even when you have a strong headline, as a rule, you will improve your chances for getting your entire letter read with strong, benefit-oriented subheads.

11:16   How and When to Use Subheads

Use subheads when you want to break a long stretch of reading matter into shorter, more readable parts; when you want to cite individual benefits or advantages; when you want to highlight a special offer; or when you want to switch from one copy point to another.

12

Copywriting: Guidelines and Techniques

A sentence should contain no unnecessary words, a paragraph no unnecessary sentences....This requires not that the writer make all his sentences short, or that he avoid all detail and treat his subjects only in outline, but that every word tell.
—WILLIAM STRUNK, JR., AND E. B. WHITE
The Elements of Style, 1979

12:01 The Writer's Involvement in Direct Mail Copy

Direct mail copy is salesmanship in print. As a rule, copy should not only be logical, clear, and concise, but it must also reflect enthusiasm on the part of the writer, and convey the feeling that the writer was also sold on the product or service offered.

12:02 Difference Between Mail-Order and Advertising Copy

As a rule, if you write copy that describes the product and invites an order, you're writing advertising copy. If your copy describes the immediate, clear-cut benefits of the product, you're writing mail-order copy.

12:03   Key Ingredient of Mail-Order Copy

As a rule, for mail-order copy to be successful it must ask the reader to perform a specific immediate action. *Immediacy* is the key word because ordering from a mail offer is usually an impulse action.

12:04   Correct Verb Tense for Mail-Order Copy

To get the reader to perform a specific immediate action, keep your benefit-oriented copy in the present tense. Let the reader know that the promised benefits will be immediately forthcoming once he or she takes the desired action.

12:05   First Paragraph Rule for Mail-Order Copy

The first paragraph in mail-order copy should emanate from the headline. The safest way is to repeat and enlarge on the headline's premise.

12:06   A Warning on Mail-Order Copy

Mail-order copy should avoid fancy language, John Caples warns. "What you have to say in your copy is more important than how you say it." (In *How to Make Your Advertising Make Money*, 1983)

12:07   Formula for Good Mail-Order Copy

Good mail-order copy, as a rule, spells out the benefits to the reader, mixing them with the features of the offer. A *feature* is a special attribute of a product or service; a *benefit* is what the product or service will do for the reader.

12:08   Most Widely Followed Copywriting Formula

Most successful direct mail copy follows the A-I-D-A formula. The *A* is for Attention. The *I* is for Interest. The *D* is for Desire. The final *A* is for Action. This is the most successful and widely used of the many writing formulas and has served generations of copywriters.

12:09   Copywriting Formula Caution

Experts offer numerous copy formulas to help you write effective selling copy. However, as a rule, you can often rely on your own creative instincts and write copy that breaks all the formula rules and still works well for you.

12:10   Copy Differences in Varying Offers

As a rule, if you're selling information, your mail offer requires an equal balance between copy, type of mailing list, and offer. If, on the other hand, you're mailing a consumer offer, you need to rely more heavily on the list and less on the copy.

12:11   Matching Writer With Broker for Better Focus

When considering a test of a successful offer to a number of marginal lists, as a rule, it's a good idea to put the copywriter in touch with the list broker first. The writer, by learning the special characteristics of the lists, can more finely tailor copy to those characteristics.

12:12   Rule for Copy Pretesting

It's a good idea to read sales copy to someone else, or have someone else read it to see if your wording delivers the impression you intended.

12:13   Copy Credibility Rule

People open mail from known sources more readily than from unknown sources. So, too, will they read copy from a credible source more readily than from one they never heard of before. As a rule, establishing credibility in your copy is critical to its effectiveness. If you're new or small and unknown, sometimes an endorsement from a well-known and trusted individual can help.

12:14   How Business Copy Differs from Consumer Copy

Business copy, as a rule, is more fact-laden, more objective, and stresses how the product or service will satisfy the prospect's business needs. It depends much less on emotional appeal.

12:15   Recognizing Dull Copy

"As a rule," says Peter Hodges, a highly regarded direct marketing consultant, "If you read the copy in any direct mail piece and you feel that it is too long, then the copy is probably too dull."

12:16   Formula for Good Ad Copy

When you plan a basic mail-order ad to run in various media, it's best to follow the Rudolph Flesch formula: "Be as simple, clear, and to the point as possible. A sincere explanation of what you have to sell and why it is worth having will be good copy anywhere." (In *The Art of Plain Talk*, 1946)

12:17   Formula for Copy Focus in Business Mailings

Copy appeals in business mailings should focus on benefits to the business rather than to the individual, since the recipient is not always the actual user or the final purchasing authority.

12:18   Best Time to Start Writing Copy

As a rule, it is best not to start writing copy until you have thoroughly researched the subject and have all of the available information at hand.

12:19   Rule for First Paragraph Length

A short first paragraph will encourage readers to continue.

12:20   Rule for Word and Sentence Length

Your copy will have greater impact if you use short words and short sentences.

12:21   Rule for Adding Illustrations to Copy

Use an illustration only if it is essential to support the copy. If it does not, leave it out.

12:22   Rule for Highlighting Features or Benefits

When a large number of features or benefits are given in the copy, they will be more readable and more effective if vertically aligned and highlighted with bullets, stars, asterisks, or boxes.

12:23   Rule for Stressing Newness in Copy Appeals

A copy appeal stressing the new and novel will be more successful than one stressing the old and dependable.

12:24 Rule for Effective Consumer Copy

Effective consumer copy must be tied to human desires—to the things people seek. What they seek, according to Victor O. Schwab, "are Health...Popularity...Praise from others...Pride of accomplishment...Self-confidence...Time...Improved appearance...Comfort...Advancement (social/business)...Security in old age...Leisure...Increased enjoyment...[and] Personal prestige." (In Kleid, *Mail Order Strategies*, 1956)

12:25 The Priceless Ingredient of Direct Mail Copy

"One of the priceless ingredients of direct mail copy," wrote Frank McGinnis, an advertising professional, "is 'Involvement'...a rather intangible and hard-to-define thing....It's the feeling you get when you read the message that it not only is directed to you, but that it involves you...and says things that apply to you personally." (In *The Reporter of Direct Mail Advertising*, January 1959)

12:26 On the Subject of Humor in Copy

As a rule, a copy appeal that attempts to take a humorous approach will be largely ineffective. "Proof," says Herschell Gordon Lewis, "is the number of times a funny advertisement wins an award but fails to sell anything." (In *Power Copywriting*, 1992)

12:27 Rule for Upping Acceptance of Follow-Up Mail

If you do lead-generating direct mail or space advertising and you mail follow-up information, you can usually avoid having such mail discarded as junk mail by adding this line to the mailing envelope: "Here Is the Information You Requested."

12:28 Rule for Mentioning Competition in Copy

It is not wise to knock your competition in copy. The space saved might be better used to tell how good your own offer is. If you must point up the shortcomings of a competitive product, do it by pointing out your offer's benefits or features that are lacking in the competition. This will not direct your reader to your competitor, and those who know the competing product will get the message.

12:29   Key Response Words in Direct Mail Copy

According to John Kremer, author of numerous books on marketing, these are among the most effective words in direct mail copy: *You, Your, Free, New, Bonus, Satisfaction Guaranteed, Order Now,* and *Success.*

12:30   Illuminating Words Will Make Your Copy Come Alive

Even without illustrative matter, as a rule, a few well-chosen words can help make your copy come alive. For example *lemon yellow* instead of *yellow; rust-resistant steel* instead of *steel; lushly illustrated* instead of *illustrated; saves you time and work* instead of a word like *useful.*

12:31   Cautionary Rule for Lifting Another's Copy

Do not lift or adapt someone else's copy for your promotion unless you are convinced that it is entirely appropriate for your type of offer.

12:32   Copywriting Sequence for Tough Assignment

Facing a difficult copy assignment for a direct mail campaign? You'll find the task easier if you do the simpler parts first, such as order form or contents. This will usually put you in a better frame of mind for creating the more difficult copy.

12:33   Way to Improve Your Best Copy Effort

"When you write a piece of copy, put it aside and read it over the next day. You will almost always be able to improve it." So says John Caples, one of the most distinguished advertising writers of this century, in *How to Make Your Advertising Make Money,* 1983.

12:34   Making Deadline When You Lack Information

When you're close to a copy deadline and you lack essential data, as a rule, it's best to write what you have and have your copy corrected, revised, or enhanced by a knowledgeable authority or expert on the subject.

12:35 Good Copywriting Idea Source

As a rule, you will find some of the best examples of good direct mail copy in the promotional mailings of the major business and professional book publishers. A single book purchase will often put you on a publisher's mailing list (at least in the subject area of the book purchased) for at least three years and, often, publishers exchange or rent their lists to other publishers for their direct mail offerings.

12:36 Improving Existing Mailing Package

As a rule, says Judy Hannah Weiss, a highly regarded circulation promotion copy pro, "Start fresh. Don't study what you're trying to beat....Think about the product and the audience and write from that. Then, after you've taken your best stab at it, go back and take a close look at the existing control to see if there's anything you missed." (In *Who's Mailing What!* January 1994)

12:37 Eliminating "Writer's Block"

As a rule, you are likely to be a better copywriter if you write more and later trim your copy down to fit than if you just stare at a blank sheet of paper and wait for the right words to come to you. Whatever the writing assignment, any words are better than no words. Any words will help you get your creative juices flowing. Chances are, by your second or third paragraph, your thoughts will begin to focus and you can zero in on your topic from then on.

12:38 Way to Get Started Writing Mail-Order Copy

As a rule, if you're new at writing mail-order copy, start with a classified ad in a publication mail-order section. If the response is substantial, that effort can turn you on to the power of writing effective selling copy like nothing else. If the response is modest, you at least get the feeling of making your words stir people to action.

12:39 Where to Learn About Writing Mail-Order Catalog Copy

If you're a beginner at writing mail-order catalog copy, you'll learn quicker by examining the copy in a number of the more than 10,000

mail-order catalogs issued regularly. As a rule, good mail-order catalog copy contains sufficient detail to help the reader reach a buying
decision and should combine fact with emotional appeal.

12:40   Time-Tested Old Rule for Mail-Order Copy Still Prevails

"A well established rule in mail-order copy," commented George P.
Metzger in his classic 1926 book *Copy*, "is that if frame of mind can be
engaged it can be held. If the reader is interested at all, he is eager for
details and will dig through any amount of 5½ point solid till he
reaches 'do it at once.'"

12:41   Pricing Freelance Copy Services

When engaging a freelance copywriter, as a rule, it's best to negotiate
a price in advance. Prices tend to be better when freelancers are not
backed up with work from other clients.

12:42   Working With Freelance Copywriters

As a rule, when working with freelancers, you will get a better job if
you furnish a rough layout with each copy assignment.

12:43   Evaluating Freelance Copy Services

When considering a freelance copywriter, as a rule, it's a good idea to
look at samples of his or her previous work—preferably for a related
product or service. You might also want to contact some of the copywriter's other clients for references.

12:44   Rule for Selecting a Writer

In *Direct Marketing Success* (1985), Freeman Gosden says "never hire a
writer without selling experience....I mean door-to-door, retail, telephone, or whatever....it must be one-to-one and with a large number
of people."

13

Testimonials, Endorsements, and Review Quotes

The reader finds it easier to believe the endorsement of a fellow consumer than the puffery of an anonymous copywriter.
—DAVID OGILVY
Confessions of an Advertising Man, 1963

13:01　Best Way to Build Confidence in Ad Claims

As a rule, testimonials from reliable or believable sources are one of the best ways to build confidence in advertising claims.

13:02　Contribution of Testimonial in Direct Mail

A testimonial gives proof of the quality, reliability, or benefit of a mail offer. If the individual giving the testimonial can be believed, the testimonial can be a powerful sales stimulant.

13:03　Testimonial Relationship Rule

The testimonial included in any mail offer should be closely tied to the interests of the audience to which it is directed. The reason: People tend to believe other people like themselves more readily than unsubstantiated advertising claims. For example: A testimonial from a doctor for medical audiences (or consumers for a health product); from an academic for a scholarly audience (prestigiously connected if possible); from a librarian to a library audience, etc.

13:04   Best Place to Insert a Testimonial

As a rule, a testimonial belongs on the flier or brochure in support of the claimed benefits.

13:05   Testimonial as Envelope Teaser Copy

A testimonial that describes or supports a main benefit will be far more effective as envelope teaser copy than a similar claim on an envelope by itself.

13:06   Using Testimonial as Substitute for Copy

When an outstanding testimonial describes a benefit better than a copywriter could, it is better to use the testimonial instead of written copy. It will carry more authority and, consequently, be more believable.

13:07   Using Lengthy Review Quote as Book Copy

In mail promotions offering scientific, technical, professional and business books, as a rule, a quote from a favorable lengthy review can often replace written copy with great effectiveness.

13:08   Length Rule for Quotes and Testimonials

As a rule, if a review quote or testimonial is well targeted to the readership, a longer quote is more effective than a shorter one.

13:09   Adding Testimonials to Successful Promotions

As a rule, you can improve response from a successful promotional effort by inserting testimonials from satisfied buyers in rollouts or reruns of the same promotion.

13:10 Source Rule for Review Quotes and Testimonials

Quotes from reviews and testimonials should always include sufficient identification to establish the credibility of the quote. For books and periodicals, the name of the review medium will suffice. For a scholarly quote, the professor's name should also include institutional affiliation and, if possible, department.

13:11 Using Photo With Testimonial

As a rule, a testimonial is stronger when accompanied by a photograph of the testimonial giver.

13:12 Testimonials Are No Substitute for Facts

Never use testimonials as a substitute for facts. People want information first, then the testimony as to its benefit, value, or reliability. Without the accompanying facts, testimonials may be viewed as shallow or unimportant.

13:13 Using Indirect Testimonials: They're Free and They Sell

Testimonials do not have to be direct quotes to have powerful confidence-building and sales appeal. Often they can be indirect or implied and still pack a powerful sales punch. For example, a textbook publisher promoting a particular text can list names of leading universities which have adopted that book for their classrooms. The implication is clear, as it would be for companies promoting a product and then listing the Fortune 500 companies already using the product. In contrast to celebrity endorsements, these do not require permission, and you do not have to pay for them.

13:14 Avoiding Testimonials That Violate FTC Rules

A testimonial for a product that is reworded, presented out of context, or used after the endorser no longer believes the statement is in violation of FTC regulations.

14

Order Forms: Design, Content, Psychological Aspects

Spend 50 percent of your time designing your order form.

—RON GREENE AND JIM PERRY
Marketing Masters, 1993

14:01 Order Form Commitment Rule

Any wording on an order form that implies less commitment than the words *order form* will enhance its effectiveness. Some popular headings include *Free Trial Copy, Trial Subscription Certificate, Sample Offer, Free Examination Requisition, Free Copy Reservation.*

14:02 Top Direct Mail Writer Avoids "Forms"

"I don't talk about Application *Forms* or Order *Forms* or Reply *Forms*," says British direct mail star John Fraser-Robinson. "I send Order Coupons. Priority Acceptance Slips. Enrollment Applications. Information Requests. Bonus Vouchers. Free Examination Offers. Privilege Invitations." (In [Andrews] *The Post Office Direct Mail Handbook,* 1984)

14:03   Feature or Benefit on Order Form

Given a choice between a feature and a benefit on the order form, it is best to opt for the benefit. It is always better to tell what the offer will do for the reader than what the offer is.

14:04   Repetition of Order Form 800 Number

As a rule, an 800 number that appears on an order form for response vehicle should also appear in the main body of the mail promotion to achieve its true potential.

14:05   Order Form Appearance Rule

An order form that looks too valuable to throw away will receive more attention than a routinely conceived one.

14:06   Preventing Shipping Errors

As many people have writing that is difficult or in some cases almost impossible to distinguish, as a rule, you can save much time and prevent shipping errors by adding these two words to every order form and coupon: *Please Print.*

14:07   Restating Offer on Order Form

As a rule, you should restate the essentials of your mail offer on the order form. It will serve as a reminder of what you told the reader in the letter and/or brochure.

14:08   Advertiser's Name and Address Rule

An order form should always include the name and address of the mailer. It will thus provide sufficient information should the rest of the mailing package be mislaid or discarded.

14:09   Restatement of Guarantee on Order Form

If you offer any kind of guarantee in your copy, as a rule, restate the guarantee on the order form or reply card to reassure the buyer that he or she is making a wise ordering decision.

14:10   Rule for Dated Signature on Order Form

Any order form involving shipment of merchandise should include a line for signature and date. Many people believe that a signature constitutes a contract. Further, when the order is from a large organization, the signature provides a point of reference.

14:11   Value of Order Form Signature

As a rule, a dated signature on an order form can be used to offer proof that a respondent placed the order should a claim arise that the merchandise was never ordered.

14:12   Residence Mailing Rule

When designing a coupon or order form for a residence mailing, always include a space for apartment number on the same line as street address. Third-class mail to multiple-dwelling addresses that lacks an apartment number often goes undelivered.

14:13   Offer Expiration Date on Order Form

As a rule, any order form containing prices or a special offer should also include an expiration or cutoff date.

14:14   Order Form Clarity Rule

Always check before printing to ensure that the order form is so worded that it provides all the information necessary to adequately identify both the merchandise being ordered and the customer.

14:15   Order Stability: Mail Orders Versus Telephone Orders

As a rule, orders received in the mail result in fewer merchandise returns than orders placed through 800 telephone numbers. The reason: A filled-in order reflects a thought-out purchase. A phone order may have resulted from impulse and the buyer may have second thoughts.

14:16   Rule for Postage and Handling Charges

The postage and handling charges you show on an order form should reflect as accurately as practicable the actual costs incurred. This is

Article 12 in the guidelines of the DMA Committee on Ethical Business Practices.

14:17   Rule for Increasing Prepaid Orders

When an order form includes a shipping and handling charge, you can substantially increase prepayments by offering free shipping with cash orders.

14:18   Allowing Space on Order Form for Customer's Telephone Number

If your order form includes two or more checkoff options, there is always a chance that none will be checked off. As a rule, when there are several ordering options always include a space for telephone number so you can reach the customer for clarification in case of problems or questions.

14:19   Purchase Order Number on Order Form

When offering a high-ticket item with a coupon order form in business mailings, it is usually a good idea to include a space on the order form for a purchase order number. This permits the order to be billed to the company or organization while correctly charging it to the individual or department that placed the order.

14:20   Credit Card Versus Check Payment

When considering order form payment options, it is worth noting that, as a rule, a credit card payment is safer than payment by personal check.

14:21   Mailer's Telephone Number on Order Form

When an order form includes multiple ordering options or ordering instructions that may raise questions, as a rule, the mailer should include a telephone number that can be called for help in completing the order.

14:22   Credit Card Relationship to Order Size

As a rule, says Bob Stone, "The average credit card order is at least 15% bigger than a cash order." (In *Successful Direct Marketing Methods*, 1994)

14:23   Best Credit Cards for Mail Order

If you plan to offer a credit card payment option on your order form, as a rule, you can get by with the two most widely held cards, Visa and MasterCard. Visa, the larger of the two, had 149.5 million cardholders in 1993, compared with 99.5 million for MasterCard and 24.3 million for American Express. (Sources: *The Wall Street Journal,* September 13, 1993, and *Business Week,* September 27, 1993)

14:24   Good Consumer Market Segments for Credit Cards

Certain segments of the consumer market are better prospects for credit card payment. Among the well-off, for example, the rate of credit card payment goes up as income level rises. Among college students, credit cards are a favored form of payment (and their pay-up rate is higher than for the general public). Among older people, credit cards are a favored form of payment (one survey of people over the age of 60 showed 56 percent favored payment by credit card over cash and check).

14:25   Use of Multiple Order Forms in Business Mailings

Even when your mail package includes an order form, as a rule, you can increase response by up to 10 percent in most business mailings by including an additional order form on the flier or brochure.

14:26   Use of Fax Numbers in Business Mailings

As a rule, a fax number is a useful ordering vehicle in any business-to-business promotion. Most businesses have fax facilities, and four out of five business-to-business catalogers accept orders sent this way. By contrast, a fax number is of little value in consumer offers; most homes have no fax facilities.

15

Response Devices: Classifications, Formats, Postage

The reply form is probably the most important enclosure in a direct mail package. It is "Where the Action is!" Therefore keep it simple and spell out the terms of the offer in easily understood language.

—VIRGIL ANGERMAN
In McLean, The Basics of Copy, 1975

15:01 Response Device Priority in Direct Mail Package

"Design the response device first," says James Lumley. "It can be a guideline in creating the other components and it makes referring to it in the letter and brochure easier." (In *Sell It by Mail*, 1986)

15:02 Effect of Color in Response Devices

As a rule, anything that sets off a response device from the rest of the mailing package will significantly increase response.

15:03   Benefit of Separate Response Device

A separate response device will be considerably more effective than one that has to be cut or torn apart from another enclosure.

15:04   Credit Card Option Suppresses Free Trial Response

On a free trial offer, a response device will draw about 15 percent fewer responses when a credit card payment option is included.

15:05   Order Form Versus Order Card

Use an *order form* when you want information leading to an order which the responder must mail back, with or without prepayment, in an envelope. Use an *order card* when you solicit orders by mail without prepayment.

15:06   Business Reply Mail Defined by Postal Service

As a rule, the word *Business* appended to *Reply Card* or *Reply Envelope* means Business Reply Mail. The U.S. Postal Service identifies Business Reply Mail as matter "that may be mailed without prepayment of postage, with fees collected when the mail is delivered to the addressee."

15:07   Why It Pays to Use Postage-Paid Response

A buying decision from a mail offer often may fail to materialize for lack of a postage stamp immediately at hand. As a rule, a postage-paid reply card or envelope will produce a higher rate of response and save orders that might otherwise have been lost.

15:08   Postage Payment as Screening Device

When building a prospect list through an offer of free literature, a premium, or a catalog, as a rule, you will be able to screen out casual or less-than-serious inquirers if you require the responder to pay the return postage on the response device.

15:09   When Response Vehicles Need Not Be Postpaid

As a rule, a postpaid response vehicle—card or envelope—is not necessary when a mailing is designed to generate orders from libraries, businesses, or institutions that use purchase orders.

15:10   Credit Card Pay Option as Aid to Prepaid Response

When an offer requires prepayment on the response device, you will, as a rule, improve dollar response by 15 to 25 percent by offering a credit card payment option.

15:11   Need for Instructions With Complicated Response

When a consumer offer invites a variety of response options, as a rule, it's best to provide step-by-step precise instructions that will make response action completely understandable.

15:12   Unique, Workable Type of Response Device

Response devices fall into four standard classifications: reply card, return envelope, coupon, or order form. However, for years some medical publishers have been using a unique type of response device that has been working extremely well. It's a sheet of perforated, gum-backed stamps, much like postage stamps. Each stamp has a recognizable book cover, together with author name and price. To order a book, the respondent removes the stamp and mails it back affixed to a paper bearing name and address. Stamps work with as few as one stamp and as many as 120 on a sheet. They are produced by Specialty Printers of America in New York City.

16

Return Envelope Usage Tips

Don't just give your prospects your
address....Make ordering as easy as
possible....Give your prospects an addressed
postage-paid envelope.
                    —TED NICHOLAS
              The Golden Mailbox, 1992

16:01 Reply Envelope Increases Cash With Order

"As a rule," says Bob Stone, "a reply envelope increases cash with order responses." (In *Successful Direct Marketing Methods*, 1994)

16:02 Reply Envelope Rule

Use a reply envelope rather than a return card when you ask for prepayment, when the offer is of a private nature, or when the response device asks personal questions.

16:03 An Important Benefit of Reply Envelope

One of the prime benefits of a return envelope is confidentiality. "You'd be surprised," says John Fraser-Robinson, one of Britain's top direct mail writers, "how often an apparently insensitive subject can be touchy enough for people to shun the use of a postpaid reply card when they'd have been happy to reply given an envelope." (In [Andrews] *The Post Office Direct Mail Handbook,* 1984)

16:04 When Business Reply Envelope Is Essential

If your order form calls for payment or credit card number, as a rule, you should enclose a business reply envelope to ensure confidentiality of the information or enclosure. Many mail order respondents will not supply a credit card number on an open return postcard.

16:05 Reply Envelope Identifiers

As a rule, the two most readily recognized aspects of a reply envelope are its size and its color.

16:06 Reply Envelopes by Other Names

As a rule, when a mailer wants the responder to pay the return postage, a *reply envelope* is supplied. When the mailer agrees to pay return postage, a *business reply envelope* is used. Some other terms used by mailers for reply envelopes are *return envelopes, self-addressed envelopes,* and *response envelopes.*

16:07 Mailings That Work Best With Postpaid Envelopes

As a rule, the postpaid business envelope is most effective when used with mailings to individuals at their home addresses. The need for a postpaid return envelope diminishes in mailings to business addresses, since respondents to business offers are more likely to enclose orders in their own business envelopes.

16:08 Business Reply Envelopes: Favored Colors

As a rule, large mailers who use colored business reply envelopes favor these three colors: light blue, pale green, and pale yellow.

16:09   Response Envelope Color as Message

You can sometimes use the color of a reply envelope to add meaning to the purpose of a mailing. A red envelope, for example, might be used with a "hot" offer or one with a short expiration date. Caution should be taken to avoid dark-colored papers that offer poor contrast with printed return addresses.

16:10   Best-Size Return Envelope for Wide Order Forms

As a rule, when considering a return envelope to accompany an order form that is the full $8\frac{1}{2}$-inch width of a normal-size letterhead, a No. 9 envelope (dimensions: $3\frac{7}{8}'' \times 8\frac{7}{8}''$) is your best choice. This size fits into a standard No. 10 mailing envelope and does not require folding of the order form. Smaller envelopes are also less convenient to handle.

17
Reply Card Usage Tips

*As a rule, the easier a card is to return, the
more cards will be returned.*
—JOHN D. YECK AND JOHN T. MAGUIRE
Planning and Creating Better Direct Mail,
1961

17:01 Reply Card Rule

The reply card is often the only part of a mail offer retained for later
reference. Therefore, it pays to repeat the benefits and essentials of an
offer on the card so that it will serve as a later reminder.

17:02 Reply Cards for Special Offers

As a rule, the reply card is one of the best places to present a special
offer or an order-increasing incentive. Magazine promotions often
increase subscription terms by tacking reduced-price longer-term subscription incentives on to subscription promotion reply cards.

17:03 What a Reply Card Must Say and Accomplish

A typical reply card must state in the prospect's language and from the
prospect's point of view that the proposition in your copy was convinc-
ing and believable enough to persuade him or her to send back the card.

17:04   Value of Customer Name on Reply Card

A reply card on which the recipient's name and address is already affixed is more effective than one which requires the recipient to print or write a name and address.

17:05   Reply Card Advantage Over Reply Envelope

As a rule, if your mail offer does not call for payment, use a business reply card rather than a business reply envelope. For some people, the sight of an envelope suggests payment of some kind is anticipated and tends to suppress response.

17:06   Reply Card Postage Rule

Postage-paid reply cards bring a higher response than those requiring a postage stamp. However, as a rule, the quality of response on inquiry cards is much higher when the prospect indicates seriousness by paying the return postage.

17:07   Value of Second Reply Card to Consumers

As a rule, response will not increase to a profitable degree when a catalog or literature offer is made to consumers and a second reply card is included with the mailing.

17:08   Reply Card With Receipt Stub

As a rule, a reply card with a receipt stub will usually draw better response than a reply card with no stub.

17:09   Credit Card Information on Reply Card

Never ask for credit card information on a business reply card. It is an open invitation to fraud and is virtually certain to curtail response.

17:10   Name and Address on Reply Card

As a rule, the name and address portion of a reply card should always be on the same side of the card as the selling message, so as to invite a logical reaction to the adjacent copy.

17:11   Reply Card Color Preferences

In color tests made as part of a catalog offer to rural households, blue and pink reply cards outpulled six other colors, with buff and yellow being the least responsive.

18

Guarantees: Importance, Content, Structure

It is a practically unbreakable rule in mail order that you must guarantee satisfaction or money back.
—JULIAN L. SIMON
How to Start and Operate a Mail-Order Business, 1993

18:01   Guarantee Importance Rule

A strong guarantee is a necessity in all direct mail selling. Every piece in your offer should stress its risk-free nature, since you are asking someone to buy an unseen product from an out-of-sight location.

18:02   Clarity Rule in Mail Offer Guarantees

As a rule, a guarantee should be the clearest, most understandable part of a mail offer. It should avoid conditions in fine print or obscure wording that can be misinterpreted and pose a danger signal to ordering risk.

18:03   Guarantee-Strength Rule

The less you are known to the mail recipient, the stronger the risk-free nature of your offer must be. However, for any audience, a stronger guarantee invariably will work better than a weaker one.

18:04   Length of Guarantee Rule

When a product is designed for very long use, or will not deteriorate in quality or value over time, you can strengthen any offer by extending the guarantee over a longer period of time.

18:05   Risk in Liberal Guarantees

As a rule, for bona fide offers, a strong guarantee will increase sales far in excess of the small number of buyers who ultimately may take advantage of it.

18:06   Matching-Guarantee-to-Offer Rule

The best guarantee is one closely matched to the nature of the product or service. For example: a guaranteed buyback at purchase price of a collectible; a money-back guarantee over a long period for a very durable product; or products that offer specified savings, a money-back guarantee if the product does not meet the specified saving over a stated time period.

18:07   Strongest and Weakest Guarantee Words

Among the strongest and most effective guarantee words: *unconditionally guaranteed, ironclad money-back guarantee, no-risk guarantee, 100 percent satisfaction guaranteed, lifetime guarantee, double your money back, no-questions-asked guarantee.* Some other widely used, but less effective guarantees, use such favored wordings as: *money-back guarantee, satisfaction guaranteed or your money back, complete refund if not satisfied.*

18:08   Conditional Guarantees

As a rule, conditional guarantees are not as effective as unlimited guarantees. However, where a conditional guarantee is necessary, a 30-day examination period usually will produce a better response than a 15-day examination period.

18:09   Ultimate in Guarantees: L. L. Bean Sets Example

Unquestionably the ultimate in risk-free guarantees is the one offered by L. L. Bean in its Christmas 1993 catalog: "Our products are guaranteed to give 100% satisfaction in every way. Return anything purchased from us if it proves otherwise. We will replace it, refund your purchase price, or credit your credit card, as you wish. We do not want you to have anything from L. L. Bean that is not completely satisfactory."

18:10   Most Popular Offer for Serial Guarantee

As a rule, the most popular guarantee for magazines or products or services sold serially is the right to cancel at any time without further obligation. When a prepayment is made, as in a prepaid subscription, repayment should be offered for any unused portion of the subscription.

18:11   Third-Party Guarantees

As a rule, a third-party guarantee can often strengthen a mailer's own guarantee. The Good Housekeeping seal of approval has been used often to strengthen product guarantees. And Publishers Clearing House in 1993 was offering four times the difference for any magazine subscription that could be bought from the publisher or elsewhere for less.

18:12   Guarantee as Clue to Customer Complaints

When complaints and customer correspondence are unusually heavy, look to the wording in your offer's guarantee. It may be that the guarantee is badly worded, or presented in a complicated manner that is not fully understood.

18:13   Making Guarantee Look Important

As a rule, your guarantee will make a much stronger impression if it is framed in an official-looking certificate border. So says Jim Kobs in *Profitable Direct Marketing*, 1992.

18:14   What Guarantee Should Include—DMA Guideline

Under the Direct Marketing Association's guidelines for ethical business practice, a guarantee should set forth terms and conditions in full in the promotion or the promotion should state how the consumer can get a copy. It should also clearly state the name and address of the guarantor and the duration of the guarantee.

19

Timing and Seasonality in Direct Mail Promotion

Seasonality is a priority subject in direct mail....For results-oriented marketers, it is important to recognize the electricity of direct mail which impacts "when to mail" as much as "what to mail and to whom."

—BOB STONE
Successful Direct Marketing Methods, 1994

19:01 Poorest Delivery Days for Consumer Mailings

As a rule, mail delivered to consumers on Saturdays and Mondays will have the poorest response rate.

19:02 Best Days for Mail Delivery

In discussions of best and worst mailing days, various direct mail practitioners generally believe that Tuesday is the most effective mail delivery day, with Wednesday second best, and Thursday, third best.

19:03 Avoiding a Monday Mail Delivery

As a rule, a bulk third-class mailing has a lesser chance of Monday delivery if mailed on Monday, Tuesday, or Friday.

19:04 Controlling Mail Delivery Day

When striving to avoid a Monday delivery, as a rule, you can better control a mail delivery day with first-class mail than with bulk third class.

19:05 Primary Direct Response Seasonal Patterns

Most direct response marketers do their big test mailings in September, as a rule, and roll out with their biggest mailings in January.

19:06 Mail Timing Rule for General Offers

As a rule, the best time to mail is when there is a need for your type of offer. If you offer products with general appeal and ones that are not tied to any particular season or seasons, you can mail effectively any time of the year.

19:07 Mail Timing Rule for Seasonal Offers

The best time to make a mail offer on a seasonal product or service is about two months before the product or service is needed. Many mailers use three months for the Christmas season because of heavier competition.

19:08 Bad Timing for Others May Be Best Time for You

No matter what you have learned about seasonality, you can never be sure for your type of offer until you have tried both the "bad" and the known good periods or seasons. Often, because your competitors may stay out of the mails during known bad seasons, this may be just the right time for a mailing—when there is less mail clutter from the competition.

19:09   Top Month for Technical, Professional Areas

As a rule, January is the best mailing month for most areas of technical and professional activity.

19:10   Consumer Seasonality Response Patterns

As a general rule, the best months for consumer offers, according to some mailers, are January, then February. The weakest month is June.

19:11   Timing for Mail to Tax Lawyers and Accountants

As a rule, the best time to test mailings to tax lawyers and accountants is right after Labor Day, with rollout in November. If you plan to mail again, mail no later than January to mid-February. March and April are poor response months for these two categories of professionals.

19:12   Seasonality for Educational Book Offers

If you mail book offers to educators, the ideal seasonal patterns for college faculty are mid-fall for the spring semester, and spring for the fall semester. For mailings to high school teachers, the first three months of the year are the decision-making months for the upcoming fiscal year.

19:13   Ideal Time for Library Promotions

As a rule, mail promotions to libraries tend to work better in July than in any other month. The reason: For most of them, it's the start of their fiscal year and they have ample funds available.

19:14   Poorest Time for Library Promotions

As a rule, late May and June are the poorest times to mail to libraries. The reason: Most library decision-makers are preparing to leave for, or are attending, the large national library conventions, such as the American Library Association meeting, or the Special Libraries Association meeting, etc.

19:15   Critical Time for Periodical Offers

In periodical subscription offers, the renewal effort is more critical than a new subscriber effort. The reason: New subscribers are often attracted by premiums or special offers, both of which are lacking for the second year.

19:16   Timing Related to Impending Price Increase

As a rule, the best time to promote a product is just prior to a price increase. For the promotion to be effective, the mailing should show the new price, and the date that it will go into effect.

20

Response Patterns in Direct Mail Promotion

There are times when most mailers should not test or even send out their regular mailings. These include just ahead or after a deadline for filing tax forms...just before or after major holidays, including Christmas...just before or after key elections.

—ED MCLEAN
The Basics of Testing, 1978

20:01　Format Influences on Response Pattern

As a rule, the format that produces the quickest response is the solo or single-item mail offer, with card packs second fastest, and catalogs slowest.

20:02　Simple Rule for Direct Mail Response

All other factors being equal, the easier you make it for someone to respond, the greater the response.

20:03　Starting Date for Campaign Tracking

For campaign tracking purposes, savvy direct marketers do not track campaigns from the mailing date or from the time the first one or two replies trickle in. As a rule, they prefer to start response tracking from the first day or two that a reasonably good number of responses are received.

20:04   Heaviest Single Day's Response From Mailing

As a rule, says Herschell Gordon Lewis, a mail-order expert, you can expect the heaviest single day's response to a mailing on the second Monday after the first order arrives. (In *More Than You Ever Wanted to Know About Mail Order Advertising*, 1983)

20:05   The Half-Life Formula for Response Estimating

The *half-life formula* is a vehicle many mailers use to estimate total response early in a mail campaign by studying total response from a like previous campaign. By determining at what point the first half of that response was received, the mailer takes the response for a like period in a subsequent mailing and doubles it to arrive at an estimated total response for the campaign.

20:06   Quality of Response Rule

As a rule, quality of response is more important than quantity of response. A free examination offer with a 1.2 percent response and a 90 percent payup rate is more profitable than a 2 percent response with a 50 percent payup rate.

20:07   Old Response Rule Now Antiquated

In the early days of direct mail, beginners were taught to expect a 2 percent return for a mailing to be successful. As direct marketing has evolved since the end of World War II, the 2 percent figure has become meaningless. In the current era, any response that is profitable is considered a good response.

20:08   ZIP Code Clustering Rule

As a rule, some direct marketers will continually review ZIP Codes that have produced favorable responses and remail on a selective basis only to high-response ZIP Codes for a particular product or offer.

20:09   Consumer Circulation Promotions

As a rule, a consumer circulation promotion mailed in January will draw about twice the response as the same effort mailed in June.

20:10   Buying Patterns for Reference Annuals

When former buyers fail to reorder references and directories that are published annually, as a rule, they are excellent prospects for the edition that follows. Many buyers and libraries order every other edition.

20:11   Response Variance From Free Exam Versus Prepayment

As a rule, the response will be at least twice as great from an offer of free examination as it will from an offer requiring some form of prepayment.

20:12   Response Estimating Rule for Solo Mail Campaign

As a rule, about half the replies from a solo mail campaign will be received about three weeks after the first meaningful response, with the remainder coming in during the following six to nine weeks.

20:13   Rule for Follow-Up Mailings to Professionals

As a rule, a follow-up mailing to a professional audience can be nearly as successful as the first mailing. Bear in mind that 98 or 99 recipients of the first mailing who did not respond will have been exposed to the offer prior to the second mailing.

20:14   Response from Business and Industrial Libraries

There is no recognizable response pattern in mail offers to business and industrial libraries. As a rule, librarians in such libraries respond to mail offers based on interest and relationship to collection irrespective of the timing.

20:15 How Many Orders per Thousand to Expect

How many orders per thousand should you expect from a direct mail effort? Because of the many variables involved, there can be no correct answer to that question. The closest answer is: "How many orders must you get to break even?"

20:16 Ignore Response Rate—Concentrate on Orders

"Ignore response rates" say Ron Greene and partner Jim Perry of Devon Direct, a top-ranking ad firm. "Just concentrate on cost per order." (In *Marketing Masters*, 1993)

20:17 When Response Rate Points to Project— Not List

If a badly conceived promotion produces an extremely poor response, and you multiply that response by 10 and the answer is still not good, you'd best drop the entire project and not waste any more time or effort on it.

20:18 Conversion Rate of Bingo Card Inquiries

Business and trade magazines sometimes place a reader service number under each advertisement and invite readers to circle a corresponding number on a bound-in postpaid reply card, called (in the trade) a *Bingo card*. Names and addresses of inquirers are forwarded to the advertisers for whom intended. As a rule, the mail-order sales conversion rate from such inquiries is extremely poor.

21

Postage and Mail Delivery Guidelines

If you're planning to mail at the third class bulk rate, you should know that such mail must contain a general message aimed at all who receive it, rather than a personal message aimed at a particular individual...and it must be for domestic delivery only.

—U.S. POSTAL SERVICE
Third Class Mail Preparation Manual,
USPS, 1991

21:01   Ranking of Postage Effectiveness

As a rule, the most-effective to least-effective ways to use postage in direct mail promotion are, in order: (1) multiple stamps, (2) single commemorative stamps, (3) single definitive stamp, (4) precancelled stamp, (5) postage meter impression, (6) printed indicia.

21:02   Metered Third-Class Versus Metered First-Class Mail

As a rule, for most promotional mailings, metered third-class postage will produce the same response per 100 pieces delivered as metered first-class postage. Reason: There is little difference in appearance between a third-class and a first-class meter imprint, and most recipients do not bother to look at metered imprints.

21:03 Metered Mail Versus Printed Postal Indicia

A metered postage mailing will outperform one with a printed postal indicia. Reason: A printed indicia invariably proclaims itself to be advertising mail, and a good percentage of advertising mail is discarded unopened.

21:04 Bulk Third-Class Message Requirement

No matter how personalized its content, a mailing must contain a general message aimed at all who receive it to qualify for the bulk third-class rate.

21:05 Way to Increase Third-Class Deliveries

As a rule, about one out of twenty pieces of correctly addressed bulk third-class mail will not be delivered. However, when the same mail bears the endorsement "Forwarding and Return Postage Guaranteed" the ratio drops to one out of thirty-three pieces.

21:06 Postage Rule for Large-Size Envelopes

If you plan to mail in a 6- by 9-inch or a 9- by 12-inch envelope, the use of actual postage stamps, as a rule, will not materially affect the readability over use of a printed or metered postal indicia. The reason: Most mail recipients know that these sizes of envelopes usually carry promotional matter.

21:07 Reasons for Third-Class Nondelivery

As a rule, most third-class mail is undeliverable for either of these four reasons: (1) incorrect address because of a relocation, (2) incorrect ZIP Code, (3) missing directionals such as N for North, (4) missing or incorrect suite or apartment number.

21:08 Third-Class Mail to Apartment Houses

When third-class mail to an apartment house lacks an apartment number, it may be treated as mail of "no obvious value" unless there is a forwarding or return postage guarantee on the mail. The mail carrier is not required to search mailboxes for an apartment number to match a name.

21:09 Postage Weight Precaution for First-Class Mail

If you're planning a first-class mailing, it's a good idea to weigh a dummy using identical materials to what you plan to print and mail to ensure that the printed piece with envelope will weigh under one ounce.

21:10 How First-Class Mail Can Pay for Itself

As a rule, the extra cost of postage for a first-class mailing to a business list will pay for itself through a higher percentage of delivery and recognition of its first-class status as being important mail.

21:11 First-Class Mail for Long-Unused List

When a list has been unused for a long period of time, as a rule, you'll get a much higher percentage of delivery with first-class mail, since first class is forwardable for up to a year after address change.

21:12 Delivery Rate: First-Class Versus Third-Class Mail

Not all third-class mail is delivered, for various reasons. As a rule, a higher percentage of any mailing will be delivered if sent by first-class mail than if sent by third-class mail.

21:13 Postage-Affixed First-Class Versus Metered Third-Class Mail

If you plan to mail first class in a No. 10 envelope, your offer will have a higher response if you use an actual stamp on the envelope instead of metered first-class postage.

21:14 Postage-Affixed Third-Class Versus Metered Third-Class Mail

As a rule, when mailing to outside or rented lists, there is little difference in response rates between postage-affixed first-class mail and metered third-class mail.

21:15 Mail-Date Spacing of Similar Lists

When a number of rental lists are known to have quantities of the same names, simultaneous multiple deliveries can be avoided, as a rule, if the mailing dates of the various lists are spaced several days to a week apart.

21:16 U.S. Postal Delivery Times

The U.S. Postal Service aims for up to three days for delivery of first-class mail, up to ten days for delivery of third-class mail. However, a mailer has no way of knowing for sure when a piece of mail will be delivered.

21:17 Heaviest Days and Week for Mail Deliveries

As a rule, heaviest mail delivery days are Wednesday, Thursday, and Friday. Heaviest mail delivery week is the first week of the month, when bills usually arrive.

21:18 Getting Postage Advance to Letter Shop

A letter shop or mailing house will usually require postage in advance of any mailing. Be sure to allow sufficient time for providing postage advance when planning a mailing on a short schedule.

21:19 Rule for Weighing Direct Mail Dummy

As a rule, when estimating the postage weight of a dummy direct mail package, it is a good idea to include a dime and a paper clip to account for the weight of the ink.

21:20 Way to Control Delivery Date on Big Mailings

If you're planning a large mailing that may have to be delivered to the post office in batches over several days, you can synchronize delivery times more evenly if you mail to the most distant deliver points first and the closest points last. (Source: Michael Spates, U.S. Postal Service, Marketing Department)

21:21   Full Identification With Nonprofit Postage

When mailing at the special nonprofit organization postage rate, the return address must show mailer's complete name and address exactly as it appears on the nonprofit mailing authorization.

21:22   Clearing Unconventional Mail With Post Office

If you plan a mailing in an unconventional size or format, make sure to clear it with the U.S. Postal Service prior to printing to ensure that it conforms to postal regulations and is mailable in the way planned.

21:23   Outgoing Postage: When Due at Post Office

Postage should be on deposit in a post office account before a mailing is brought to the post office. However, when you mail using a printed postal indicia, the money need not be paid until the mail is delivered to the post office.

21:24   Ensuring Prompt Reply-Mail Deliveries

Before a mail campaign, the postage account at the post office should be checked to ensure it has sufficient funds for the campaign's incoming reply mail postage. If funds are insufficient in the account, incoming mail will be held up.

21:25   Establishing Mailing Date With Bulk Third-Class Mail

As a rule, the date supplied by the letter shop is not the actual date of a bulk third-class mailing. The true mail date is the one on the postal receipt issued and signed by a postal employee. The postmark on that receipt bears the date the mail was released by the postal acceptance unit for dispatch.

21:26   Limitations of Bulk-Mailing Permit

A bulk-mailing permit enables mailing only at the post office where the permit is held and then only if delivered to the bulk-mail acceptance unit during operating hours.

21:27   Checking on When and How Mail Was Delivered

The best way to get a positive check on *if* and *when* a mailing was delivered and in what condition, is through the use of a mail monitoring service. A monitoring service provides the mailer with an individual identifiable decoy name and address in one or more cities which you add to your mailing list. When the piece in your mailing is delivered, the monitoring service's agent returns it to you by first-class mail, unopened. Such monitoring also alerts you to unauthorized use of your list.

21:28   Warning on Mailing "Overs" With Postal Indicia Imprint

You are breaking the law if you distribute any mailing piece with a printed postal indicia on it. Federal law says only the U.S. Postal Service can distribute mail bearing a printed postal indicia.

22

Budgeting Tips for Direct Mail

Don't paint yourself into a corner with your direct marketing budget....Always allow for contingencies, and then allow for slippage within slippage.

—BOB DAVIDSON
*McGraw-Hill Publications Company,
in 1986 talk at Professional Publishers
Marketing Group Meeting*

22:01 Rule for Meeting or Beating Campaign Budgets

You'll come in on or under budget with most direct marketing campaigns if you add an additional sum on to the estimated cost at the outset to absorb cost overruns and unanticipated contingencies.

22:02 Budget Planning as Ingredient for Success

Careful budget planning and budget monitoring are essential prerequisites for any successful direct marketing enterprise. So advises Joseph Dunn in the *DMA Fact Book,* 1983.

22:03 Bulk of Promotion Budget to Target Market

As a rule, the bulk of any promotion budget should be directed to the target market. Only after target market potential has been exhausted should budgeted funds be spent on secondary and tertiary markets since these are the least cost-effective markets.

22:04 Budgeting for the "Echo Effect"

If yours is an established organization whose products are sold not only through your own mail efforts but also through retail stores and independent distributors, budgeting for direct-response promotions must factor in the hidden, indirect, or "echo effect" sales generated through these sales outlets. These "echo effect" sales can be as much as 12 to 20 times the response directly traceable to the original direct mail efforts.

22:05 Budgeting for "Lifetime Value" of Subscriptions

When budgeting for subscription products, whether periodicals or newsletters, it is important to bear in mind that the cost per order can be higher than the subscription price. That's because, as a rule, the true value of the order is income over the life of the subscription, and not just for the first year.

22:06 Promotion Budgeting for Subscription-Based Products

Promotion budgeting for subscription-based products should, as a rule, always take into account that selling more to existing customers is infinitely less costly than trying to find new ones.

22:07 Approaching a Large, Good List With Small Budget

When you find a large, good list for your offer but cannot make large mailings because of budget restrictions, as a rule, there are two readily workable approaches: (1) Mail to as many names as your budget will permit, starting with the lowest ZIP Codes. Then, as you are able to afford more later, just start with the next higher number. (2) Mail only to those states where you presently do the most business.

22:08   Rule for Estimating Value of Mail-Order Customers

How much can you afford to spend to get a new mail-order customer? A good yardstick is the "Simon Rule" (Julian L. Simon in *How to Start & Operate a Mail-Order Business*, 1987): (1) take a random sample of active and inactive customers, (2) add up amount of their total dollar purchases, (3) divide by total number of orders placed in the sample, and (4) multiply by the percentage representing your average profit margin.

22:09   Flexible Budgeting as Way to Build Customer Base

Once you have established the value of a new customer over time, your direct marketing budget should be sufficiently flexible to enable you to go after as many new customers as you can get at an acceptable cost.

23

Credit and
Collection Tips

No legal experience is more common to
marketers than bad-debt problems....One way
to buy "insurance" is to use a standard credit
card payment option....Then [the credit card
companies] absorb your bad debts after they
approve the orders.
—ROBERT J. POSCH
The Direct Marketer's Legal Adviser, 1993

23:01   Way to Reduce Bad Debt on Trial Orders

As a rule, you can reduce bad debt with free trial offers by requiring
orders to be dated and signed. Unsigned orders should be returned to
customers; about two-thirds will sign and return—an indication of
serious interest.

23:02   How to Make Collection Letter Pay
Dividends

As a rule, it is good business to offer a related item with the first collection letter for an unpaid purchase. Most mail-order buyers are honest people who forget to pay or misplace a bill and need a reminder.
They usually pay up with that letter.

23:03   Best Signature for Collection Letters

As a rule, a male name on a collection letter will have a greater impact than a female name.

23:04   Way to Improve Collection Letter Impact

A "Return Requested" notice on a collection letter has been found to have increased impact. So advises Rick Friedman, periodical circulation professional. Adds Friedman, "this wording makes the debtor feel he can't hide from you and that you know the letter was received."

23:05   Way to Improve Impact of Collection Series

As a rule, collection letters have more impact when copy, format, and envelopes are varied from one time to the next. Avoid form-letter appearance or duplication.

23:06   Collection of Bad Debt by Phone

When seeking collection of a bad debt by phone, as a rule, calls should be between 9 a.m. and 8 p.m. No mention should be made of the bad debt to anyone but the debtor. This is in compliance with federal debt collection practices.

23:07   How Writing on Order Can Cut Losses

As a rule, you can often cut your losses from bad debt by examining the writing on incoming orders. Watch for childish-appearing writing, nearly illegible writing, or orders written in pencil. Ask yourself if this is the kind of writing you might reasonably expect from the type of prospect to whom you sent your mailing.

23:08   Bad Debt a Fact of Life for Free Exam Offers

With business and professional free examination offers, there will always be a certain percentage of nonpayers. That percentage may vary greatly from one occupational group to another. Worst payers, generally, are small businessmen, people in real estate, and mail-order entrepreneurs. Best payers among professional occupations: scientists and engineers.

23:09   Way to Go When All Else Fails

When all else fails with your collection efforts, use the services of a professional collection agency. They cost you nothing. Payment is based on their successful results, and they use professional methods, confidential sources of information, and highly effective procedures.

23:10   Rule for Refunding Credit Balances

As a rule, credit balances over $1 must be refunded to customers after the lapse of a seven-month period to comply with federal regulations. (Credit balances under $1 may be written off.)

24

International Direct Mail: Planning and Distribution

International direct marketing is growing as more and more companies find out that good ideas, products, and marketing cross national borders without difficulty.
—PETER J. ROSENWALD
*In (Nash) The Direct Marketing
Handbook, 1984*

24:01 International Aspects of Successful Offers

As a rule, a direct mail offer that has worked well in domestic markets will work equally well to similar audiences in international markets.

24:02 Pricing in International Promotions

As a rule, international mail promotions will not encounter sales difficulty when prices are shown in U.S. currency.

24:03 English Language in International Promotions

International mail promotions for books, periodicals, and information services should be in the English language. Use of any other language may suggest to the recipient that the offer will be supplied in the language used.

24:04 Jargon in International Mail

When planning an international mailing, as a rule, it is a good idea to get someone not American-born to review your copy to ensure that it does not contain jargon that will not be understood by foreign readers.

24:05 Planning for Single Foreign-Country Mailings

If you're planning an active, continued mail campaign to a single foreign country, you're likely to be much more successful if you first obtain newspapers, magazines, and sample direct mail packages from that country and study them for guidelines and popular usage in that country. Then, before attempting a launch, get the opinion of a native of that country.

24:06 International Mail Response Device Rule

In international mail promotion, a separate response device will be as much as three times more effective than one which is attached.

24:07 Address-With-Name Rule in International Mail

Including a person's name in the return address will improve response in international mail promotions.

24:08 Response in International Library Mail

It is not necessary to include a reply card in international library promotions. Foreign libraries, as a rule, will respond on their own order forms.

24:09   Addressing for Middle East Promotions

Mail promotions aimed at professionals in the Middle East work best when mailed to a job function rather than a name. In many jobs there, the job turnover rate is as much as 50 percent a year.

24:10   Testimonial Value in International Offers

If you mail to German or Japanese markets, as a rule, your offer will do better if it includes testimonials that provide proof of the quality of your offering.

24:11   Type of Testimonials in International Mail

As a rule, in international mail, use only testimonials by internationally respected authorities, or individuals associated with internationally respected institutions.

24:12   Rule for Pretesting International Lists

Many business and professional periodicals have substantial international circulations. As a rule, if you have done well with their domestic circulation lists, the foreign names on these same lists will also do well for you.

24:13   International Postage Saver

As a rule, it will be less expensive and more efficient to have a flier inserted and distributed with a U.K. or European business or professional periodical than to mail it separately.

24:14   Inserts in Foreign Periodicals

As a rule, if you have your mailing piece distributed as an insert in an appropriate professional periodical, your cost for the insert mailing will be about one and one-half times the advertising page rate for that periodical (more if the weight of your insert affects the periodical's mailing cost).

24:15   Currency Rule for International Promotions

International promotions will be more successful if you accept payment in pounds sterling, Canadian dollars, or Japanese yen, as well as in U.S. dollars.

24:16 Way to Prevent Bad Debt on International Offers

When you receive overseas orders without prepayment, as a rule, it's best to send a pro forma invoice and ship only after payment is received.

24:17 Credit Card Rule in International Promotions

As a rule, be sure to include a credit card payment option on the order form in international promotions. It provides a convenient vehicle for payment in U.S. currency.

24:18 Cost Saver Rule for International Promotions

When the same catalog or promotion piece is used for both domestic and international mailings, you will greatly reduce postage costs if you substitute lightweight paper for the international mailing components.

24:19 Foreign Postal Service Rule on Self-Mailers

As a rule, most foreign postal services require that self-mailers be enclosed in an envelope. The only exception is postcards sent first class, or air mail.

24:20 Mailings to Third-World Countries

As a rule, surface mail to third-world countries tends to be very unreliable. Promotional mailings to those countries should be sent by air mail.

24:21 Source of Reliable International Lists

Foreign rental lists are often out of date and sometimes lack names of specific individuals. As a rule, the most reliable and accurate source of foreign lists are the foreign paid subscribers to specialized U.S. publications.

24:22 Cautionary Rule on Foreign-Address Lists

When renting international lists, make it a firm rule to inspect each list to ensure it meets U.S. Postal Service requirements, before releasing it to your mailing house. Current USPS requirements call for only the country name on the fourth or bottom line of a foreign address, in capital letters, and not abbreviated. If the address comes with a postal code, the code must be on the line above the country of destination.

24:23   International Mailing List Costs

As a rule, international mailing lists are considerably more costly to rent than U.S. lists.

24:24   Return Address Requirement in International Mail

For any international mailing, as a rule, be sure to include "U.S.A." as part of the return address, in addition to the ZIP Code.

24:25   Special Printing Requirement for Canadian Mailings

With new legislation that became effective in 1993, every piece of a mailing to Canada from the United States must state in at least 7-point type "Printed in the USA" on it. This includes outer envelope and reply card. If the USA imprint is omitted on any piece, the entire mailing will be delayed in Customs and assessed a duty tax unless proof of country of printing can be established.

24:26   Using "Free" in Canadian Mailings: A Note of Caution

If a planned mailing to Canada includes a free offer with a purchase, as a rule the offer will be in violation of Canadian consumer law which defines *free* as requiring no purchase to obtain the item. "So, if a premium is offered to first-time buyers," says Mark Morin of Direct Marketing Strategies of Quebec (in *DM News*, November 15, 1993), "it is a gift with purchase and you cannot use the word 'free.'"

24:27   Canadian Mailings: Pricing Guidelines

As a rule, mailings to Canadian consumers work best when the offer is priced in Canadian dollars. However, those price endings that work well in U.S.-priced offers, such as $19.95, $24.95, and $29.95 will have equally strong appeal to Canadians.

24:28   International Marketing Seasonality

As a rule, the three biggest months for sales to international markets are April, June, and July.

PART 2

Card Packs: A Comprehensive Understanding

25

The Card Pack: Its Impact as a Tool of Direct Marketing

The most important factor in successful card pack advertising is its ability to sell several related products to the same customer.

—BILL NORCUTT
Secrets of Successful Response Deck Advertising, 1984

25:01   Astounding Growth of the Card Pack

As a rule, the card pack is by far the fastest growing area of direct marketing and so successful is this easy-reply format that nine out of ten direct marketers who try the card pack return to this medium again.

25:02   Origin of the Card Pack Concept

This direct marketing concept, which originated in 1959 as a *card deck,* burst into prominence as a highly effective direct marketing tool in the 1980s, fueled largely by its adoption as a book promotion tool by publishers for professional and reference books and materials. The term *card pack* was introduced in 1985 by former McGraw-Hill marketer John Stockwell, a pioneer in card pack marketing and currently a card pack consultant, and it is now the term favored by the majority of users. A few pre-1985 users that still favor *card deck* include Standard Rate and Data Services for its directory listings, and Prentice-Hall for its 14 "Target Marketing Card Decks."

25:03   Understanding the Card Pack: How It Works

The *card pack* is a collection of business reply postcards ($3\frac{1}{2}''\times 5\frac{3}{8}''$) with an advertising message on one side and the advertiser's address on the other so that it can be returned to the advertiser, usually postage-paid. In the traditional pack, cards are stacked in a deck and mailed bulk rate in a sealed poly envelope to a defined audience. The recipient selects cards of interest and mails them back to the advertiser. Response is usually quicker and higher than from any other direct marketing format.

25:04   The Two Classifications of Card Packs

As a rule, card packs are either proprietary or co-op.The *proprietary* pack has a single sponsor who makes a variety of offers, each on one card. Heaviest proprietary deck users are business and professional book publishers, who may offer 40 to 60 books for free examination in one deck on 40 to 60 different reply cards. The *co-op* or *cooperative* card pack sponsor is, as a rule, a trade magazine publisher who sells single-card participations to advertisers on the credibility and profile of the magazine's circulation list. The co-op pack publisher coordinates all marketing and production activity.

25:05   Card Pack a Speed-Reading Medium

As a rule, says John Hudetz, CEO of Solar Press, the world's largest producer of card packs (over 250 million a year), "the card pack allows the buyer to speed-read through dozens of products in less than a minute....The offers read like miniature billboards."

25:06   Greatest Success Area for Sponsored Card Packs

Since the early 1980s, sponsored card packs have enjoyed their greatest success among business and professional book publishers. Numerous publishers mail to their various constituencies, and to other lists of known book buyers in the same subject areas, on a regular basis. The recipients—business executives, scientists, scholars, and engineers— have indicated in various mail-preference surveys that the card pack is a favored mailing format for offers of books for free examination.

25:07   Why Card Pack Is Favored by Business Catalogers

The card pack is valued by business catalogers because it permits fast, extremely low-cost mailings and provides a quick-response vehicle for testing various mailing lists and offer elements prior to mailing more costly catalogs.

25:08   Card Pack Versus Catalog With Same Products Offered

As a rule, a multiproduct card pack will substantially outpull a catalog offer with the same product mix. However, the catalog order can be returned with mailing label affixed for list-cleaning purposes, and it also provides ample space for those products that cannot be sold on the limited space provided on a postcard.

25:09   Card Pack Readership Versus Space Advertisement

As a rule, when given a choice between a paid space advertisement in a specialized business magazine and participation in a card pack mailing to the same circulation, you should choose the card pack because the same offer in a card pack will achieve a much higher degree of readership.

25:10   Criteria for Risk-Free Card Pack

As a rule, you can launch a cost-effective card pack with as few as 20 cards, provided you have products or services appropriate for a targeted audience and accessibility to outside lists that you know to be effective.

25:11   Major 1990s Innovation in Card Pack Packaging

The introduction of a new packaging format, the side-by-side (S/S) pack, was made possible by a 1991 U.S. Postal Service ruling. Use of this new format dropped the mailing cost of a card pack from the higher "flat" category to the lower letter category. With the S/S format, packs of 12 to 64 cards, approximating 60,000 in circulation, are packaged in two side-by-side piles in a single 6- by 9-inch envelope and bulk mailed at the lower letter rate for mail under $\frac{1}{4}$ inch thick.

25:12   Card Pack Cost Comparison With Other Formats

The cost per thousand for each card in a card pack is much lower than virtually any other form of direct marketing.

25:13   Why Business Packs Outpull Consumer Packs

Business card packs consistently do better than packs mailed to consumers. One big reason is that business packs have good pass-along readership, while consumer packs at residential addresses have none.

25:14   How Often to Mail Packs to Professionals

Studies have shown that, as a rule, sponsored mailings of card packs to professional audiences are most effective when they are issued three times a year. However, in one McGraw-Hill study to buyers of engineering and technical books, responders indicated they would prefer to receive four to six a year.

25:15   Headline on Card Is Key to Card's Success

As a rule, a recipient will scan a pack of 50 to 60 cards in one to three minutes. Unless the headline on the card stops the reader, the card is wasted.

25:16   Headline or Illustration

As a rule, when limited space permits either a headline or an illustration on a card, a strong headline will outperform an illustration.

25:17   Card Pack Packaging Options

Most card packs are enclosed in clear or printed polywrap. This material is stronger, less costly, and easier to fill than paper envelopes. (The polywrap is formed around the pack of cards at the time of packaging.) Other packaging options include pearlized poly, metalized polypropylene, and demetalized polypropylene. Printing on the outer wrapping can be in up to six colors.

25:18   The Newer Polywrap for the 1990s

The favored packaging material for card packs was originally polyethylene plastic, but by late 1993, with newer technology, card pack producers had switched to polypropylene ("polyprop"), which they found to be clearer than polyethylene, more durable, and fresher-looking after traveling through the mails.

25:19   Way to Increase Pass-Along Readership

If you mail card packs to business, industrial, or institutional audiences, as a rule, you can improve response by including a "pass-along" request in a cover-card message. Most publisher card packs contain a message to this effect: "Please circulate the cards you don't select to your associates."

25:20   Card Pack Lead-Time Requirement

As a rule, most card pack printers require three to four weeks once all the artwork and final film are received. Changes in copy can often be made up to a week before mailing.

26

Card Pack Marketing Guidelines

When you start your own card pack, not only can you reserve half the pack for your own offers, but you could also pay for the costs of the entire mailing by selling the remaining cards to noncompeting companies.
—JOHN KREMER
Ways to Market Books, 1989

26:01 Rule for Measuring Pack Response Rate

If you plan to promote your products by card pack, you can consider such offers successful when they produce 2 to 3 times their overall cost in direct orders.

26:02 Influence of Card's Position in Pack

As a rule, cards in the first half of a pack tend to work better than those in the second half. However, seasoned pack marketers claim a super offer, no matter where positioned, will usually do well.

26:03 Seasonality for Businesses and Institutions

As a rule, card packs work best to individuals in businesses and institutions during the first and third quarters of the year. Most large mailers test in the third quarter and roll out early in the first quarter following.

26:04 Indirect Sales Generated by Card Packs

As a rule, says Glenn Matthews, a mail marketer, card pack mailings of work-related materials to professional individuals in institutions and industry will generate as much dollar sales volume through institutional or business purchase orders as from cards returned from the mailing. This view is based on results of three tests, each to 50,000 professionals, in different interest areas.

26:05 Copy-Length Rule for Card Pack Sales

As a rule, high-priced products that require lengthy, detailed copy will not sell through card packs, where the selling story must be limited to 100–150 words. However, a card pack works extremely well for lead generation for such items.

26:06 Getting a Low-Priced Item in the Card Pack

As a rule, when it is not cost effective to place a low-priced item in a card pack, you can cut the cost factor in half by placing two low-priced items back to back on the same card and having the buyer provide the return envelope and postage.

26:07 Advantage of Proprietary Over Co-Op Deck

A key marketing advantage of the proprietary card pack over the co-op pack is that response and test results can be quickly evaluated since all cards are returned to the same address.

26:08 Reducing Return Postage Costs in Proprietary Deck

You can cut down on return postage costs in a card pack by enclosing a master order card on which the respondent can list the various order numbers that identify individual cards in the pack.

26:09 Way to Get Return Payment With Card Packs

You can still use a card pack type of offer even when you require return payment. Just include a postpaid business reply envelope with the loose pack of cards, or include an order form and have the respondent furnish the return envelope.

26:10   Optimum Size for Card Packs

As a rule, the optimum size for an effective card pack is not under 30 cards nor over 90. However, Aspen Publishers mailed packs with 100 cards for many years and found this count highly effective for its publication offerings.

26:11   Benefit of Horizontal Card Printing

As a rule, most card pack users print their copy across the width of the card. Aside from the fact that this is the way most people hold postcards for reading, it also allows for a strong headline across the top in an oversized, bold type.

26:12   Using Illustrations: Two Marketers' Views

Two seasoned card pack marketers have mixed views on the need for an illustration on a card. Says John Stockwell, "I use an illustration when it looks interesting." Counters Betty Connor, "I always use an illustration. People want to know what they're getting."

26:13   Illustrations for Very Small Spaces

If an illustration is essential and the space is too small for a halftone to show sufficient detail, use a line drawing.

26:14   Graphic Symbol With Phone Number

As a rule, if you include a phone number on a card, putting an illustration of a telephone next to the phone number will result in an increase of phone responses.

26:15   Unsigned Free Examination Requests

Where a card pack free examination offer requires a signature, as a rule, three or four of every 100 respondents will omit the signature or forget to sign. It's a good idea to return such cards and request the signature before making shipment.

27

Card Pack Design Factors That Influence Response

The most exciting part of any card pack program is watching the orders come in. Yesterday, a stack of cards came in that was 8" high—that's about 1,000 orders from a mailing to our house list.

—ROBERT LUEDTKE
In Bodian and Luedtke, Beyond Lead Generation: Merchandising Through Card Packs, 1986

27:01 Influence of Packaging on Response

As a rule, a card pack mailed to a rental list in a polybag, clear or printed, will produce better results than the same offer in a paper envelope. For mailings to customer lists, however, the type of envelope or wrapping has little influence on response.

27:02   Higher-Cost Envelope Increases Response

As a rule, a card pack mailed to rental lists in printed foil polywrap—a silver-colored metalized polyester—will increase response, but at a much higher packaging cost.

27:03   How Offer-Type Influences Response Speed

As a rule, responses from an inquiry card will be returned more quickly than cards that offer something for sale.

27:04   State-of-the-Art Card Pack Response Technology

The easier an advertiser makes it for a recipient to respond, the greater the chances for a response. Card pack technology took a giant leap forward in the early 1980s with the introduction of the Six Shooter—an insert with outgoing card packs containing six peel-off labels bearing the recipient's name and address, which the recipient could use on returned cards. By late 1993, the technology had been advanced to permit card packs to be mailed with a postcard-size insert, with three to twenty-two return labels bearing the recipient's name and address.

27:05   Influence of Taped Business Card on Response

When a card in a business card pack solicits inquiries, rather than orders, as a rule, you can boost response with the instruction "Tape Business Card Here" to replace the fill-in information requested of the recipient.

27:06   Influence of Layout on Response

As a rule, you will do better with a card printed the horizontal way than with a card printed the vertical way.

27:07   Influence of Second-Color Ink on Response

For most card pack offers, says Ralph Holcomb, a card pack consultant, adding a second-color ink will not increase response to a recognizable degree.

27:08 Influence of Color Background on Response

Cards in a pack printed on a yellow-colored background have virtually the same response as cards printed on the normal white background.

27:09 Influence on Telephone Numbers on Response

As a rule, in a card pack offering the inclusion of a telephone number on a card will not influence response. However, it may be helpful for clearing up ordering questions on higher-priced items.

27:10 Negative Influence of Pay Option

As a rule, adding a credit card pay option to a free examination offer will suppress response about 15 percent.

27:11 Influence of Separate Order Card in Pack

As a rule, including a separate order form or order device with a card pack will increase response in nonconsumer packs.

27:12 Card Pack Response Pattern Breaks Rule

A long-held view of most direct marketers is that multiproduct offers depress response. However, card pack response patterns disprove this view. Despite competition from the accompanying cards, as a rule, individual card responses are usually considered highly satisfactory for the modest investment per card involved.

27:13 When Four Colors Will Help Response

While one color of ink is the most economical choice for most card pack offers, Robert Luedtke, a mail-order cataloger and heavy card pack user, says you should consider four colors when you have a high-priced item and color will greatly enhance visual impact. He claims a 30 to 40 percent increase with four-color cards on selected high-priced offers.

27:14   Blank-Card Response Rate for Card Packs

As a rule, about 10 to 15 of every 100 cards received back from a free examination card pack mailing will be blank. However, when the card pack mailing is to doctors or other high-level professionals, the quantity of blank cards is greatly reduced (for medical specialists it's as little as 1 percent).

27:15   Indirect Sales Response From Card Packs

In the mid-1980s, card pack mailings by publisher John Wiley to professionals included selected test-card offers for slow-selling books with fixed sales patterns. Postcard returns on the test-card offers were poor to nil. However, indirect sales of the tested books eventually produced income far in excess of their card-pack participation costs.

27:16   Seasonality Influence on Consumer Card Packs

As a rule, card pack mailings to consumers at home addresses show no seasonality patterns and will be effective virtually any time of the year.

27:17   Card Pack Versus Catalog Response

As a rule, a free examination offer on a card in a card pack will produce as much as twice the response as a listing of the same product in a catalog, but with considerably more bad debt.

28

Co-Op Card Packs: Participation Practices and Procedures

What you're really buying in a co-op card publication is a mailing list in the form of a postcard.

—DAVE FLORENCE
In Bauer, How to Publish a Card Pack, 1988

28:01 Audience for Co-Op Card Packs

As a rule, most co-op packs are mailed to highly targeted audiences by business-to-business trade publications, or by business-to-business catalogers. Relatively few card packs are mailed to consumers.

28:02 What a Co-Op Pack Is

"As a rule," says Dave Florence of Direct Media Group, in (Bauer) *How to Publish a Card Pack*, 1988, "what you're really buying in a co-op card publication is a mailing list in the form of a postcard. Without a good list, good response is virtually impossible."

28:03 Rule for Judging Co-Op Card Pack Rates

Advertising or participation costs in co-op card packs may vary widely with different publication sponsors. However, as a rule of thumb, the more highly targeted the audience the higher the cost-per-thousand rate. Do not be surprised to find a highly targeted co-op pack charging many times more per thousand names than a big-circulation trade magazine sponsored co-op pack.

28:04 Co-Op Card Pack Premium Position

As a rule, the top card in a co-op pack will produce a 10 to 15 percent better response than placements elsewhere in the pack. Co-op pack sponsors, aware of this phenomenon, usually charge a premium for this position.

28:05 Co-Op Card Pack Charges for Premium Positions

As a rule, the top and bottom cards in a co-op card pack are priced at a premium. The top card is usually from $100 to $400 over the single-card participation cost, or 10 to 20 percent more than the single-card insert rate. The bottom card premium cost is somewhat less than the top card.

28:06 New Deck-Sorting Procedure Rotates Position Exposure

A 1990s state-of-the-art innovation in co-op card packs from Solar Press—made possible by emerging technology—is the "card shuffle." Explains Frank Hudetz, CEO at Solar Press, "Traditionally, cards in a pack have been in a set sequence that favored advertisers in the upper half of the pack. With the new 'card shuffle,' selected cards can be rotated on a regular basis throughout the pack. This allows equal position exposure for all the rotated cards, making it possible for five or ten advertisers to enjoy the top card position in various segments of the same co-op mailing."

28:07 Use of Duplicate Card in Same Deck

If your single-card participation in a co-op deck is producing a high rate of response, as a rule, adding a duplicate card with the same offer may also be cost-effective. Bear in mind, some co-op decks offer a reduced rate for buying two or more cards.

28:08 Using Fax Number in Conjunction With Phone Number

If you show your fax number in close proximity to your phone number in a business co-op mailing that seeks inquiries, as a rule, about 25 percent of your inquiries will come through the fax number.

28:09 Another Way to Find Co-Op Packs

"The best way to find co-op packs," says Bill Norcutt, "is to run a card in one offering products related to yours. Then sit back, and let the decks find you. If you let them call you first, you'll be in a much stronger position to negotiate [a better price]. (In *Secrets of Successful Response Deck Advertising*, 1984)

28:10 High Readership of Co-Op Card Packs

The largest proportion of co-op card packs are published by specialized business publications and mailed to their subscribers. As a rule, nine out of ten recipients of these co-op packs always look through the postcards they receive.

28:11 Sponsor Recognition as Response Factor

Your offer will usually draw a better response in the card pack of a business or professional sponsor that is widely recognized or respected than in a lesser-known or unknown sponsor's pack.

28:12 Co-Op Card Cost in Publication-Sponsored Pack

As a rule, the rate charged for participation in a co-op card pack sponsored by a business publication is the same for publication advertisers and nonadvertisers.

28:13 Way to Save on Co-Op Card Pack Participations

If you regularly mail your own card packs, as a rule, you can save substantially by overprinting your best performing cards and inserting them in other co-op packs at a reduced per-card cost.

28:14   Cost-Cutting Technique for Co-Op Participation

When the single-card cost of a co-op card pack participation is deemed too expensive for a single product offer, consider an A-B split, using two different offers. You are thus able to test the entire circulation at half cost for each offer.

28:15   Estimating Rule for Affordability of Co-Op Pack

You can estimate whether you can afford to offer your product in a well-targeted card pack by using these percentages for anticipated response: for inquiry card responses, from $1\frac{1}{2}$ to 2 percent; for outright orders, not more than $\frac{1}{2}$ percent.

28:16   Formula for Estimating Co-Op Pack Responses

As a rule, about 45 percent of the total response from a co-op card pack mailing will come in from two and one-half to three weeks after the mailing date. An additional 45 percent will be received during the three weeks following.

28:17   Return Postage Preference in Industrial Co-Ops

As a rule, nearly 90 percent of industrial co-op card pack advertisers make their response cards postpaid.

28:18   Use of 800 Numbers on Industrial Co-Op Cards

Most of the advertisers in industrial co-op card packs who do not pay return postage generally include an 800 number. This is because they prefer to deal with inquiries on a more personal level.

28:19   Way to Deal With High-Quality Pack Illustrations

Nearly all card packs are printed on high-bulk vellum paper that does not allow for high-quality illustrations. As a rule, when a high-quality illustration is essential on a co-op card, some advertisers preprint their own insert card on special paper and pay a special insert charge over the normal participation rate.

28:20   Velox Rule for Card Pack Illustrations

If you're submitting camera-ready art for a card pack participation, as a rule, your illustration will conform to requirements and reproduce well if you use a 110-line screen velox in position.

28:21   Value of Sponsor Name in Co-Op Offers

As a rule, says Peter Hodges, a highly regarded direct marketing consultant, "the best way to start a co-op card pack in any specialized area is under the auspices of a recognized publication in the field. It gives the pack a sense of professionalism to show that it is tied up with a reputable publication."

28:22   International Co-Op Card Pack Availabilities

U.S. advertisers may now purchase participations in a wide range of business, professional, and consumer co-op card packs in Canada, in a multicountry European package, and in such individual countries as Belgium, France, the Netherlands, Switzerland, and the United Kingdom. For details on international advertising participation, contact John Brennan of Solar Direct, a division of Solar Press, at 1-800-323-2751, extension 2075.

28:23   Rule-Breaking Co-Op Card Is a Winner

As a rule, card packs work best when an advertiser keeps to one offer per card. However, there was an instance in 1982 where 28 offers were made on a single card by publisher John Wiley. The *Journal of Chemical Education* sent a co-op pack to subscribers simultaneously with the mailing of its September issue. The periodical carried a Wiley advertisement describing 28 different books or book sets in detail. The Wiley card in the JCE co-op card pack just listed the 28 books, with checkoff boxes for ordering free examination copies and space for the respondent's name and address. The experiment paid off.

28:24 Co-Ops Merit Publisher Attention

Folio, the magazine for magazine publishers, urges its readers to consider sponsorship of cooperative card packs for two reasons: (1) Packs attract buyers who respond better to a direct marketing approach than to advertising. (2) It doesn't take very many cards in a pack to reach profitability. (April 15, 1993)

28:25 The Many Names of Cards in a Card Pack

Generically, the cards in a card pack are *response cards*. However, publishers of co-op card packs use a variety of terms for such cards including: *action cards, ad cards, direct action cards, information cards, news action cards, post cards/postcards, product cards, query cards, sales lead cards, target cards, targeted cards.*

28:26 Directory of Card Deck Advertising Sources

Most ad agencies seeking information on co-op card pack availabilities subscribe to *Card Deck Advertising Source* (before 1994, known as *Card Deck Rates and Data*). Issued twice a year in March and October, it contains about 1000 listings in more than 115 markets with full participation details. If you have a co-op pack and want a free listing, write to Standard Rate and Data Service, 2000 Clearwater Drive, Oak Brook, IL 60521, att: Stan Getz, Editor.

28:27 Directory of National and International Co-Op Card Packs

A comprehensive directory of co-op card pack availabilities in the United States, Canada, and numerous European countries is published by Solar Press, 1120 Frontenac Road, Naperville, IL 60653. Each entry has comprehensive information, as supplied by the publisher. The directory is published annually with frequent updates. It is bargain-priced at $9.95. Call: 1-800-323-2751.

PART 3

The Art and Science of Mailing List Usage

29

Mailing Lists: Approaches and Techniques

A mailing list is the names and addresses of prospects and/or customers who have something in common, whether it be previous buying habits, occupation or other attributes.
—WILLIAM S. RUBIN
In (Burns) Mailing Lists:
A Practical Guide, 1984

29:01 General Categories of Lists

Most mailing lists generally fit into three broad categories: (1) customer and prospect lists owned by a business and used regularly in the normal course of business; (2) rented lists compiled from publicly available sources; (3) response lists encompassing all individuals who have responded to an advertised offer, whether buyers, subscribers, or inquirers.

29:02 Weakness and Strength of Compiled List

The chief weakness of a compiled list is that there is no way of knowing whether any of the names on it will be responsive to a mail offer.

However, with geographic and psychographic options available with many compiled lists, the chances of reaching a well-targeted list are greatly enhanced.

29:03   Cautionary Rule for Response Lists

As a rule an offer of a response list does not necessarily indicate mail-order buyers. Under the "response" label, some list owners offer names of inquirers or subscription expires. Ask for the source before ordering.

29:04   Buyer-List Classification by Selling Medium

Buyer lists in direct marketing fall into three identification categories: (1) direct mail sold lists, (2) space sold lists, and (3) phone sold lists. The name of the list identifies the medium through which the sale was made.

29:05   Mail-Order Buyer Versus Mail-Responsive List

When considering two seemingly identical lists for a rental, as a rule, you'll do much better with a mail-order buyer list. The "buyer" list indicates each name has made a purchase from a mail offer. The "responsive" list indicates a response, which may have been a purchase, an inquiry for more information, or a request for a salesperson to call.

29:06   Mail-Responder Lists Versus Compiled Lists

As a rule, a mail-responder list will outperform a compiled list in the same area and, therefore, is more likely to warrant the added rental cost.

29:07   List Recency Rule

The more recently a name has been added to a list or has recorded some activity within a list, the more likely it is to be responsive to a mail offer. Conversely, the older a name on a list, or the longer a period since it recorded some activity, the less responsive it is likely to be.

29:08 Prospect List-Building Rule

The best way to generate new names for a prospect mailing list is to offer something free that is related to the type of offer you are likely to make at a later date.

29:09 List-Use Frequency

The best rule for list-use frequency: Mail as often as the list continues to be profitable.

29:10 Prospect List Frequency of Use

As a rule, a productive prospect list should not be used more than twice a year. However, testing will sometimes show that more frequent uses are still cost effective.

29:11 When Keeping a Prospect List Doesn't Pay

When you mail to a business or professional list on an annual basis, or even less frequently, as a rule, it is cheaper and more beneficial to rent a same-interest list from an outside reliable source and start with fresh names each time you mail.

29:12 Selection Rule for Special-Interest Lists

People with like interests, according to Martin Baier, a marketing professor, tend to have like buying habits. It follows, as a rule, that an appeal or offer that works well with one special-interest list will work reasonably well with another list of individuals known to have the same special interest.

29:13 Mailing List Affinity Rule

The greater the affinity or logical connection between the name on a mailing list and the mailing offer, the greater the chances for the mailing's success.

29:14 Weak Offer or Weak List: Which Is Worse?

As a rule, a weak offer will work with a good mailing list. However, a good offer to a bad list will inevitably fail.

29:15 Rule for Maximizing Small-List Yield

When a small list produces an unusually high response, as a rule, it should be remailed to on a cyclical basis until repeat mailings cease to be cost-effective.

29:16 Faculty List Deterioration

As a rule, college faculty directories change about 20 percent each year. New courses are constantly being added to the nearly 5000 already taught, and as a consequence, college faculty directories become obsolete in one semester. It is always best to rent current faculty lists from such reliable college sources as CMG Information Services in Wilmington, Massachusetts, which updates faculty lists every semester.

29:17 Rule for Segmenting Lists by Age Group

Many products have more appeal to people at certain age levels, or at certain levels in their career path. If this applies to your type of offer, as a rule, you'd best use lists that offer age segmentation options and mail only to appropriate age groups.

29:18 Magnetic Tape List Specification

If you plan to order a list on magnetic tape, the most commonly used tape is 9-track 1600 BPI. Most computer addressing installations can work from this type of tape without difficulty.

29:19 Primary Rental List Source

As a rule, any list rental search should start with a look into Standard Rate and Data Service's *Direct Marketing List Source* (prior to 1994 called *Direct Mail List Rates and Data.*). The directory, updated every other month, gives full details on more than 10,000 rental lists in over 220 market classifications. Back copies may sometimes be found in libraries.

29:20 Most Complete List Information Source

As a rule, the most complete source of information for any rental mailing list is the *list data card* (also called *data card* or *information card*), which is prepared and distributed by the list owner or manager. It often provides more detailed information than may be found in SRDS *Direct Marketing List Source,* including attributes of company or offer from which list was derived, demographic and psychographic characteristics, average purchase amount, and percentage of men and women.

29:21 How and Why to Use List Keys

Always add a key to each list used in a mailing for tracking purposes. Use of keys will enable you to identify response from each list and/or from a particular segment within a list. The key is usually on the mailing label, reply card, or other response device.

29:22 Knowing and Using List Segmentation Options

As a rule, before engaging in list rentals, beginning direct marketers should acquaint themselves with and take advantage of the numerous rental list segmentation options that can help to improve direct mail performance. These segmentation options include geographic, ZIP Code area, sex, age, marital status, occupation, habits, lifestyles, and buying or behavior patterns.

29:23 List Procedures That Reduce Mailing Costs

Two ways to reduce mailing costs on volume mailings are (1) a merge-purge of lists to eliminate duplications, and (2) fine-tune list segmentation to reach prime prospects only.

29:24 Rule for Success in Direct Mail

Success in direct mail promotion, according to Frank Paulo of SRDS *Direct Marketing List Source,* depends on three things: (1) mailing lists, (2) mailing lists, (3) mailing lists.

30

Rental Lists: Practices and Procedures

The best creative idea and the soundest copy may go to waste if the right list is not available.

—DAVID OGILVY
Ogilvy on Advertising, 1983

30:01 List Rental Clearance Rule

To ensure timely delivery, place your list rental order at least one month in advance of your planned mailing date. (Most list owners specify 10 to 15 working days.)

30:02 Mailer Responsibility in List Rentals

As a rule, a list rental agreement makes the mailer directly responsible to the list owner for payment. Payment for a rental by the mailer to the list broker constitutes payment to the list owner.

30:03 List Rental Payment Requirement

Initial list rentals almost always require prepayment. Subsequent orders usually provide net 30-day terms (and sometimes only highly rated companies are offered this option).

30:04 Key Elements of List Rental Order

Any list rental order should always include these key elements: (1) mailer's name and purchase order number, (2) quantity of names wanted, (3) list selections, (4) key coding for tracking purposes, (5) proposed mailing date, (6) a "ship to" address.

30:05 One-Time Use Rule for List Rentals

Mailing list rentals are for one-time use only by the original renter, unless agreement has been made in advance for more than one use. In rare instances, a compiler may sell a list outright with no use restrictions.

30:06 Mailing Date Clearance Rule

Once you have an approved mailing date from a list owner, you must clear any new date with the owner if you do not mail on the date for which approval was given.

30:07 Right-of-Refusal Rule

The list owner has the right to accept a list rental order under any terms he or she wishes, or to refuse a rental request for any reason.

30:08 Cautionary Rule for Compiled List Rentals

When ordering a list compiled from a directory, be sure to ask the year of the directory. Most directories are about 20 percent obsolete within a year and a list from a two- or three-year-old directory is likely to have a greatly reduced rate of deliverability.

30:09 Sample Mailing Piece Requirement

As a rule, many list owners and managers require one or two sample mailing pieces before approving a list rental. Try submitting a reasonably accurate dummy if the mailing piece has not yet been printed.

30:10   Rule for Test Rentals

When a segment of a larger list is rented for testing purposes, the rental order should clearly indicate that it is a test order. Mailer should also provide specific instructions on how the order is to be segmented and whether the list owner should keep a record of names supplied to prevent duplications should there be subsequent rentals from the same list.

30:11   Rule for When to Stop Using Outside List

When you mail to the same outside list repeatedly, as a rule, most of the buyers on that list will wind up on your house list. You can more quickly determine when to stop using that list by mailing your own list at least one week before each usage. The outside list buyer names will then get on your house list, and there will be fewer and fewer orders from the outside list.

30:12   Overcoming Rental Request Turndown

When a rental request is refused for competitive reasons, offer an exchange of your house names for theirs. This will indicate, as a rule, that the rental request poses no threat.

30:13   Reciprocity Rental

As a rule, some list owners will rent to competitors only on a reciprocal basis, that is, an equal exchange of the competitor's house list names.

30:14   Alternative to a Competitor's Customer List

As a rule, when you are refused a customer list rental for competitive reasons, you may be more successful if you ask to rent the list owner's prospect list.

30:15   Eighty-Five Percent Rule in List Rentals

Direct marketing professionals who computer-match names with other lists and purge duplications will try to arrange in advance to pay for only 85 percent of the names rented. This is to make up for the names eliminated through such matches. This type of discount is called a *net-name arrangement.* It was originated in 1971 at a Direct Marketing Idea Exchange (DMIX).

30:16 Potential for Yearly Volume Discount

If you intend to use a list or lists from the same company regularly, as a rule, you can reduce rental costs by inquiring about a yearly volume discount.

30:17 Verifying List Continuation Order

Here is a rule of thumb for determining whether the second or continuation order for a mailing list contains essentially the same names as those in an original test: Order the test names in ZIP Code sequence, starting with the lowest number. Before the test mailing, photocopy the last sheet or two of names. When reordering from the same list, have the second order start with the lowest ZIP Code numbers on your photocopy. When the names are received, match them against the photocopy. They should be essentially the same names.

30:18 Rule for List Re-Use

"If your first run through a list was very good," advises Bob Martin, a former Prentice-Hall marketer, "rest it for 90 days and then remail excluding the buyers. As a rule of thumb, you can expect a drop in response from your first run of about 33 percent."

30:19 Using List History as Guide to Future Use

When you rent lists on an ongoing basis, as a rule, you should keep a list history of each list and record results after each mailing. Such records can be an indicator of what lists work best for what offers and provide you with a guide to the overall efficiency of each list.

30:20 ZIP String Rule for Small Lists

As a rule, you can speed the delivery of a large mailing by grouping various small lists into one ZIP string, that is, merge them into one continuous ZIP Code sequence. This form of list formatting is mandatory for mailing at third-class bulk rates.

30:21   List Count Verification Rule

The list count supplied from a data card prepared by the list owner
may be accurate at the time it is prepared, but it is subject to con-
stant change. Therefore, as a rule, you should verify all quoted
rental list counts supplied before proceeding with any mailing print
order.

30:22   When Rental Lists Overlap

When you plan to use two different rental lists that you suspect have a
high degree of overlap, you will improve response if you space the
mailings of the two lists a week or two apart.

30:23   Duplicate Delivery Influence on Response

As a rule, delivery of duplicate pieces of the same mailing at the same
time will not increase response.

30:24   List Duplication Quality Rule

The larger the number of duplications between a rented list and your
house list, the better the list, since it offers evidence that the names on
the rental list have interests similar to those of your customers.

30:25   Way to Feminize Male List

If you have an offer for women and the list you want has only men's
names on it, as a rule, you can still use the list by adding *Mrs.* to the
front of each name.

30:26   Gender Selection List Rule

When a list rental order calls for gender selection, as a rule, all names
on the list identified by initials will be skipped.

30:27   Telemarketing List Clearance Rule

List rental orders should clearly indicate planned telemarketing
usage. Some list owners will not permit telephone solicitation from
their lists.

30:28 Databases and Database Lists

A *Database* is a mingling of many mailing lists in a central computer so that information on any of them is shared, as from a single record. A *Database List* is a list drawn from a database.

30:29 Database Rental Rule

When you rent from a database that includes one or more lists you already rent from participants in the database, you should always request suppression of the lists you are already using.

30:30 Cautionary Rule for Rental Lists

You can avoid costly errors if you scan each rental list before sending it to your mailing house to ensure that it contains the type of names you rented and conforms with your order instructions. So advises Peter Hodges, a highly regarded direct marketing consultant.

30:31 Way to Track Unkeyed Rental Lists

As a rule, the best way to check the response from an unkeyed rental list is to order a duplicate copy of the list and check off the names of the responders.

30:32 Rule for Large or Small List in Same Field

When faced with your choice of either a large list or a small list in the same field or activity, your choice should depend on your follow-up plans. If you plan to follow up with a second, larger mailing, opt for the larger list. If not, use the smaller list.

30:33 Validity of Deliverability Guarantees

As a rule, a deliverability guarantee by a list compiler such as 93 percent or 95 percent is no guarantee that anywhere near that percentage of the list is deliverable. The likelihood is that a far greater percentage will never be delivered, particularly on compiled lists where in many instances the original directory source was as much as 20 percent out of date by the time it was published.

30:34   Way to Save on Same-Source Small-List Rentals

As a rule, you can avoid minimum list rental fees for several small lists from the same list company by having them merged into one continuous ZIP string. A pitfall of this practice is that the merged lists will all bear the same list key and cannot be identified separately for tracking purposes.

30:35   Overcoming List Rental Minimum

List companies usually designate a minimum order size—either a minimum number of names or a dollar minimum such as $100. If your list requirement is below the minimum, consider trying two different but compatible lists to make the minimum.

30:36   Judging List by Competitor Use

A good yardstick for ascertaining in advance whether a potential rental list is appropriate is to find out whether any of your competitors have used it and, if so, how many times, and how often.

30:37   Choosing Between Update Guarantees

As a rule, if a list company uses the term *guaranteed delivery* in lieu of giving a precise updating frequency, it is likely that the list is updated or recompiled annually.

30:38   List Rental Confirmation Form

As a rule, once a list order confirmation form has been signed and returned by a list renter, it is considered a contractual agreement between the renter and the list owner.

30:39   Rule for Payment of Cancelled Order

If a list rental order is cancelled for any reason after work has started, the renter is required to make reasonable payment to the list owner for work already done.

30:40   Publicizing Your List for Rental Availability

The easiest and cheapest way to make known that your house list is available for rental is to have it listed in SRDS *Direct Marketing List Source*. The listing is free. All you need to do is complete the SRDS listing questionnaire. This is the primary list information source for most list brokers.

30:41 List Seeding for Improper Usage

As a rule, most owners of rental lists seed each list with decoy names to signal whether the list was improperly used under terms of the rental agreement. The owner is alerted when the rented list is subjected to unauthorized, improper, or repeat usage.

30:42 Cutting-Edge Technology in List Formats

An innovative new list format for list owner/renters is CD-ROM. List owners may now maximize revenues by selling their lists on CD-ROM with either of two profit capabilities: (1) sale of the list with a "clock" that limits use to one year, (2) sale of the list with a metering capability that charges customer for each name retrieved. The CD-ROM list format was pioneered by American Business Information Inc., P.O. Box 27347, Omaha, NE 68127.

30:43 Direct Marketers Are Also List Purveyors

As a rule, most successful direct mail advertisers are also in the mailing list business as well, that is, they treat their mailing lists as separate profit centers through list rentals to others.

31
Rental List Characteristics

A list rental can be a form of market research....Many companies are able to improve their own selection of rental lists by monitoring the successful outside usage of their house file.

—ROSE HARPER
Mailing List Strategies: A Guide to Direct Mail Success, 1986

31:01 List Rental Verification Rule

Because list suppliers may send the wrong list, as a rule, it is best to scan each rental list to ensure it conforms to your instructions before sending it to the mailing house.

31:02 Alternative List Rental Formats

In addition to the standard four-up Cheshire label format, most list renters provide a variety of alternative addressing options, always at additional cost. These may include: heat-sensitive four-up Cheshire; three-up Cheshire; one-up north-south Cheshire; peel-off (pressure-sensitive); magnetic tape (either 800, 1600, or 6250 BPI); galley or sheet list; 3 by 5 cards; two-up telemarketing cards; second originals; simultaneous duplicate of list order.

31:03   Standard List Rental Format

As a rule, most rental lists are supplied on four-across (four-up) east-west Cheshire labels. These are on ungummed, continuous paper, and are affixed by machine at your mailing house. Each label measures 1 by 3.44 inches, with print area limited to 30 characters.

31:04   Deliverability Potential for Rental Lists

As a rule, the more frequent the update, the greater the mail deliverability potential. When like lists have different update frequencies, select the list with the most frequent update cycle.

31:05   Key Word That Ensures Current Names

As a rule, the key word in all rental orders of buyer, member, or subscriber lists should be *active*. By ordering only active buyers, members, or subscribers, you will be mailing to buyers during the past 12 months, currently active members, or subscribers who have paid for and are currently receiving subscriptions.

31:06   Age Factor in List Change Rate

If you rent lists by age grouping, you should know that, as a rule, stability increases with age. For example, the annual address-change rate for 25- to 39-year-olds will be about four times as great as for those in the 45- to 64-year age bracket.

31:07   Mail-Order Buyer Responsiveness Rule

As a rule, people who have made a purchase from a mail offer are more likely to make another purchase from a mail offer. Consequently, a list of known mail-order buyers will usually outperform any response list which may not necessarily be buyers, or any compiled list.

31:08   Mail-Order Buyer Recency Rule

The more recently a mail-order buyer has responded to a mail offer, the more likely that individual is to respond to another mail offer. When renting a list of mail-order buyers, the more recent the names on the mail-order buyers list, the greater its chances for success. List owners sometimes will sell mail-order buyers for the last 30, 60, or 90 days, or within the last year. These are called *hotline* names and the lists are known as *hot lists*.

31:09 Meaning of *Merge* and *Purge*

A *Merge* is to combine two or more lists into a single list utilizing the same sequential order. A *Purge* is to identify and eliminate duplicate or undesirable items from a file, or unwanted names from a mailing list. (From Bodian, *NTC's Dictionary of Direct Mail*, 1990)

31:10 Most Usual Reason for Merge-Purge

The most usual reason a direct marketer turns to a merge-purge, as a rule, is to eliminate duplicate names and addresses on outside or rental lists that already appear on a house list. It is usually done through an outside service bureau, although some large mailers may have an in-house computer service department that will do the job.

31:11 Primary Product of a Merge-Purge

As a rule, a merge-purge produces two kinds of names: unique names, and duplicate names. The *unique name* is one that appears on only one of the many lists in the merge-purge. A *duplicate name* is one that is found on two or more lists. It indicates a multiple buyer (or multibuyer) who has bought from two or more companies whose names were matched in the merge.

31:12 Best Names in Merge-Purge of Mail-Order Buyers

When a merge-purge is made of various mail-order buyer lists for elimination of duplications, as a rule, the duplicate names eliminated are the best names, since they are known multiple buyers of mail-order products.

31:13 High Duplication Indicator in Merge-Purge

As a rule, a high percentage of duplication between a particular rented list and your house list in a merge-purge suggests the two lists have similar profiles and, therefore, the rented list should be highly responsive to your offers.

31:14 Merge-Purge Duplication Discount

If you are going to merge-purge a rental list against your own, as a rule, some managers will give you a small discount for names on the rental list which duplicate those you already have.

31:15 Three Primary Purposes of a Merge-Purge

A merge-purge has three primary functions, says Robert M. Daniels of Mailing List Systems (in *The Merge/Purge Fact Book,* 1988): (1) to combine data from various mailing lists, (2) to identify and potentially eliminate duplicate names for a single mailing, (3) to create a marketing database.

31:16 Small Lists Unsuited for Personalization

Small rental lists, as a rule, are not available on magnetic tape and, therefore, cannot be used for merge-purges, or personalized letters.

31:17 Magnetic Tape Minimums

As a rule, be prepared to order a minimum of 10,000 names if you want a list supplied on magnetic tape. Some owners or compilers will not supply this format in a lesser quantity, and a few may even set minimums at 15,000 or higher.

31:18 List Geographics

As a rule, *geographics* in a list segmentation refers to separation of a list in terms of geographic or political subdivisions such as ZIP Code, sectional centers, cities, counties, states, and/or regions.

31:19 List Demographics

As a rule, *demographics* in list segmentation refers to what an individual is or does and includes such things as sex, age, marital status, occupation, income, family size, and education.

31:20 List Psychographics

As a rule, *psychographics* in list segmentation means subdivision of the list in terms of people's lifestyles and attitudes.

31:21   List Selections: Lists Within Lists

As a rule, a *list selection* is any part of a mailing list with identifiable special characteristics which can be extracted and used independently. *Direct Marketing List Source* recognizes a list selection as "any part of a list which is also available for rent."

31:22   Choosing and Using Best List Selection Options

If you offer a product specifically aimed at gender, age, family type, lifestyle, or income level, as a rule, you'll do best when you use rental lists that offer selection options in such categories as: gender, age, marital status, head of household, presence of children, income range, length of residence, type of dwelling, home ownership, home value, school years attended, and recency of name on list.

32

Customer and Prospect Lists: Effective Uses

The house list stands as the single most important asset in direct response. Because of the dependence on repeat orders, the most important task is the maintenance and intimate knowledge of the house list.
—JAMES F. LIPSCOMB
*In (Burns) Mailing Lists:
A Practical Guide, 1984*

32:01 House List Always First Choice

Virtually all direct marketers agree that a house list will, as a rule, produce a much higher response than any other list. That's because people like to order by mail from someone they know and can trust. With customers, you have demonstrated the quality of your product or service and have built a bridge of trust.

32:02 House List as Most Precious Asset

"For most direct marketing companies," says Ed Nash in *Direct Marketing*, 1986, "their house list is their single most precious asset—the one whose loss could put them out of business."

32:03   Quick Quality Identifiers for Customer Lists

As a rule, the two quick quality identifiers for any customer list are (A) *best*—those who have bought from you more than once, and (B) *second best*—those who have bought from you only once.

32:04   House List Versus Competitors' Lists

While a customer or house list customarily produces a better response than any rented list, with rare exceptions, a direct competitor's list, or a database list that includes buyers from several of your competitors, may sometimes surpass your own.

32:05   Next Best List After Your House List

As a rule, next to your own house list, the second most responsive list for you to use is that of a firm that sells products or services closely related to your own.

32:06   RFM Formula: A Way to Identify Your Best Customers

As a rule, the best prospects on any customer or house list are those who make frequent purchases in significant amounts. Identifiable by computer search, they fit into the RFM formula, recency of purchase, frequency of purchase, and monetary amount of purchase. (The RFM formula was introduced in the 1930s by the big mail-order houses.)

32:07   How RFM Formula Helps Save Money

As a rule, the RFM formula works best when mail-order catalog houses assign points in each of the three categories: recency of purchase, frequency of purchase, and monetary value of purchase (monetary may be amount of money spent in a specific time period or in total). To avoid waste circulation, points are assigned in each category and catalogs are then mailed only to those who get the most points and are deemed the most likely to buy again.

32:08   Easiest Way to Expand Prospect List

One of the easiest ways to expand a prospect list for a mail-order operation is to ask for the names of friends or associates on the back of the order envelope, or on a removable stub attached to the order envelope.

32:09 Another Proven Way to Get High-Quality Prospect Names

Another successful way to get high-quality prospect names is to send a simple, modestly worded thank-you note after you receive an order or inquiry. In it, ask for the names of others the respondent thinks might be interested in the same product or service. "Don't be surprised," advises Harry B. Walsh of Ogilvy & Mather, Inc., "if the names you get back turn out to be the best you can mail." (In [Barton] *Handbook of Advertising Management*, 1970)

32:10 Getting Customers to Help Update House List

An economical way to update or correct a customer list is with a coupon on the back of the envelope of a scheduled mailing. It should ask the customer to mail back both the coupon and address portion of the envelope, indicating desired changes. A popular heading for this type of address correction request is: "Are your name and address correctly shown on the face of this envelope?"

32:11 New-Name Acquisition Rule

The key to any successful continuing direct mail operation is new-name acquisition. As a rule, if a program does not gain at least as many new names as it loses each year, it is likely to fail.

32:12 House List Cleaning Rule

As a rule, a house list should be cleaned at least once every six months. Add "Address Correction Requested" to envelopes to receive address corrections back from the post office.

32:13 Income from Customer List Rentals

Often the key to profitability for a direct marketing company is the income it derives from renting its customer lists to other direct marketers.

32:14 House List Rental Frequency Rule

As a rule, when you mail regularly, you can still rent your house list up to 26 times a year if you limit rental mail dates to one week before and one week after your own mailings. When you have a special mailing, make the time gap for outsiders a littler wider.

32:15   Charging Criteria in House List Rentals

If you rent your house list, as a rule, you can charge more for this year's customers than for last year's customers and more for multiple buyers than for one-time purchasers. And if you segment names by recency of purchase, you can charge even more for customers who have made a purchase within the last 30, 60, or 90 days. The latter are referred to as *hot line* names.

32:16   Free Listing to Generate Income From House List Rentals

If your list is available for rentals, you should list it without cost in the Standard Rate and Data Service bimonthly publication *Direct Marketing List Source* (formerly *Direct Mail List Rates and Data*). Be prepared to complete and return a questionnaire giving details of your list and to certify the accuracy of data submitted. Write to Direct Marketing List Source, 2000 Clearwater Drive, Oak Brook, IL 60521.

32:17   Payment Rule for Mailing List Exchanges

As a rule, no money is involved in mailing list exchanges when done between principals. However, when arranged by a list broker, the principals may have to split the list broker's commission.

32:18   House List Protection in Rentals and Exchanges

The rental or exchange of any house list, as a rule, requires the recipient's written agreement to abide by the various conditions of the rental or exchange that will ensure the confidentiality of the list.

32:19   Exchange Requests From Competitors

It is best to avoid list exchange requests from direct competitors and, instead, to consider exchanges only with those offering closely related products or services.

33

Compiled Lists: Effective Uses

A good compiled list has defined characteristics and covers comprehensively all names within those characteristics. Comprehensiveness is the key to differentiating between a compiled list and a response list.

—E. G. LONGBOTTOM
In (Andrews) The Post Office Direct Mail Handbook, 1984

33:01 Compiled List Advantages

Compiled lists offer these advantages over response lists: less cost to rent, usually lower minimum quantities, no mailing sample requirement, and only one name per address.

33:02 Unreliability of Compiled List Counts

As a rule, the list count given in a compiler's catalog or on a list data card is a very rough estimate of the true count and must be verified.

33:03 One Way to Identify a Compiled List

As a rule, when a guarantee of deliverability is mentioned in connection with a list, it is a compiled list. A response list never makes any claims as to deliverability.

33:04   Compiled List Versus Mail-Order Sold List

As a rule, a compiled list may not be as effective as a mail-order sold list. However, it may offer more selection options.

33:05   Rule for Directory-Compiled Lists

If you plan to use lists compiled from directories, it's always best to go to the source of the directory, like a professional society for a list of professionals active in the society's prime activity, or the telephone company for a telephone company list. A spokesperson for Illinois Bell once reported in a *DM News* article that there were nearly 10,000 changes on their lists for every business day, from a name universe of 3.38 million.

33:06   Rule for Checking Compiled List Source

When renting a compiled list, it is always a good idea to ask its source. If the list is from a directory, ask the year of the directory and when, if ever, the list was last updated. Many compilers do not correct lists between directory editions. Instead, they recompile when each new edition is issued. Occasionally, they may, on slow-moving lists, recompile from every second or third edition.

33:07   When Compiler's Source Is an Unknown

When a compiler is unable to provide a compilation date or source, it may be because the list was assembled from a number of different sources and updated from yet other sources.

33:08   Cautionary Rule on Compiled List Rentals

There's always the possibility of renting the same names on a compiled list from two different compiler sources, each using a different list name. It's always a good idea to ask the list supplier to give the specific source of the list and methods of compilation to avoid such a duplication.

33:09   Principal Causes of Compiled List Duplications

There are two principal ways in which you can rent different-named compiled lists and get identical names: (1) when several compilers pool resources to compile a list and then each markets it independently of the other; (2) when a compiler wholesales a list to several other compilers, who may, in turn, offer these lists under different titles.

33:10   Compiled List Versus Mail-Responsive List

As a rule, a mail-responsive list in any business or professional area will almost always outperform a compiled list with the same characteristics.

33:11   Compiled List Updating Procedures

As a rule, list compilers who offer mailer credit for "nixies" or nondeliverables do not use them to update their lists. Most of these sources compile from telephone and other types of annual directories and prefer to recompile annually or as new volumes are issued rather than to update existing lists.

33:12   Deterioration Index Shows How Lists Age

The *deterioration index* for any compiled list is the approximate or estimated annual percentage rate at which a compiled list of any group having distinguishing characteristics goes out of date or ceases to be responsive to a direct mail effort (adapted from Bodian, *NTC's Dictionary of Direct Mail*, 1990). A directory with an annual deterioration rate of 20 percent could have been compiled in 1991, produced in 1992, and published in late 1992 with a 1993 cover date. In such a case, a 1993 compiled list from that directory might be two or more years out of date.

33:13   Compiled List Deterioration Rule

As a rule, the rate of deterioration or nondeliverability varies with a list's source. A consumer list could deteriorate as much as 25 percent in a year, while a list of dentists at their address of practice may deteriorate very little.

33:14   Business List Locator Rule

As a rule, there is an SIC (Standard Industrial Classification) number for virtually any type of business you may want to reach. While most list compilers offer business SICs with four digits, some compilers refine lists to six digits to identify narrow subgroups within the larger business area for more precise mail targeting.

33:15   Sequence for Storing Compiled List

When compiling a list you intend to use repeatedly, keep it in alphabetical sequence by name to facilitate subsequent location of names for cleaning or changing.

33:16   Compiled List Names Dilemma

Most brokers use the lists in the SRDS *Direct Marketing List Source* (formerly, *Direct Mail List Rates and Data*) as their primary list source. As a rule, the list name in the SRDS publication is the one supplied by the owner-compiler. As many compilers use the same source data, identical lists from the same source data may or may not have the same name.

33:17   House List Selection Priority

"In selecting lists," advises Howard Flood of the McGraw-Hill List Management Center, "choose house list first, response lists next, and compiled lists maybe." (at Professional Publishers Marketing Group (PPMG) meeting, NYC, September, 1986)

34

Tips on Business Mailings

Most business lists are segmented by industry or line of business. The U.S. Government's Standard Industrial Classification Code (SIC), a numerical coding system that classifies the total economy in different industry segments, is used for this purpose.
—DIRECT MARKETING ASSOCIATION
DMA Fact Book on Direct Marketing, 1983

34:01 Business List Versus Business-Compiled List

A business list, as a rule, is any list of names at business addresses, or a list of individuals with a business-associated interest. A business-compiled list is a list of names at business addresses usually taken from telephone books and various directories. *The Directory of Directories,* published by Gale Research Company of Detroit, lists over 5100 directories which provide compilation sources.

34:02 Addressing for Older Business Lists

If a business list is more than two years old, as a rule, the rate of delivery will be much higher if you mail to a job title or job function rather than to a named individual.

34:03 Business Title Addressing Rule

As a rule, when using a business list with a three-line address, you should always add a fourth line containing either a department, a job title, or a job function.

34:04 Reaching Business Decision Makers

As a rule, you can reach virtually any decision maker in a business organization by mailing to a firm name and address and adding a carefully focused title. Job-title or job-function lines work best with compiled lists.

34:05 Reaching High-Level Executives of Unknown Title

When a mailing is intended for a high-level corporate individual of unknown title, as a rule, you'll be more likely to reach him or her by addressing your mailing to "President" or "Chief Executive Officer." Whoever does the mail screening for the top executive will usually buck the mailing piece down to your intended prospect.

34:06 Multiple Mailings to Same Business Address

For business-to-business high-priced offers, consider multiple mailings to the same address with different titles. As a rule, many of such purchases involve the decision maker, the buyer, and the user.

34:07 Business-to-Business List: Comparison With Consumer List

A business-to-business list differs from a consumer list in this key aspect: The consumer list offers products or services to individuals for their own use. The business-to-business list offers products or services to a business for its own use, for producing other products, or for resale to other companies, institutions, or government agencies.

34:08 Way to Expand Business-to-Business Customer List

As a rule, you can expand a business-to-business customer list by eliminating the name of a particular individual and replacing it with various job titles at the same business address.

34:09   Vehicle for Increasing Business List Response

As a rule, any mailing to a business or professional address will enjoy a measurably larger response—both traceable and indirect—when it includes a routing slip or pass-along request.

34:10   Using Stamps to Increase Business List Response

When mailing to a business list, you will enjoy greater response if you use multiple precancelled stamps on the outer envelope. The stamps give the envelope the kind of personal look that helps get it past secretaries and into the hands of decision makers.

34:11   Mail Format for High-Level Corporate Executives

When mailing to a list of high-level corporate executives, your effort will be more effective if you plan for a mailing that looks more like a personally typed letter and less like a promotional piece.

35

Tips on Mailings to Professionals

Some compiled lists are segregated into categories defined by the source. Members of associations have a common denominator— they are all CPAs or electronics engineers for example. That may be all you need to sell a specialized item useful only to a class of customers by occupation.

—HERMAN HOLTZ
The Direct Marketer's Workbook, 1986

35:01 Professional List: Address Rule

Mail to professionals at their professional address if the offer is related to their professional practice. Mail to their home address if the offer is lifestyle related.

35:02 Mailing-Address Preference of Professionals

Most business and medical professionals prefer to receive business mail at their place of work. This was the finding of a study of one million professionals by Erdos and Morgan Inc. Research Service.

35:03   Professional Mail Pass-Along

As a rule, mailings to professionals at their business address have an added advantage over mailings to residence addresses in that they may be shared with or passed along to associates.

35:04   Lists of Professionals Who Buy by Mail

Mail-order book buyers in the academic, library, and health-care professions are often good prospects for related mail offers. The primary mailing list source for mail-order book buyers is CMG Information Services, P. O. Box 7000, Wilmington, MA 01887-7000.

35:05   Alternative to Mailing to Job Function

Some industries employ many individuals with the same job function. Consequently, to reach multiple individuals within such an organization, it may be better to advertise in a specialized periodical than to mail to a job title. Example: *C&E News* reaches several thousand chemists at DuPont.

35:06   Professional Association Membership List Source

When a rented list from a professional group works well for you, as a rule, there are related organizations whose names will often do equally well. These organizations can be located in *The Encyclopedia of Associations,* published by Gale Research, Detroit, Michigan. It is available in most libraries.

35:07   Way to Overcome List Rental Prohibition

When a professional association or society list is vital to your ongoing marketing efforts and the organization will not rent its membership list to outsiders, you can sometimes qualify for list rental by taking out a membership, or an associate membership.

35:08   Easy Way to Secure Certain Professional Lists

When a professional association or society does not rent membership lists, sometimes their periodical or journal includes an annual membership directory issue which you can obtain as part of a paid subscription.

35:09 Best Way to Target College Professors

As a rule, virtually any college professor in the United States can be reached in his or her school by course taught, type of school (two-year or four-year), by size of school enrollment, and many other factors. Faculty list selections for close to 5000 courses are available from CMG Information Services, P.O. Box 7000, Wilmington, MA 01887-7000.

35:10 Reliability Warning on Older Professional Lists

"The older the information on a list," Ray Lewis is quoted as saying (in Bodian, *Book Marketing Handbook,* volume two, 1983), "the more likely it is to be obsolete....For engineers, nurses, scientists, college professors, and other highly mobile professional groups, the general annual rate of change is about 20%. The 'deterioration index' for any such list would be 20% times the age of the list in years."

35:11 Annual Address Changes in Professional Groups

This author's 1983 research revealed the following annual address change rates for various professional groups: landscape architects, 24 percent; attorneys, 17 percent; book publishing industry, 25 percent; U.S. business, 20 percent. These figures can serve as a useful indicator of annual change in professional mailing lists compiled from old data.

36

Tips on Medical and Health-Care Lists

Because location has so much to do with building up a good practice, lists of doctors and dentists are subject to a small annual percentage of change.
—HARRY A. BELL
Getting the Right Start in Direct Advertising, 1946

36:01 Most Accurate Medical Lists

As a rule, medical lists rented from American Medical Association (AMA) Masterfile authorized agents are the most accurate for any business or professional group. They are updated weekly.

36:02 Address Rule for Mailings to Physicians

Use a physician's home address when you're selling products related to hobbies, leisure activities, investments, and nonpractice related offers. When such offers are directed to the medical office, a high percentage are usually discarded without being opened.

36:03   Physicians as Mail-Order Book Buyers

As a rule, younger doctors are better mail-order book buyers than older doctors for books intended for personal use. Older doctors, however, are more influential in terms of library acquisitions and textbook adoptions.

36:04   Way to Make Medical Offer More Effective

As a rule, when the offer is to a medical doctor, be sure to save the most important benefit for the postscript. Reason: Physicians tend to read the postscript before the letter.

36:05   Ink Color Rule for Medical Promotions

A medical promotion has a better chance of being looked at if it is printed in blue rather than black ink.

36:06   Necessity for Making Physician Mail Interesting

If you can't make a mailing to physicians extremely eye-appealing, don't mail it. One study indicated that doctors discard about 40 percent of the "uninteresting" mail promotions they receive without examining them.

36:07   Season to Avoid Mailing to Physicians

Physicians will look at interesting-looking mail all year round, but show the least interest during the Christmas season.

36:08   Best Age Group for Nonmedical Specialty Mailings

If you mail to medical doctors in any interest category outside their primary medical specialty, as a rule, your rental list will be more responsive if you specify doctors under the age of 55.

36:09   Most Mail-Responsive Names on M.D. Lists

As a group, the most mail-responsive names on any medical doctor list are those out of medical school five years or less.

36:10   Best Timing for Nurses Market

As a rule, nurses are most responsive to mailings sent between September and April.

36:11   Health-Care Industry as Largest U.S. Professional Group

The field of health care with more than 5 million names is the largest and most diverse professional group reachable through mailing lists. The lists are all carefully segmented. Registered nurses represent 2.2 million of the total. Most health-care lists can be found in SRDS *Direct Marketing List Source*.

36:12   Dental List Distinctions

Dental lists, as a rule, are provided at the professional address unless otherwise requested. Other dental list distinctions include specialty and number of hours per week at chairside.

36:13   Dentists as Mail-Responsive Individuals

As a rule, the approximately 125,000 actively practicing dentists in the United States are well above average income and tend to be responsive to business and personal mail offers, as well as offers related to their dental practice.

37

Periodical Circulation Lists

A circulation list is a list of regular recipients
of a periodical, including paid subscriptions,
and controlled or qualified recipients.
　　　　　　　　—NAT G. BODIAN
　　　　NTC's Dictionary of Direct Mail

37:01　Most Responsive Magazine Subscription Lists

As a rule, the most responsive lists for magazine subscription promotions are subscription lists of other magazines or newsletters.

37:02　Getting the Most Out of Circulation Lists

The way to get the most out of a periodical circulation list rental is to specify "active subscribers" on your rental order instead of just "subscribers."

37:03　Best Segment of Magazine Subscription List

If you rent magazine subscription lists, as a rule, your offer will do better if you rent only that portion of subscriber lists that have responded to mail subscription offers. Many magazines segment by-mail subscribers from those who subscribed by other means or received a gift subscription.

37:04 Rule for Getting Subscriber List After Turndown

As a rule, when a periodical refuses to rent its active subscriber list, sometimes you can come back and get a list of "expires"—that is, people who have let their subscriptions for the previous year run out.

37:05 Controlled or Paid Circulation: Quality Comparison

As a rule, when lists are available from *paid* and *controlled circulation* periodicals in the same field or profession, the quality of the paid circulation list is usually higher. A paid subscriber is a mail-order buyer, whereas controlled circulation subscribers receive the publication free of charge on the basis of their titles or occupations.

37:06 Periodical List Deliverability: Paid Versus Controlled

As a rule, a paid circulation subscription list is cleaner and has a higher rate of deliverability than a controlled or compiled circulation list because paid subscribers have an ongoing financial interest in receiving delivery.

37:07 Periodical List Follow-Up Mailing Rule

As a rule, if a periodical subscription list produces a high rate of response on an initial mailing, a follow-up mailing to the same list about 30 days after delivery of the first mailing will usually produce 40 to 60 percent of the initial response.

37:08 Pull of "Expires" List Compared With Outside lists

As a rule, a list of a periodical's expires of recent years will work as well as most outside rented lists.

38

Tips on Consumer Lists

Consumer lists are names always at home addresses...names resulting from a common inquiry or buying activity...names resulting from a general or specific purchasing interest...or names compiled from public records.

Adapted from Nat G. Bodian, NTC's Dictionary of Direct Mail, 1990

38:01 List Availability of U.S. Consumers

As a rule, more than 90 percent of the approximately 92 million U.S. households are reachable by mail through various available response and compiled consumer lists.

38:02 Largest Consumer List Reaches 160 Million

One of the largest and most sophisticated consumer lists at the end of 1993 was the Database America Consumer File from Database America, Montvale, NJ 07645. It included 85 million households representing 160 million individuals. The list has ZIP-plus-four addresses and 20 selects, including homeowner, telephone number, known mail-order buyer, and credit card holder. Rebuilt quarterly, the compiler,

Database America, guarantees full-postage refund for undeliverables from its ZIP-plus-four records.

38:03 Way to Eliminate Waste in Consumer Mailing Lists

As a rule, there is a way you can eliminate names of consumers who do not want to receive advertising mail. A list of people who have indicated they do not wish to receive such mail is available on magnetic tape from Mail Preference Service, the Direct Marketing Association, 6 East 43rd Street, New York, NY 10017.

38:04 Usual Residential List Selection Options

As a rule, the selection options usually available for a residential list include: head of household by name, single or multiple family dwelling, average income, age of individual, age and number of children.

38:05 Annual Rate of Consumer List Decline

As a rule, about 16 out of every 100 persons change their address every year. That's why it's important to check the currentness of the consumer lists you rent. (Source: U.S. Census Bureau data, as reported in *The New York Times*, December 12, 1994)

38:06 Importance of Apartment Number in Consumer Lists

Residence mailings to individuals living in multiple dwellings often go undelivered because they lack apartment numbers. Be alert for apartment numbers in residence list rentals.

38:07 Enhancing Residential List Deliverability

When using residential lists, you can save a piece addressed to a former occupant by adding a second line after the name line of the address reading, "or Current Resident."

38:08 Way to Reduce Consumer List Nondeliverables

About two-thirds of the more than 40 million movers in the United States each year are renters. The other movers are home owners (or home buyers). If you mail to consumer lists, you should be able to cut your nondeliverable or "nixie" rate by about two-thirds by using lists of home owners only. (A Census Bureau analysis revealed that 9.4 percent of home owners moved in the 15 months prior to the 1990 census, compared with more than 40 percent of renters during the period. Source: *The New York Times,* December 12, 1994)

38:09 Way to Reach Consumers With Highest Discretionary Income

Consumers over age 60 have the highest discretionary income in the United States. Over-age-60 consumer lists represent excellent prospects for all types of products designed to make life healthier, more enjoyable, and more comfortable. Age-60-plus consumers respond to health-related offers, music, continuity clubs, jewelry and fashion accessories, apparel, book clubs, gardening, subscription offers, collectibles, and housewares.

38:10 Most Responsive Consumer Age Group

College-age students are the most responsive consumer group for direct mail offers. College-age students are responsive to offers for books, casual clothing, video tapes, sporting goods, and photo supplies, in that order.

38:11 Mail Responsiveness of Consumers Over the Age of 50

"Of consumers over the age of 50, 40 percent had bought something through direct mail during the past three months compared to only 16 percent who purchased by phone." So say Carol M. Morgan and Doran J. Levy in *Segmenting the Mature Market,* 1993. (In this same book, the authors claim this same market segment throws away 17 percent of the direct mail they receive unopened.)

38:12 Pull of Country Dwellers Versus City Dwellers

"As a rule," says Ted Nicholas in *The Golden Mailbox,* 1992, "lists of country dwellers outpull lists of city dwellers."

38:13   Free Trial Offers to Consumer Lists: Cautionary Note

As a rule, consumer lists should not be used for free exam or free trial offers. Such offers work best when mailed to business addresses or to professional individuals in business or organizational environments.

38:14   Consumer Lists for Puerto Rico: Cautionary Note

As a rule, consumer lists with standard three-line addresses that follow USPS guidelines for the 50 states are not applicable for consumer addresses in Puerto Rico. Therefore, if you plan to include any Puerto Rican addresses in any mailing list database, be sure such addresses adhere to the special USPS address requirements for Puerto Rico, or your mail going to Puerto Rico will not be deliverable as addressed.

38:15   Response Potential for Hispanic Consumer Lists

As a rule, Hispanic households respond to direct mail offers at three times the rate of Anglo households. One reason: Hispanic households receive just 13 pieces of direct mail a year compared to 300 pieces of direct mail to Anglo households. In the decade ending in the year 2000, Hispanic households are expected to grow by 48 percent to about 10 million. (Source: *Solar Reflections*, February, 1994)

39

Contributor and Fund-Raising List Tips

If you are to touch your prospect's pocketbook,
you must first touch his heart.
—MARGARET M. FELLOWS AND M. H. KOENIG
In Kobs, Profitable Direct Marketing, 1992

39:01   Yield Criteria for Fund-Raising Lists

As a rule, fund-raisers have three yardsticks for measuring yield from a particular fund-raising list: (1) rate of response or percentage of return, (2) dollars returned for each dollar spent, (3) average dollar contribution per donor.

39:02   Classes of Fund-Raising Lists

As a rule, fund-raising lists are divided into two classifications. If contributions originated from a fund-raising effort, the list is a *responder list*. If contributions originated from a charity appeal, the list is a *donor list*.

39:03 Multiple-Cause Rule

Contributors to one cause are usually good prospects to contribute to another cause as well.

39:04 List Know-How of Fund-Raising Professionals

As a rule, states the *DMA Fact Book*, "most direct marketing fund-raisers know from a given list how many will donate...how long they will donate...and what the affordable acquisition cost is by source."

39:05 Age Factor in Charity Appeals

As a rule, with increasing age, people become more responsive to charity appeals.

39:06 Contributor List Quality

The larger the donation, as a rule, the better the prospect. Large contributors not only give more, but give more frequently as well.

39:07 Contributor Lists Often Better Than Indicated

As a rule, a large percentage of contributors give more than once to a cause they consider worthy. Therefore, even a low response rate from a contributor or donor list may prove extremely profitable over time.

39:08 How Gender Contributor Lists Work

When contributor lists are available by gender, as a rule, women tend to be better givers for most appeals. However, when aiming for major contributions, male-addressed appeals tend to produce better results.

39:09 Rule for Using Fund-Raising List With Other Offers

A list of donors will not be responsive to other types of mailings that are not directly related to the cause to which they contributed. Such mailings might include, for example, a magazine whose editorial content is directly related to the fund-raising cause, or a political magazine for a politically related donor list.

39:10   Business List Selection for Charity Appeals

As a rule, a list of small companies in a prospering industrial classification will offer better prospects for a fund-raising appeal than a like appeal to larger companies in the same activity. Small company lists are readily obtainable by industrial classification as well as by number of workers employed within that classification.

39:11   Fund-Raising Affinity List Rule

A list of business firms having some connection with the nature of a charity or fund-raising appeal will be more responsive than a list of like-size companies with no relation to the appeal.

40

Testing: Basics and Guidelines

There are two kinds of tests: (1) Tactical tests;
(2) Approach tests. Tactical tests [mainly]
include testing of lists, timing, non-
duplication, plotting response
patterns....Approach tests include testing the
offer and copy.

—ED MCLEAN
The Basics of Testing, 1978

40:01   Rule for Regional Mailings

If you plan a direct mail test of a specific geographic region or of a limited number of states, as a rule, you will draw your best response from
the states closest to your address as shown.

40:02   Rule for Evaluating New-List Test Results

Always test one or more proven lists at the same time that you test
new lists so that you can have comparative results.

40:03 Percentage Formula in Large-List Testing

As a rule, you can't get hurt with a large mailing list when you test with 5 percent and, if successful, follow up with 20 percent more. If that works, you can mail to the remaining 75 percent.

40:04 Response Drop-Off From Rollout After Test

As a rule, the response rate from a rollout to the balance of the list after a successful test mailing will usually be lower than the response from the test.

40:05 Test Minimums for Judging Response Results

If you're looking for a 2 percent return, you can get by with a test of as few as 2500 names. However, if you expect a 1 percent response, you should mail to at least 5000 names. Either way, you should aim for 40 to 50 responses per list or list segment to be able to "read" results. (Source: *Newsletter on Newsletters*, December 15, 1986)

40:06 Rule for When to Skip List Tests

As a rule, a small, highly targeted list does not have to be tested. If you're trying to sell a book on organic chemistry and you have a list of 3000 organic chemistry book buyers, what is there to test?

40:07 Large-List Minimums

When you wish to test a very small segment of a large list, be prepared for minimum list requirements usually of 5000 names, but often 10,000 names.

40:08 One Way to Meet Large-List Minimums

As a rule, a very large list with a minimum test requirement that is too large for you may be feasible if you can test several different segments of the list that add up to the minimum.

40:09 Most Reliable Cross Section of Large List

As a rule, Nth name selection is probably the most reliable cross-sectional sample you can get from a list for test purposes. In this method portions of a list are selected in a set numerical pattern, such as every tenth name, etc.

40:10 ZIP Code Random Selection List Test

As a rule, you can prevent remailing to the same names after an Nth-name selection test if you opt instead for a test of the list using a random selection based on the last one or two digits of the ZIP Code. If the test is successful, you eliminate the ZIP Code test numbers when you roll out to a larger portion of the list, or to the entire list.

40:11 Testing in ZIP Sequence

When testing a segment of a larger list, a good way to ensure that you are getting a true cross section is to order a list segment in ZIP sequence.

40:12 Best Segmentation for Regional Test

The best approach for doing a regional test of a very large list, as a rule, is to select the names for the region or states in which coverage is desired and then do an Nth name select (every 5th name, etc.) for the names in that region only.

40:13 Test Speed-Up Rule

Response from any direct mail test can be speeded by mailing first-class instead of third-class.

40:14 Rule for Avoiding Duplication After Test

When you subsequently mail to an entire list after testing one or more segments, you can avoid duplication to earlier-mailed names by requesting that previously mailed names be suppressed.

40:15   Rule for Repeating to List Test Segments

Test segments of large lists are usually skipped on the rollout mailing. However, when the test produces an unusually high rate of response, it usually pays to include the test segment of the list in your rollout.

40:16   Test Rollout Quantity Rule

High-volume mailers who test a small segment of a large list will not remail or rollout to more than ten times the test quantity.

40:17   Test Rollout Segmentation Rule

When you plan to mail only to certain segments of a large list, make it a rule to do list testing of only those list segments you intend to roll out to.

40:18   Erosion Rate from Test to Rollout

As a rule, there is an erosion of response of about 20 percent from test to rollout on any large list.

40:19   When Response Diminishes From Test to Rollout

Sometimes a list that does marginally well in a test will fail miserably on a later continuation mailing. As a rule, the reason may be in the age of the names on the list. As list names get older, they lose effectiveness.

40:20   Testing to Counteract House List Erosion

As a rule, experienced mailers try to include one or more test lists with each mailing to counteract the normal erosion of their house lists.

40:21   Test Rule for Periodical Subscriptions

In periodical subscription promotions that involve a trial subscription, rollout after a test of a large list should evaluate not only initial response, but also payup rate at the end of the trial offer.

40:22   Rule for Determining List Response Rate

The response rate from any list is never a given. It depends on the offer and is arrived at for a particular offer only through testing and retesting.

40:23   Response Period of Most Test Campaigns

As a rule, you can count on about 95 percent of the response in a test campaign in eight to twelve weeks after receipt of the first response.

40:24   Price Test Rule

The highest response in a price test will not necessarily come from the lowest price.

40:25   List Testing Through Package Inserts

As a rule, the package insert offers an easy and relatively inexpensive way to test a list. Such inserts, which are put into outgoing packages along with ordered merchandise, get the attention of the customer when he or she opens the package.

40:26   Copy, Price, and Offer Test Packaging

As a rule, for copy, price, or offer testing, it is better to test two mailing packages on several lists, than to test one package on one list.

40:27   Price Testing

As a rule, the lowest price may not always be the most responsive price in a mail offer. If you're into testing, try different prices in split tests on the same lists to see which of two or more price variations produce the best results.

40:28   Rule for Evaluating Split-Test Results

As a rule, results from split tests should not be considered seriously unless the differences are substantial.

40:29   Variable Testing Rule

Variable testing in any direct mail effort should be limited to one test at a time for the results to be valid. Mixing two tests in the same mailing will dilute the results for each test and prove nothing.

40:30   Measuring Value of Test Results

As a rule, a test does not have to produce a profitable result to be of value. One can often learn more from a failed test than from a mildly successful one. Rose Harper said it best in *Mailing List Strategies*, 1986: "No test is ever a failure if you learn something from it."

40:31   Sure Indicator of Repeated Test Successes

"When you receive the same mailing over and over...you can be reasonably sure," say Kenneth Roman and Jane Mass, "that it has been proven in testing." (In *The New How to Advertise*, 1992)

40:32   Retest Rule for Marginal Lists

When a highly touted list gives marginal test results, as a rule, if you retry the list using only the "hotline" names the second time, you'll get much-improved results. (*See 31:08*)

40:33   Simple Way to Test Small List Segments

When you wish to test tiny mailing list segments that are too small to be keyed cost-effectively, as a rule, you can solve this problem by color-edging the response cards of each list segment with different color marking pens or crayons.

40:34   Best Way to Test Internationally

"The best way to test internationally, says Chris Page, "is through a relationship with a direct mail company overseas that is familiar with the intricacies of local and international markets." Page, a British-born vice president, international, of Direct Media, Inc., in Greenwich, Connecticut, adds, "Don't make the mistake of assuming everyone does things the way we do them in the U.S." (In *Catalog Age*, March 1992)

PART 4

List Brokers, Compilers, and Managers

41

List Brokers: When and How to Use Them

The list broker makes all the necessary arrangements for one company to make use of the list of another company.
—ROBERT J. POSCH
The Direct Marketer's Legal Adviser, 1983

41:01   Functions of List Broker

The list broker is a marketing professional who researches the list availabilities for a mailer's product or service and then makes recommendations based on availabilities and the broker's professional judgment or prior experience with the lists recommended. The broker will also assist with subsequent evaluation of a list's performance.

41:02   Advantage of Working With a List Broker

As a rule, a principal advantage of working with a list broker is that you can tap into his or her knowledge of lists used by other clients that have performed exceptionally well for particular types of offers or merchandise.

41:03   Financial Benefit of Working With a Broker

"Because a broker generally knows (and is trusted by) most of the principal list owners, managers, and mailers, he can generally obtain terms and concessions which might not be available to mailers working alone." So says Rose Harper in the DMA Monograph, *Mailing Lists: A Practical Guide*, 1984.

41:04   Which is Better—One Broker or Several?

As a rule, you will get much better service if you work with a single broker who has an intimate knowledge of your market and your offerings than you would by working with two or more and comparing recommendations of each before ordering lists.

41:05   Criteria for Selecting the Right Broker

If you plan to deal with a list broker, as a rule, you will do better if you select one that has a good reputation and proven track record in the markets you are trying to reach. He should also have a reputation for service and on-time list delivery, as well as an intimate knowledge of computer processing and mailing procedures.

41:06   Broker Result Discussions Confidential

As a rule, when you discuss mailing results with a broker, he will use the information only as an aid in assisting your future list selections. The broker may, however, indicate to others that the lists you tested were reordered.

41:07   Rule for Identifying Customer for Broker

As a rule, the more clearly you define your typical customer for your list broker or compiler, the better he or she is able to research other lists for prospects bearing a similar profile for you to test.

41:08   How List Brokers Are Compensated

The list broker works for the mailer, but is paid a commission, usually 20 percent, by the list owner. The list broker never charges the list renter for research, list recommendations, or location of new list sources.

41:09 How Broker Can Create Market for Product

When you believe you have a good mail-order product, but are unsure of a market, as a rule, a good broker can assemble a group of lists known to have worked for related products and create a potential market for your offer.

41:10 When You Need a List Broker

"As a rule of thumb," advised Freeman Gosden in *Direct Marketing Success*, 1985, "use a list broker when the choice of lists is wide; use a list owner when the choice is segmentation within a list."

41:11 Type of List Broker to Select

As a rule, business lists tend to be considerably smaller than consumer lists. Consequently, if you mail primarily to business addresses, be sure to select a list broker accustomed to working with and knowledgeable in smaller business lists.

41:12 Important Advantage of Dealing With a Broker

One big advantage of using a list broker for a potential new project is that if the broker's research finds that the market is too small for your project, he may suggest that you scrap the project.

41:13 Lead Time Needed for Broker-Arranged Orders

As a rule, a list broker needs at least ten days to place an order with a list owner and get the list run off. Unless the list broker is local, add the time necessary for list delivery on to that period.

41:14 Broker's Responsibility for List Delivery

As a rule, the list broker will ensure that the list rentals he has arranged will be delivered on a timely basis.

41:15   Brokers: Primary Source for Lists

As a rule, direct marketers rely more heavily on personal contacts with list brokers than on any other source. Personal contacts with list managers is second, and the SRDS publication *Direct Marketing List Source* (formerly *Direct Mail List Rates and Data*) is third.

41:16   List Brokers Are Also Often Managers

As a rule, many list managers include a department or division which specializes in list management.

41:17   Primary Source of Broker List Information

As a rule, most list brokers rely on SRDS *Direct Marketing List Source* (formerly *Direct Mail List Rates and Data*) as their primary source of list information. Personal contact with list managers ranks second.

41:18   Getting Names of List Brokers

The best place to get names of list brokers—unless you can find out who your competitor uses—is the Direct Marketing Association (DMA), at 6 East 43rd Street, New York, NY, 10017. They'll give you names in your area, or perhaps in your specialized business interest. You may also find some broker names listed in the Yellow Pages of your nearest big-city phone directory under "Mailing Lists."

41:19   Checking Broker Qualifications

You can use these steps to check the qualifications of the broker you're considering: (1) ask broker for client references; (2) call the references and ask about their list success; (3) question whether their overall experience was satisfactory; (4) ask for names of others they know who also used the broker; (5) call the other references and ask about their experience with the broker. (Adapted from "Work Smart with List Brokers" in *Sales and Marketing Strategies & News*, Sept./Oct. 1993)

42

List Compilers: When and How to Use Them

The quality of the recommendations compilers make is a reflection of the "tools" you provide them to work with....Know your customers better than you know yourself.
—CHUCK ORLOWSKI
In (Nash) The Direct Marketing Handbook, 1984

42:01　Compiler's Sources of Lists

As a rule, virtually all compiled lists come from the following sources: the 5200-plus directories published annually—telephone directories, both white pages and yellow pages; government publications, both federal and state; census data; trade show registrations; warranty cards; registration lists; trade journals; college catalogs and class schedules; telephone research.

42:02　The Triple Role of Some Compilers

In some instances, the list compiler is also the list manager and the list broker. Like a list broker, the compiler knows which lists have worked well for clients and is happy to share this knowledge with customers.

42:03   Compilers as Market Specialists

As a rule, compilers tend to specialize by market. Some compilers favor business and professional markets only. Others compile lists only in the consumer market.

42:04   Difference Between Compiler and Broker

Where list brokers, as a rule, represent all mailing list owners, the list compiler normally represents only those lists owned and maintained by the compiler's company.

42:05   Functions of Compiler With Single Large List

When a list compiler represents a single large list, his intimate knowledge of various segments of that list enables him to recommend certain test segments he believes closely match a client's customer profile.

42:06   Compiler Considered as List Owner

As a rule, a list compiler acts as a list owner when dealing with a mailer or with a list broker. Where a compiler satisfied an order with a list obtained from another compiler, the compiler-supplier is still considered the list owner.

42:07   How Compilers Work From Customer Specs

As a rule, a compiler will compile and supply names on order to any specifications supplied by a customer or a potential customer.

42:08   Way to Discover Compiler's List Source

As a rule, you can learn what source a compiler has used for a list by looking under "Source" in the entry for that list in the SRDS *Direct Marketing List Source* (formerly *Direct Mail List Rates and Data*). This can be helpful when you have two or more lists of potential interest and you want to learn which, if any, originated from the same source.

42:09 Compiler Rule for List Maintenance

A list compiler has total responsibility for the maintenance and promotion of any compiled list offered for rental.

42:10 Compiler Attitudes Toward List Maintenance

As a rule, most list compilers find it easier to recompile annually or periodically than to update compiled lists on a regular basis.

43

List Managers: When and How to Use Them

The list manager is an employee of a list owner or an outside agent responsible for the use by others of specific mailing lists.
—DIRECT MARKETING ASSOCIATION
DMA Fact Book on Direct Marketing, 1983

43:01 Primary Role of List Manager

As a rule, the primary function of a list manager is to handle all the details of outside rentals for a list owner. The manager's job is to "sell" the list as well as to handle all details of record keeping, billing, and accounting. The list manager may be an in-house employee of the list owner on salary, or an outside list management company working on commission.

43:02 Specialized Consumer List Management

Some consumer list management firms will specialize in a particular area, such as fund-raising, periodicals, or high-ticket mail-order catalogs. If you do consumer mailings, it will be worth your while to investigate the list management firms that specialize in your interest area.

43:03   The Wider Role of an Outside List Manager

Some outside list management firms may represent from 100 to 200 different lists. As a rule, most tend to specialize in either business lists or consumer lists.

43:04   How List Manager Serves Broker

The list manager serves the list broker by recommending specific lists, or specific segments within a large list, which meet the criteria supplied by the broker on behalf of a client and which the manager, from intimate knowledge of the list or lists managed, believes will have a good match with the broker client's product or service.

43:05   When to Deal With a List Manager

When you use very few lists and in modest quantities, as a rule, you will get more help by working directly with list managers than by going to a list broker.

43:06   Manager and Broker Responsibilities: A Comparison

A list manager's primary function is to "sell" the owner's list and maximize rental income. A list broker's function is to help a mailer find the most appropriate list. As a rule, you should work directly with a list manager only after you are sure the manager's lists are the most appropriate lists for your purposes. A list manager can clue you in to the most appropriate selection options within the lists managed and the various computerized formats in which the lists may be supplied.

43:07   Dual Role of Professional List Managers

As a rule, says Ed Burnett in Bodian, *NTC's Dictionary of Direct Mail*, 1990, "all professional list managers broker as well as manage lists."

43:08   List Manager Often Also List Broker

A list management firm marketing the house list of a mail-order business may often also be its list broker. When renting his client's house list to outsiders, the firm collects the typical manager's commission as compensation. When acquiring outside lists for the same mail-order business, the firm is acting as a broker and collects the broker's commission from the owners of the lists the firm is acquiring for the firm's client.

43:09   When List Performance Falters, Talk to Manager

As a rule, when a known, successful list starts to give poor or radically changed results, it may be worth a talk with the list manager. Ask if anything has changed in the list owner's operations. Sometimes list quality may be affected by company changes in marketing strategy, pricing, advertising approach, or pricing structure.

43:10   Compensation of List Managers

Only when list rentals are significant and can cover salary and overhead does a company employ an in-house manager. As a rule, list management is handled by outside professional list management companies. Their management income is derived from rental commissions, usually 10 percent. Commissions may vary, however, depending on degree of manager involvement and scale of management services rendered to the list owner.

43:11   Profile of List Manager's Employer

A list manager serves a list owner either as an employee or as an outside agent. The list owner, as a rule, is a developer of a list of names with something in common, acquired through promotional activity or by compilation. Occasionally, a list owner may acquire a list outright through purchase from a list developer.

43:12   List Manager Channels of Promotion

As a rule, the primary channels through which a list manager will promote a list are personal calls on prospective customers, telephone contacts, newsletters, space ads, and direct mail promotion.

PART 5
Telemarketing

44

Telemarketing Basics

One advantage of telemarketing is that you
get instant response.
—LINDA PINSON AND JERRY JINETT
Target Marketing for the Small
Business, 1993

44:01 Primary Incentive for Telemarketing

As a rule, one of the primary incentives for getting into telemarketing is its low start-up cost. Most firms get into telemarketing by using the services of an outside service bureau.

44:02 Telemarketing Name Recognition Rule

As a rule, telemarketing works best when the calling company is known to the person called, or is a present or past customer.

44:03 Best Way to Start in Telemarketing

When considering an in-house telemarketing operation, as a rule, it is best to start with an experienced outside service to see how they do it.

44:04   Telemarketing Capital of the United States

As a rule, you'll have less trouble finding a telemarketing service in Omaha, Nebraska, than in any other city of the United States. The city of 339,000 has 27 telemarketing firms that provide jobs for more than 10,000 local residents.

44:05   Key Advantage of Telemarketing

A big advantage of marketing by telephone is its complete flexibility. As a rule, a test of any list can be accomplished in a relatively short time. Also, necessary changes can be made in price, terms, and copy approach as warranted early in the test.

44:06   Suggestion for Starting In-House Program

If you're new to telemarketing and plan to start a program in-house, as a rule, it will be beneficial to contact a local telemarketing service for either training assistance or recommendations in obtaining qualified telemarketing personnel.

44:07   Telemarketing Relationship Rule

Once you've established a telephone relationship with a customer, you can go back to that customer by phone again and again.

44:08   Telemarketing List Affinity Rule

When seeking outside lists for telemarketing, look for lists of buyers who have responded to offers for similar products or services.

44:09   Telemarketing List Frequency Rule

A telemarketing list should not be used more than once for the same offer, and not more often than every three months for a different offer.

44:10   Mail-Responsive Lists for Telemarketing

As a rule, a list that performs well for a mail offer will do considerably better in a telemarketing effort.

44:11 Telephone Numbers for Telemarketing

Always be sure to have all the telephone numbers before the start of a telemarketing campaign. If the list is not available with numbers, either use in-house staff or an outside lookup service.

44:12 List Budgeting for Telemarketing

Not all business lists are available with telephone numbers. Consequently, when budgeting telemarketing list costs, include the cost of telephone-number lookups by independent search services and any additional fee should a sheet listing be requested with rental lists.

44:13 Lists That Qualify for Telemarketing

As a rule, any mailing list that produces more than a 2 percent response is a potential list for a telemarketing test, provided the product lends itself to telemarketing and the price is high enough to warrant such an effort.

44:14 Consumer Telemarketing: Best Hours to Call

As a rule, the best time period for calling consumers at home is between the hours of 5 p.m. and 9 p.m.

44:15 Evaluation Rule for Telemarketing Test

Within a 10-hour test it is usually possible to ascertain whether an intended telemarketing campaign has any potential.

44:16 Telemarketing Response Versus Direct Mail

"As a general rule of thumb," says Ed Nash (*Direct Marketing*, 1982) "telephone responsiveness can average ten times that of direct mail— as high as 25 to 35 percent of all calls made."

44:17 In-House Telemarketing Value Rule

It will not be cost-effective to engage an in-house telemarketing staff if you're selling products with an order value of less than $75.

44:18 Product Value Rule for Telemarketing Service

It probably will not be cost-effective to sell a product through an outside telemarketing service if it has an order value of less than $100.

44:19 Checking Outside Service for Specific Campaign

If you plan to engage an outside telephone answering service in conjunction with a particular campaign, as a rule, you should call the service at the outset of the campaign to ensure that incoming calls are processed in strict accordance with your instructions.

44:20 Business-to-Business Telemarketing Cost

As a rule, when a telemarketing call replaces a sales call, the average cost is $10 for a completed call. The personal visit by a salesperson, by contrast, could cost a company as much as $800.

44:21 Prompt Delivery Is Crucial in Telemarketing

An important rule of telemarketing: Never hold up orders. The sooner you get the product into your customer's hands, the more likely the customer is to recall placing the order. If the product sold is priced high enough to warrant the expense of overnight delivery, this type of service is most effective.

44:22 Telemarketing Edge Over Other Forms of Advertising

The advantage that telephone marketing has over advertising and direct mail is immediacy. When an offer is not clear to the prospect or customer being called, the telemarketer can answer questions at once; when a customer or prospect raises objections, the telemarketer can respond to them as they arise; when additional information is requested to clarify an offer, what might take days or even weeks by mail can be addressed over the telephone in a matter of moments.

44:23 Telemarketing as a Growth Industry in the United States

Telemarketing is the fastest-growing segment of the U.S. economy. Sales of goods and services by telephone reached $300 billion in 1993. Contrasted with telephone sales a decade earlier, this was a 535 percent increase. Telephone sales in 1983 were $56 billion. (*Source:* "Sorry, Wrong Number," *Time* magazine, September 13, 1993)

44:24 Telemarketing as a Growth Industry in the United Kingdom

The telemarketing industry in the United Kingdom in late 1992 was estimated at 4.5 billion pounds (roughly 6.75 billion U.S. dollars) and employed several hundred thousand people making and receiving calls. This, according to Simon Roncoroni, a London telemarketing consultant, in *Direct Marketing International,* October 1992.

45

Prospect Lists
for Telemarketing

*A telephone call takes less time than a
canvass, is more personal than a letter, costs
less than both (unless long distance) and
provides fairly close personal contact with
your prospect.*

—JAY CONRAD LEVINSON
Guerrilla Marketing for the Nineties, 1993

45:01   Businesses as Prospects for Telemarketing

As a rule, more than 80 percent of all telemarketing revenues are generated from pitches to other businesses.

45:02   Effective Way to Get Telemarketing Prospects

"One of the more effective and time-tested ways to find telemarketing
prospects," says Phillip Mahfood (in *Teleselling*, 1993) "is through
prints ads placed in trade publications aimed at [the target] industry."
Adding a clip-out coupon, he says, compels the prospect to supply
the envelope and postage, an indication of being serious about the
offer.

45:03 Effective Quantity for Telemarketing List Test

As a rule, says Bill Good of Telephone Marketing, Inc. (in *Prospecting Your Way to Sales Success*, 1986), a test list order should not be more than a thousand names. You will certainly know well before a thousand if the list has potential. (*Author's note:* Some telemarketing lists have minimums of 1500.)

45:04 How Big a Telemarketing List to Rent

When you plan a telemarketing campaign from a very large list that has proved successful in tests, how large a list should you buy for follow-up? One telemarketing pro has a formula which he says works well for him: Estimate how many calls you can make in one week and multiply that total times eight.

45:05 Recommended List Format for Business Prospecting

The recommended list format for telephone business prospecting is the 3- by 5-inch telemarketing sales card. This card format is available from a number of business list compilers. On request some business list compilers will also include such information as SIC business category, sales volume, number of employees, and telephone number with area code.

45:06 Most Convenient List Format for Teleselling

As a rule, when you rent a list for telephone selling, you should ask for the names on a sheet listing. This provides the telemarketer with the names on sheets, one address to a line, usually with 50 lines to a page. There is an additional charge for this list format.

45:07 List Classification for Telemarketing Buyers

As a rule, lists of people who buy through telemarketing solicitation are classified as *mail-order buyers* although, technically, the term applies to those who have ordered and paid for a product or service bought through the mail.

46

Reminders for Telephone Marketing

Telemarketing works best when you are selling
an expensive product that demands lengthy
explanations and personal selling skills.
—TED NICHOLAS
The Golden Mailbox, 1993

46:01 Benefits of a Prepared Telemarketing Script

As a rule, a prepared telemarketing script works best because it enables the caller to sound knowledgeable, cover essential points, and test the message against a message with different variables and get measurable results.

46:02 Successful Telephone Selling Rule

The key to all successful telephone selling is to always be sure you are speaking to people who are capable of making an ordering decision.

46:03 Way to Upgrade Telemarketer Effectiveness

As a rule, the better informed the telemarketer is about the offer and its benefits, the more effective his or her sales pitch will be.

46:04 Basic Rule of Telemarketing

Sincerity and courtesy are the basic rules of telemarketing. It is best to avoid a pitch that attempts to be clever, tricky, or gimmicky.

46:05 Effect of Caller Gender on Telemarketing Success

As a rule, comments Dr. Gary S. Goodman, a telemarketing consultant, gender has no effect on telemarketing performance (in *Reach Out and Sell Someone*, 1983). He adds, however, that females selling products closely associated with femininity seem to fare much better than male callers. Conversely, he says further, males seem to have more success with "macho" or heavy industrial products.

46:06 Modulating Telemarketing Pitch to Sound Natural

A telemarketer should strive to speak in his or her natural voice and not like someone reading a script. A good way to accomplish this, says Bill Good (in *Prospecting Your Way to Sales Success*, 1986) is to have the telemarketer practice the script many times and then record the last reading. Later, play it back against a recording of the person speaking naturally.

46:07 Idea for Getting the "Very Best" Telemarketing Reps

As a group, says Dr. Gary S. Goodman, a telemarketing consultant and training expert, unemployed actors make the very best telemarketing representatives. "They appreciate the job because they are out of work frequently. They are often excellent communicators who can adjust to different people on the phone. They take criticism constructively, and they respond quickly to suggested changes." (in *Reach out and Sell Someone*, 1983)

46:08   Low-Cost Source of Telemarketing Reps

A good way to save time and money in recruitment of telemarketing representatives is to contact the employment offices at nearby colleges. College employment services can provide a good talent pool of trainable help, and they can prescreen candidates in keeping with your requirements before recommending them to you.

46:09   Telemarketing Pitch Procedure

As a rule, any telemarketing pitch will have a better reception if the name of the calling company and the reason for the call are given first.

46:10   Telemarketing Pitch Success Indicator

A telemarketing pitch that is producing results after the first 50 calls will, as a rule, continue to work well after 500.

46:11   Test Sample Size for Large Telemarketing List

When you're planning a test of a large telemarketing list, advises Ernest Roman of CCI Telemarketing, as a rule, "an effective test can be accomplished with as few as 500 calls." (In *DM News*, November 15, 1994)

46:12   List Size Rule in Telemarketing

If like offers have worked well with larger lists, as a rule, a list of as few as 500 names can be used for a telemarketing campaign.

46:13   Acceptance Rate of Telemarketed Free Trial Product

As a rule, only about 25 percent of the people who agree to accept a product for free examination through a telemarketing offer will wind up buying it.

46:14   Advance Letter in Business Telemarketing

As a rule, in business telemarketing a sales letter sent to prospects in advance of a call will enhance the effectiveness of the call. The letter gives the telemarketer a reason for making the call, and it provides the prospect with information that can be discussed during the call.

47

Inbound Telemarketing With 800 Numbers

800 service, first introduced by AT&T in 1967, is popular for ordering by mail and from catalogs....Such services have increased dramatically during the last ten years.

—JOEL LINCHITZ
The Complete Guide to Telemarketing Management, 1990

47:01   800 Number Versatility

The 800 number is the most versatile response device ever conceived for direct marketing. It can be used in every direct marketing application, in all advertising media and in all forms of communication, with products or with services.

47:02   800 Number as Instant Response Device

As a rule, a toll-free 800 number provides the best means for instant customer responses, without apparent cost, at the moment of greatest advertising impact. This, according to Robert J. Posch in *The Direct Marketer's Legal Adviser*, 1983.

47:03   Adding 800 Number With Special Offers

As a rule, when your offer includes a premium or special benefit for prompt response, including an 800 number will substantially increase the number of responses by telephone.

47:04   Using 800 Numbers for Prepaid Orders

As a rule, 800 telephone numbers work well in mail promotions and space advertising that require prepayment by inviting payment by credit card. Here's how best to say it in print: "To charge your purchase by phone, call toll free: 1-800-000-0000—and use your credit card!"

47:05   800 Number Use for Orders Only

When the 800 number is only for credit card orders, as a rule, you can eliminate unrelated calls by preceding the 800 number with: "For Credit Card Orders Only, Call:"

47:06   Fax Number Appended to 800 Number

When order forms are complex or include numerous checkoff items, it is helpful to include a Fax number under the 800 number. The Fax number, as a rule, should be in smaller type and in a lighter typeface than the bold-faced 800 number.

47:07   Using Hours With 800 Numbers

As a rule, 800 numbers in mail or print ad offers should always include calling hours. In business offers, "Call during business hours" is usually adequate. However, for consumer offers, hours should be stated. With service bureaus that provide round-the-clock service, numbers are usually accompanied by "Call toll free 24 hours:" or "Call 24 hours a day, 7 days a week:"

47:08   Identifying 800 Area Coverage

If your 800 number is for a limited geographic area, as a rule, always include the area covered. If the 800 number is for out-of-state calls only, be sure to include that information so that in-state callers will not be sidetracked.

47:09 800 Number Exposure Time on TV

As a rule, it takes a TV viewer a minimum of 15 to 20 seconds to record an on-screen 800 number after a sales pitch. Exposing the 11-digit number for a lesser time can result in lost orders.

47:10 No-Cost Way to Increase 800 Number Calls

As a rule, one of the most effective and frequently overlooked locations for an 800 number is in a new-product news release. When an 800 number appears in such an announcement, especially to a targeted audience, it will often produce better results than an advertisement for the same product in the same publication.

47:11 Value of a Memorable 800 Number

As a rule, 800 numbers will work even better when they are very memorable. George Walther, in *Phone Power*, 1986, cites a company with a phone number that was hard to track that shipped rose bouquets on order. When their number was changed to 1-800-LD-ROSES, sales went up 67 percent in one year.

47:12 800 Number Enables Catalog Customers to Get Delivery Data

Starting with its 1993 Christmas catalog, L. L. Bean began informing its customers that they could now use the 800 Customer Service number to learn the exact date their order would arrive. The change was brought about by a change in delivery carriers from UPS to Federal Express.

47:13 800 Number With Outside Answering Service

When using an outside answering service with 800 telephone number promotions, as a rule, you should call the number periodically and check on how the calls are being handled. Alert the answering service management about any problems. Often these problems involve a single operator and are not known to management.

47:14   Cautionary Note on 800 Calls

As a general rule, orders received over a toll-free 800 number should be viewed with suspicion when the caller fails, or hesitates, to supply a telephone number, an area code, or a ZIP Code; when the caller provides an address at a military base or prison; or when the caller sounds like a child.

47:15   How 800 Numbers and Credit Cards Influence Orders

For mail-order merchandise offers, as a rule, orders will increase by 30 percent when the mail marketer includes an 800 number and accepts major credit cards. About half of all the orders will come from the 800 number.

47:16   Affordability of 800 Numbers

You can easily afford an 800 number, if you heed the advice of Laura Hinze of Conversational Voice Technologies, Gurnee, Illinois. Advises Ms. Hinze, "800 service is available from a myriad of carriers....Installation doesn't require technical know-how or significant fees. Cost per minute averages 18 cents [and] there is no minimum time frame for installing a number, nor is there a minimum call volume" (in "Ask the Experts," *Sales and Marketing Strategies & News*, Sept./Oct. 1993).

47:17   Advantage of Outside Agency for 800 Service

The main advantage of using an outside agency in conjunction with 800 telephone service is that, as a rule, such agencies provide 24-hour service, and arrangements can be made for billing on a per-call basis. Most have large staffs and multiple phone lines—a particularly important advantage for direct marketers who use broadcast advertising.

PART 6

Printing, Production, and Letter Shop Procedures

48

Paper: Usage and Economies

Any size of paper listed in a manufacturer's sample book is considered a standard size. Standard sizes are the most economical to buy.
—JUDY PICKENS
Copy to Press, 1985

48:01 Cheapest Way to Buy Paper—But Not Always

As a rule, buying paper in bulk from the manufacturer is the cheapest way to obtain paper. However, if the printer charges for warehousing and bringing the paper to press, the price advantage may be diminished. Further, buying in bulk for long-term use is not recommended as paper deteriorates in storage.

48:02 Advantages of Buying Paper Through Printer

As a rule, when you buy paper through the printer you gain the advantage of the printer's bulk buying power. Further, the printer may get prompter delivery and will handle ordering and follow-up orders as needed, as well as warehousing until needed.

48:03 Getting Paper Samples for Job Planning

Even when your paper needs are small and you do not buy directly from the paper company, as a rule, they will promptly supply you with samples on request, knowing that when you do make a paper choice, you will specify their paper to your printer.

48:04 Soliciting Printer Recommendations on Paper

As a rule, it's a good idea to solicit the recommendations of your printer on quality, weight, texture, and color before making a final selection on paper for a planned promotion.

48:05 Way to Reduce Paper Costs

Before specifying a special type or grade of paper for a mailing campaign, it's best to see what the printer stocks that may be its equivalent. Many printers buy certain papers in skid quantities at bulk prices and can often supply the equivalent to special papers at prices considerably less than what your specially ordered paper would cost.

48:06 Cautionary Role on Paper Substitution

When you select and specify paper for a job and your printer recommends a just-as-good substitute, as a rule, it's a good idea to ask for and examine a sample and compare it with your choice before giving the go-ahead to make the switch.

48:07 Judging Paper From Printer's Stock

As a rule, paper is the most expensive element in a mail promotion. If you plan to use paper from a printer's stock, first look at printed samples of other jobs done with the same paper and judge how the printer handles it.

48:08 Paper Size for Greatest Economy

As a rule, you will produce printed jobs more economically if you use paper sizes that are in multiples of 8½ by 11 inches, as most printing presses can accommodate these dimensions.

48:09   Rule for Maximizing Printing Efficiency

Sometimes a slight change in the dimensions of a planned printed promotion can substantially reduce paper waste and costs. Plan job sizes
that make efficient use of available equipment and materials.

48:10   Paper-Folding Rule for Printed Promotions

If you plan your printed promotions so that the first fold is with the
paper grain, it will fold more easily and cleanly.

48:11   Rule for Printing Paper Spoilage

When supplying paper for a printed job, allow at least 10 percent
extra for spoilage in printing, folding, and binding, as well as for
overruns.

48:12   Reply Card Thickness Rule

If your planned mailing includes a tear-off reply card, as a rule, you
should verify that the paper stock meets U.S. Postal Service thickness
requirements (at least .007 of an inch) before printing. The maximum
allowable thickness is .0095 of an inch.

48:13   Detecting Paper Grain

As a rule, offset paper, when moistened on one side, will curl with the
grain.

48:14   Cautionary Rule for Printing Paper Changes in Same Job

To prevent problems at the post office, never permit a printer to use
different weight papers for a job that will go out as a single mailing.

48:15   Cautionary Rule for Printing Paper Thickness

Using a thinner paper (lower basis weight) can reduce paper costs, but
it has a pitfall: The thinner the paper, the greater the likelihood of the
printing on one side of the sheet showing through to the other side of
the sheet (reduced opacity).

48:16   Way to Reduce Catalog Paper Costs

As a rule, you can substantially reduce paper costs for a catalog offering a large variety of lower-priced products requiring lots of descriptive matter and/or illustrations by printing on tabloid-size newspaper stock.

49

Ink Use: Tips and Preferences

The Pantone Matching System® is an industry-wide formula system for coordinating (ink) color choices between printer and ink specifier. It comprises over 1,000 standard ink colors that may be specified by number.
Pantone Color Specifier, 1994

49:01 Most Effective Ink Color in Printed Promotions

The most effective (and most preferred) way to communicate a printed message is with black ink on white background. Other colors may seem more attractive. However, high-intensity colors break reading concentration. Bright colors tend to make the lines merge and make reading more difficult.

49:02 Ink Color Specifications

As a rule, color specifications for any printed job should specify a number from the Pantone Matching System (PMS) palette of over 1000 standard color choices.

49:03   Ink Color Specification for Beginners

If you're new to printing and unfamiliar with the Pantone Matching System, do not instruct your printer to use "sky blue" ink or "fire engine red" ink. Either give the printer an actual sample of the color you wish, or borrow his *Pantone Color Specifier 1000* for that purpose.

49:04   Ink Color Rule for Printed Promotions

When producing a printed promotion in more than one color of ink, the darkest color ink should always be used for the main message, lighter colors for emphasis.

49:05   Ink Color for Photographs

As a rule, when printing a promotion piece in black ink and a second color, it is usually best to print all the photos in black.

49:06   Ink Color Rule for Blocks of Reverse Type

When planning a block of reverse type against a second-color background, avoid light colors that do not give a readable contrast.

49:07   Ink Selection for Colored Paper

As a rule, if you're printing your promotional flier on colored paper, be sure the ink will be dark enough on the paper to afford sufficient contrast for legibility.

49:08   Second Color in Sales Letters

If you plan to use a second ink color in a sales letter, as a rule, it's best to restrict the second color to a few lines or a few key words.

49:09   Second-Color Preference for Sales Letters

If you're using two colors of ink in a sales letter, as a rule, the best second color is red.

49:10   Sales Letter Text in Light Color Inks

If you're using a light second color in the text of a sales letter, as a rule, it's best to use a bolder typeface for the second-color text than for the black-ink text.

49:11   Color Bars as Eye-Catchers and Identifiers

A vertical bar of color on the face of a mailing piece can be a strong magnet in drawing attention to it. Henry Hoke, Sr., founder of *Direct Marketing* magazine, first used a color bar as a mailer identifier in postcard mailing promotions in the mid-1940s. The vertical bar was one-eighth of an inch wide—a red bleed along the card's left edge. In recent years, Herschell Lewis used the color bar idea on mailing envelopes. He used vertical bars along the left edge, favoring blue and brown inks over black and green.

49:12   Beneficial Ink Combinations in Mail Orders

As a rule, says L. Perry Wilbur, "many executive order forms use blue or green ink on a white background, or black on a gold background....Some ink color combinations that work well for mail-order operators: blue on white paper; red and black on white paper; blue or black on canary paper; black on pink paper." (In *Money in Your Mailbox*, 1993)

49:13   Beneficial Use Rule for Second-Color Ink

When adding a second color to any direct mail piece, a few well-chosen lines or spots of color will be more visually appealing than one big splash of color.

49:14   Use of Color to Improve Mailing Impression

As a rule, you can maximize the impression of your message by making the mailing look expensive through the use of four-color printing.

49:15   Gender Ink Preferences

Studies have shown that ink color preferences vary from one sex to another. Males, as a rule, prefer blue ink, while females prefer red ink.

49:16   USPS Ink Requirement: If It Glows, It Won't Go

As a rule, inks used to print mail pieces should not be fluorescent or phosphorescent. This is to ensure that no ink glow will exist which may cause malfunctions at the post office during facer-canceler operations. A way to check for fluorescence or phosphorescence is by illuminating a printed sample with an ultraviolet light in a darkened room to determine if there is any perceptible glow. You may also submit a printed sample to the Executive Director, USPS Engineering Support Center, 8403 Lee Highway, Merrifield, VA 22082-8101. (*Source:* USPS Publication 25, 1988)

50
Typography: Selection Guidelines

Types have personalities to an extent...a
delicate type may work well in a brochure on
fine glass, and rugged type for machine parts.
But matching the character of a typeface to the
subject matter ought not to be overdone.
Readers are generally unaware of type style
differences.
How to Plan Printing, S. D. Warren Co., 1978

50:01   Essentials of Type Selection

As a rule, one should consider three elements when selecting a type-face: (1) a typeface in character with the message you wish to convey, (2) a face that makes a good impression on the eye, (3) a face that is easy to read and comprehend.

50:02   Typeface Identification Rule

As a rule, it is best not to approve a typeface on the basis of a verbal or catalog identification. What might be a medium-weight face in one type supplier's font could be boldface in another's. Always look at type samples first.

50:03   Fitting Copy With Capital Letters

Capital letters tend to run much wider than lowercase letters. Consequently, as a rule, when copyfitting, it is best to allow $1\frac{1}{2}$ to 2 units per capital letter to ensure a perfect fit.

50:04   Type Readability Rule With Benday Tints

When you plan to show type in reverse on a benday tint background, as a rule—depending on the typeface used—the tint should be a high-enough percentage to give a readable contrast.

50:05   Rule for Fitting Copy

A quick rule of thumb for fitting copy is to find typeset copy similar to what you plan to use and count all the words in a square-inch block. Then count the number of square inches your advertising copy will occupy. Through multiplication, you can estimate the maximum number of words your copy must be to fit the available area.

50:06   Column-Width Readability Rule

A block of copy set in two narrower columns will be read much more quickly than copy set in one wider column. The narrower the column, the greater the readability.

50:07   Typeface Selection for 800 Phone Number

When selecting a typeface to show an 800 phone number in a print or mail promotion, as a rule, it's best to choose the boldest typeface possible that will not distract from the surrounding print matter.

50:08   Typesize of Boxes and Bullets

Boxes (squares) and bullets (large dots or circles) are the two most widely used symbols in promotional typography. As a rule, they should be no larger than the height of x in the adjacent alphabet, or, preferably, smaller.

50:09 Rule for Using Dashes

Dashes are used in many ways in promotional typography. As a rule, use an en dash when you want to replace the word *to* or *through* as in "Offer valid January 1–30" or "Supply on 4 across East–West Cheshire labels." Use an em dash when you want to indicate missing material, or to replace a colon. Use a ¾ em dash with condensed typefaces in place of an em dash. Most promotional typography has word spacing on either side of it when an em dash is used.

50:10 Rule for Killing Widows in Type Composition

Widows in type composition are not bad; in fact they sometimes improve readability. However, if you're intent on killing off a widow—that's the single word or syllable that falls over onto a separate line by itself—you can often do it by eliminating a word or phrase earlier in the last sentence. Avoid adding words to prevent widows; they tend to dilute copy.

50:11 Avoiding Look-Alike Promotions

If your competitor uses a readily recognizable typestyle in mail promotions, as a rule, you should use a different typestyle so your efforts won't be confused with your competitor's.

51
Type: Legibility and Readability

51:01   Type Readability and Legibility

As a rule, in typographic usage, *readability* and *legibility* are used interchangeably. However, according to composition consultant Frank J. Romano (in *The TypEncyclopedia*, 1984), *legibility* deals with ease of reading and perception of the message communicated, whereas *readability* refers to writing style and the resulting ease with which the information is understood.

51:02   Typeface Readability

As a rule, typefaces with serifs can be read more easily than sans serif typefaces.

51:03 Readability of Lowercase Type

As a rule, type set in all lowercase letters or in cap and lower-case is easier to read than type set in all-capital letters.

51:04 Letterspacing as Aid to Readability

When you use type set in all-capital letters and it seems difficult to read, as a rule, you can improve readability by spacing between letters.

51:05 Readability of Boldface

Text type has greatest readability when set in regular typefaces. Blocks of text set in boldface generally have greatly reduced readability and this typeface should be used sparingly.

51:06 When and Where to Use Reverse Type

Reverse copy is acceptable for small copy blocks or occasional headlines, but, as a rule, it should be avoided for body copy. Body copy in reverse both slows and diminishes readability.

51:07 Rule for Choosing Best Face Among Look-Alikes

When choosing between two typefaces that look very much alike, you'll do better if you select the typeface with the greatest x-height. The higher the x-height of a typeface, the better its readability.

51:08 Headline Typesize Rule

Headlines set in lowercase will be more readable than headlines set in capital letters only. Readability of type set initial caps with lowercase falls somewhere in between.

51:09 Heavy or Ultra-Bold Faces in Headlines

A heavy or ultra-bold typeface is often highly effective for a headline. But such faces should be limited to one or two lines, as a rule, so as not to affect readability.

51:10   Typesize Rule for Subheads

As a rule, subheads are more readable if set in a heavier-weight type-face than the accompanying text.

51:11   Paragraph Spacing

As a rule, you can increase type readability by adding space between paragraphs.

51:12   Right-hand Margin Composition Rule

When typeset composition is set ragged right, it tends to be less formal and more eye-appealing than a justified right margin.

51:13   Lists of Facts

When you are listing features or benefits, setting them off with bullets, squares, arrowheads, or asterisks will help readability.

51:14   Ideal Type Widths for Preventing Eye Strain

Columns wider than 2 to 3 inches pose a strain on the eyes of the reader and are less likely to get read.

51:15   Printing Background Readability Rule

When text matter is printed on colored paper or over a color or benday background, the smaller the typesize the lighter the background should be.

51:16   Type Selection for Coated Papers

Avoid using lightface sans serif typefaces on high-gloss paper stock. Such stock reflects glare and such typefaces are extremely difficult to read.

51:17   Typeface Variety in Printed Promotions

In planning a printed promotion, "Use but a few typefaces for your text," says typographic expert Bill Gray (in *Tips on Type,* 1983). "Some of the best designers use just one or two."

51:18   Typesize Rule for Older Readers

Most older people (professionals included) require glasses for reading. It is a good idea to keep this in mind when planning a promotion to upper-level professional audiences. This holds true for mailings to any older consumer audience.

52

Printing and Production Hints and Economies

*In selecting a printer, you want to see that
what the firm has done before is similar to
your needs. The last thing you want is to have
a printer experiment with you.*
—FREEMAN F. GOSDEN, JR.
Direct Marketing Success, 1985

52:01 Way to Locate Reliable Printer

If you're new to direct mail and need help in locating a reliable printer, as a rule, you'll be able to get recommendations from either the
artist who's preparing your first piece or from the list broker you're
working with for your mailing lists. Get estimates from more than one
source and examine samples of their work.

52:02 Printing Quotations

As a rule, any printing quotation is valid for 30 days.

52:03   Comparing Printing Quotes

As a rule, price quotes from various printers cannot be compared unless they are based on identical written specifications and job requirements.

52:04   Involving Printer to Reduce Costs

You can sometimes reduce printing costs by involving your printer in the design plans. As a rule, a good printer will be able to make suggestions that can increase effectiveness or lower costs.

52:05   Time Needed for Job Completion

As a rule, allow at least seven to ten days for a printer to complete a job. Rush jobs can cost you more. Jobs that allow a printer much more time may get you a better price.

52:06   Spoilage Rule for Print-Order Quantities

As a rule, always add an allowance to any print-order quantity to make up for spoilage, or for printing industry-permitted underruns.

52:07   Using Gang Run to Cut Printing Costs

A *gang run* means printing two or more pieces from the same sheet at the same time. If you can arrange to print two or more promotion pieces at the same time on the same press-run, as a rule, you can materially cut the printing cost of each job.

52:08   Rule for Minimizing Mailing Costs

As a rule, the more aspects of a printing and mailing that can be handled by a single source, the lower the cost is likely to be.

52:09   Rule for Setting Printing Completion Date

A printing order that gives a specific completion and delivery date will get better attention than one with less specific instructions. It will also ensure that the completed job reaches your mailing house in advance of the scheduled mailing date.

52:10   Cancellation of Printing Orders

As a rule, any printing order may be canceled at any time by written notice, but the printer must be compensated in full for any work or services performed on the job up until the time the cancellation notice was received.

52:11   Claims Against Printers or Mailers

If you believe you have a valid claim against a printer or mailer, as a rule, you lose any right to that claim if it is made more than ten days after completion of the order. A claim should always be submitted in writing.

52:12   List Verification for Print Orders

When designing a promotion around one or more large mailing lists, it is a good rule to reverify the list counts before setting the print quality.

52:13   Self-Mailer Postal Indicia Positioning

When checking a self-mailing folded dummy, as a rule, always check the position of the printed postal indicia to ensure that it is printed on the correct side. If it is not, it will not meet postal regulations.

52:14   Self-Mailer Sealing Rule

As a rule, a folded self-mailer will stay folded in the mail without the need for a seal or staple.

52:15   Way to Prevent Extra Charge for Press Proofs

As a rule, if you request press proofs of a printing job and are not physically present at the time the form is made ready on the press, you will have to pay an extra charge to the printer for the lost press time.

52:16   Economical Way to Save on Revised Reprints

If you're planning a multipage or multipanel brochure for a major mail promotion and reprints will require updated information, as a rule, you can save on reprint costs by positioning the copy requiring future changes in a single panel or on a specific page.

52:17 Way to Save on Envelope Printing

As a rule, you will save considerably if you buy directly from an envelope manufacturer based on yearly anticipated needs. You get the price advantage of the larger quantity, and you can schedule deliveries in quantities as needed during the year.

53

Letter Shops: Locating and Working With Them

I look for a lettershop that's compatible with handling our type of business. This depends on the size of the mailing, frequency of mailings, turn-around time necessary, location of lettershop compared to our printers, and, also, ultimately, price.

—MICHAEL BARON
In Schwartz, Mail Order! How to Get Your Share of the Hidden Profits That Exist in Your Business, 1982

53:01 Way to Locate Reliable Letter Shop

Unless the printer is doing the mailing for you, after printing, you'll need a letter shop or mailing house. For leads, turn to the artist who designed your mailing piece, the printer who will print it, or the list broker who will supply the mailing lists. Ask for names of letter shops that deal with accounts similar to yours so that your job won't slip through the cracks in a large mailing house.

53:02 Letter Shop Selection Based on Equipment

As a rule, it's best to select a letter shop whose equipment is compatible with your type of mailing. Not all letter shops have the equipment necessary to deal effectively and economically with all types of mailings.

53:03 Necessity for Dealing With Recognized Letter Shops

If your rental lists are to go directly to the letter shop, as a rule, you should be sure to use either a well-established shop or one identifiable through directory listings or affiliation with direct mail organizations. Some list owners will ship rental lists only to recognized letter shops.

53:04 When More Than One Letter Shop May be Advisable

When you wish to get a large mailing out on a specific date and your letter shop cannot do it all in one day, as a rule, you can accomplish your mailing objective by having two mailing houses each do half the mailing simultaneously.

53:05 Letter Shop Location Selection

As a rule, for greatest convenience and best service, it's best to use a letter shop close to home rather than one in a distant city that might be a little less costly.

53:06 Identification Rule for Letter Shop Deliveries

Take extra pains to ensure that all the components for a scheduled mailing are clearly marked so that they can be easily identified and assembled after delivery to your letter shop.

53:07 Packing Rule for Shipments to Letter Shops

Letters shops often have a preference for the form in which they receive mailing materials. You should clear in advance whether your mailing house prefers delivery in cartons or on open skids, and then indicate this in your packing instructions to your printers.

53:08   Letter Shop Permit Use

As a rule, you do not need to get a bulk mailing permit if your mailings go though letter shops. You can use the letter shop's bulk rate permit.

53:09   Letter Shop Mailing Verification

As a rule, you can learn the exact date of a letter shop mailing and the exact quantity of pieces mailed by examining a copy of the post office receipt that the letter shop gets when it deposits your mailing for delivery. Such receipts also show type of piece mailed, weight of a single piece, rate, and total postage.

53:10   Need for Extra Mailing Envelopes

As a rule, when you supply a letter shop with an exact number of envelopes for a planned mailing, it will be insufficient to complete the job. Always include an extra supply of envelopes to make up for short counts and envelope spoilage.

53:11   Machine Insertability in Mail Processing

When planning any mail promotion, as a rule, you should check with the mailing house to ensure that all the components are machine insertable. Machine insertability makes mail processing less expensive.

PART 7

Mail-Order Space Advertising Techniques

54

Space Advertising: Basic Approaches and Procedures

Unlike general advertising...direct response advertising, as used by direct marketers, must be measurable and accountable in terms for response, as well as in the generation of customer lists and data.

—MARTIN BAIER
Elements of Direct Marketing, 1983

54:01   Fastest Way to Start in Mail Order

As a rule, the fastest way to start in mail order is with a direct response space advertisement. It will usually generate action more quickly and at lower cost than a mailing.

54:02   Way to Judge Good Mail-Order Media

As a rule, when a publication is heavy with mail-order advertising, it usually is a good indication that mail-order ads work well in that publication.

54:03   Way to Get Lowest Newspaper Ad Rate

Newspapers usually have different advertising rates for different classes of advertisers. As a rule, the highest rate is the national rate. The mail-order rate ranks among the lowest. Be sure to specify "Mail-Order Rate" on your advertising insertion order. Certain magazines also have lower rates for mail-order ads.

54:04   Lead-Time Needed for Newspaper Ads

If you plan a mail-order advertisement for a particular issue of a newspaper, as a rule, you should allow for sufficient time for the ad to be cleared for compliance with the paper's mail-order guidelines. Newspapers may sometimes ask an advertiser to add a street address to a post office box number, or to clarify a claim made in an ad.

54:05   Best Day for Newspaper Mail-Order Ads

As a rule, Sunday is the best day for newspaper mail-order advertising. Circulation is usually much larger on Sunday, and Sunday papers are more carefully read.

54:06   Influence of Weather on Mail-Order Ad Response

As a rule, Sunday mail-order ads enjoy a better response on rainy and bad-weather days than on clear-weather days.

54:07   Response Duration for Newspaper Ads

As a rule, about 95 percent of the response from a newspaper mail-order ad will be received within three weeks after the ad appears.

54:08   Low-Cost Way to Test a Mail-Order Medium

One of the most economical ways to test the mail-order pulling power of a publication is with a classified ad. Sometimes a well-worded classified ad can outpull a display ad.

54:09   Newspaper and Magazine Ad Deadlines

If you plan a mix of classified advertisements in both newspapers and magazines, you should be aware of the great difference in deadline times between the two mediums. You can place a ready-to-run ad in some newspapers two to three days prior to publication, or by Wednesday noon for Sunday. By contrast, some magazines want your advertisement by the tenth or fifteenth of the second month preceding publication.

54:10 Allowing Extra Time for Publication-Set Ads

If you're inexperienced in mail order and want a newspaper to set your advertisement, as a rule, it's a good idea to allow at least four weeks before you want the ad to run. This time allowance will get you a better-composed ad, and you will have a chance to see and correct proofs and make last-minute copy or price changes.

54:11 Way to Get Pub-Set Ad to Meet Requirements

If you request that the publication set your advertisement and provide precise instructions on how you want it set, as a rule, the subsequent advertisement will closely conform to your expectations. If you confirm in advance the typefaces available and specify them, you will get exactly what you ask for.

54:12 Speed and Cost of Space Versus Direct Mail

As a rule, you can reach more of a market more quickly and for less cost through space advertising than by direct mail.

54:13 Mail-Order Ad as Quick Pretest of Mail Offer

If you're not sure whether a product is good enough for a mail offer, as a rule, you can get a quick indication of sales potential with a small mail-order ad in a daily or weekly publication.

54:14 Direct Mail Copy Suitability in Ads

As a rule, copy that works in direct mail will work equally as well in a publication mail-order advertisement.

54:15 Way to Make Expensive Ad Space Affordable

When a desirable publication is too expensive for your advertising budget, you can often advertise in a geographic or demographic edition of the same publication at a small fraction of the full rate. *The Wall Street Journal*, for example—one of the best publications for mail-order offers to upscale business audiences—has a number of regional editions.

54:16 Buying Advertising Space on Per-Inquiry Basis

If you have a mass-appeal item, there are some publications that will run your advertisement on a per-inquiry basis. That means the publication runs the ad without a fixed payment and you pay only for the inquiries or sales that the advertisement attracts. Such arrangements, called *PI deals*, usually require that the responses go to the publication for control purposes.

54:17 Estimating Costs With Per-Inquiry Advertising

"In dealing with PI ad outlets," says Tyler Hicks (in *Mail Order Success Secrets*, 1992) "listen to the estimates the media person gives you....Often they can tell within a few hundred how many inquiries you'll get."

54:18 Media Selection Rule

When considering media for mail-order advertising, as a rule, it's best to use a business publication for business-type offers, and a consumer publication for consumer-product offers.

54:19 Saturation Coverage of Space Ads

As a rule, a space ad in a business or professional journal will give much greater saturation coverage than direct mail in many fields (law, accounting, and architecture, or the various branches of engineering). Although these firms are a single entry on a specialized mailing list, they employ numerous members of the same profession, often at various levels within the organization.

54:20 Advertising Link for High-Ticket Business Offers

The most highly targeted business lists often fail to reach corporate prospects whose decisions are essential for high-ticket offers. These high-level types are more likely to see an offer when it is advertised in a business publication in their field. Consequently, for offers that may involve higher-level decision makers, it is often a good idea to link a major business mail offer with advertising of the same offer in a related business publication.

54:21 Highest Ad Readership Page

As a rule, in a specialized business magazine, the page facing the table of contents has the highest readership. A study by Cahners Publishing company of readers in 32 business magazines indicated that 63 percent read business magazines from front to back, while another 27 percent go straight to the contents page to look up pertinent articles. Thus, an advertisement facing the contents page gets 90 percent of the magazine's readership.

54:22 Response Cycle for Monthly Publication Advertisements

As a rule, a direct-response advertisement in a monthly magazine will usually produce about half its total response within a month after publication.

54:23 Repeat Rule for Monthly Publication Ads

A mail-order ad that pulls well in a monthly publication will continue to be effective if re-run in the same publication several times.

54:24 Border for Small-Space Mail-Order Ads

As a rule, a small-space mail-order ad in any publication will be more effective if enclosed in a border. The border tends to focus the reader's eye on the ad and, in effect, increases readership.

54:25 Response Contrast in Half- and Full-Page Ads

As a rule, a one-half page ad will be two-thirds as effective as a full-page ad in the same publication.

54:26 Response Increase: Single to Double Page

As a rule, you will not double response for a successful mail-order ad by going from a single page to a two-page spread.

54:27   Readership of Bleed Ads

As a rule, a one-page bleed ad in a specialized business magazine will be read by 25 percent more readers than a conventional one-page ad.

54:28   Relationship of Ad Headline to Response

When advertising a mail-order product in a print medium, as a rule, the headline and opening paragraph represent 85 percent of the pulling power, and the rest of the ad the remaining 15 percent.

54:29   Copy Length Rule for Mail-Order Ads

In mail-order ad copy, as a rule, long copy performs better than short copy.

54:30   Effect of Testimonials in Mail-Order Ads

As a rule, testimonials to claims tend to increase response to a greater degree in mail-order advertisements than in straight ad copy.

54:31   Writing Copy for Widely Different Media

When it is not possible to write copy to fit a particular advertising medium, as a rule, "there is only one type of copy for widely different media," says Rudolph Flesch (*The Art of Plain Talk*, 1946). "Be as simple, clear, and to the point as possible. [Such] copy may lack sophistication...but it will do the work."

54:32   Way to Locate Association and Society Publications

As a rule, if you need quick information on association or society publications, you will find it within the organization's listing in Gale's *Encyclopedia of Associations*, available in most libraries.

54:33   Exchanging Names for Ad Space

Mail-order advertisers can sometimes save money on advertising by exchanging one-time use of customer names for advertising space. This works best with small-circulation periodicals.

54:34   Split-Run Ads as Vehicle for Testing

As a rule, a mail-order advertiser has a sure way of testing one offer, product, copy approach, or format against another in a publication. It's called a split-run test, in which each of two variations runs in a different half of the publication's issue or edition. Many magazines offer split-run testing.

54:35   Formula for Judging Media Effectiveness

John Kremer offers a virtually foolproof way to learn about mail-order media effectiveness. He advises you to look for publications in which offers similar to those you plan are advertised over and over again. "If your competition is currently advertising and was also advertising at least six months ago, chances are the advertiser is doing well and making money." (In *The Complete Direct Marketing Sourcebook,* 1992)

55

Advertising: Positioning Strategies

The location of an ad in a magazine is very important....If special rates are not mentioned for particular locations, you can sometimes get them just by asking.

—WILLIAM A. COHEN
Building a Mail Order Business, 1991

55:01 Way to Select Best Location in Advertising

Any location in a periodical or newspaper that is viewed by a high percentage of the publication's readership is a good position for an advertisement.

55:02 Importance of Mail-Order Ad Positioning

When an ad is designed primarily to generate mail orders, position of ad is often as important as copy.

55:03 Right-Hand Versus Left-Hand Page Readership

An advertisement placed on a right-hand page usually will attract more readers than one on a left-hand page.

55:04　Best Ad Position in Business Periodicals

As a rule, an advertisement in a specialized business periodical will attract the most attention on the page facing the table of contents.

55:05　Rule for Paying Premium for Good Ad Position

When an ad produces an unusually high yield due to special positioning, it's worth paying the publication a position charge to guarantee the same spot for subsequent insertions.

55:06　Way to Avoid Paying Special Position Charges

As a rule, unless you are advertising in a designated mail-order section with its own rates, if you specify a particular position in a publication you may have to pay a position charge. If, however, you state on your insertion order "would appreciate" a certain location, you will not have to pay the position charge if you get it.

55:07　Best Positioning for Fractional-Page Ads

When placing fractional-page ads, as a rule, a top-of-page position is more effective than one on the bottom of the page.

55:08　Positioning Ad Illustration to Lift Response

As a rule, the location of an illustration in an advertisement can influence response. If the illustration is particularly impressive, place it at the top of the advertisement where it will be readily noticed and draw attention to the ad copy.

55:09　Way to Limit Loss in Newspaper Ad Campaign

In planning a newspaper ad campaign, as a rule, you stand to risk the least if you start with the lowest-cost newspapers and, as the offer continues to prove itself, work up to the higher-priced newspapers with subsequent insertions.

56

Mail-Order
Advertising:
Coupon Guidelines

*There is no formula for how large a coupon
should be, or at what size its effectiveness
decreases....As a rule, you should make your
coupon as convenient as possible for the
customer to fill in.*

—HAROLD P. PRESTON
Successful Mail Selling, 1941

56:01   Coupon Rule for Mail-Order Ads

When you advertise in the mail-order section of a newspaper or magazine, you do not need a coupon. Readers know mail orders are being
solicited. Just include the words *Write to* over your address.

56:02   Coupon Format Rule

Seasoned mail professionals say that the best coupon is one that is rec-
tangular in shape, that is surrounded by dashes with corners joined,
and that stands out from the surrounding printed matter.

56:03   Coupon Positioning in Ad

Order coupons, as a rule, go in the lower right-hand corner of the ad. However, if an ad is running on a left-hand page, the coupon should be at the left so as to be on the outside. The coupon should never be in the middle.

56:04   Coupon Position on Page

As a rule, response in a coupon-bearing ad is improved when the coupon is close to the bottom of the page and the reader does not have to cut a hole in the page or remove the entire page.

56:05   Coupon Size

As a rule, your ad with coupon will enjoy a better response when the coupon is large enough to be comfortably completed by hand.

56:06   Advertiser's Name in Ad Coupon

As a rule, coupon response is increased when the advertiser's name and address are included in the coupon.

56:07   Ad Coupon Readership in Magazines

In many full-page magazine mail-order ads, readers have a tendency to skip from the headline to the order coupon. Consequently, as a rule, the coupon should be a miniature version of the ad's offer, with sufficient detail to make the sale by itself.

56:08   When to Omit Periodical Ad Coupon

When you run a mail-order ad in a periodical you know to have a high pass-along rate, as a rule, it's a good idea to omit the coupon so as not to deter pass-along readers who might be turned off by the missing coupon.

56:09   Coupons in Archival Journals

If it is necessary to include a coupon advertisement in an archival journal, because of reader reluctance to deface such a periodical, it is useful to include an instruction to this effect: "To order, complete and return a photocopy of this coupon."

57

The Role of
800 Numbers
in Ads

*The basic reason for an 800 number is to
solicit incremental orders that would not have
been generated without this marketing
motivator.*

—ALLAN CAPLAN
*In (Nash) The Direct Marketing Handbook,
1984*

57:01   800 Number Effect on Ad Recognition

Advertisements bearing an 800 phone number are usually noticed by
20 percent more people than those lacking one. This was the finding of
a Cahners Publishing Company ad readership study.

57:02   800 Number Versus Regular Telephone Number

As a rule, at least twice as many people will respond to an 800 number
in an advertisement as will call a regular telephone number—all other
factors being equal.

57:03   800 Response Relationship to Typesize

As a rule, increasing the typesize of an 800 number in an advertisement will increase response through that number.

57:04   Rules for Displaying 800 Numbers Effectively

Always include the "1" in front of an 800 number and have it set in boldface type. The preferred way to show it is 1-800-000-0000. Avoid using 1 (800) 000-0000. Using brackets around an area code, to some, implies a long-distance call.

57:05   Speed of Response With 800 Number

As a rule, adding an 800 number to an advertisement can generate orders the day the publication is delivered, where mail response may take one or more weeks.

57:06   Words for Increasing Sunday Phone Response

In tests involving ads in Sunday papers or supplements, adding the words *including Sunday* to the line "Call seven days a week" over an 800 telephone number increased response by one-third.

57:07   800 Number as Order Coupon Replacement

As a rule, when an advertisement with a free examination offer does not contain an order coupon, an 800 number will be an effective replacement.

57:08   800 Number Placement in Advertising

As a rule, the best position for an 800 number in a newspaper or magazine ad is in the lower right-hand corner where a coupon would normally appear. When used jointly with a coupon, the 800 number should appear directly above the coupon.

Appendix A

Mailing List Compilers: A Selected List

The following compilers offer lists through *Direct Marketing List Source*, a publication of Standard Rate and Data Service.

ABC Advanced Business Compilation
2101 Corporate Blvd.
Boca Raton, FL 33431

Abstract/Records Service, Inc.
20450 Walnut Dr.
Walnut, CA 91789

Addressing Unlimited Inc.
14621 Titus St.
Van Nuys, CA 91402

Alfa List Co.
3903 Frontier
Dallas, TX 75214

American Business Lists, Inc.
P.O. Box 27437
5711 S. 86th Cir.
Omaha, NE 68127

American Church Lists, Inc.
P.O. Box 1544
Arlington, TX 76004-1544

American List Council, Inc.
88 Orchard Rd.
Princeton, NJ 08543

Ed Burnett Consultants, Inc.
100 Paragon Dr.
Montvale, NJ 07645

CMG Information Services
187 Ballardvale St.
Wilmington, MA 01887

Compilers Plus, Inc.
466 Main St.
New Rochelle, NY 10801

Customized Mailing Lists, Inc.
1906 Field Rd.
Sarasota, FL 34276

Demographic Systems Incorporated
2 Executive Dr.
Fort Lee, NJ 07024

Dun & Bradstreet Information
  Services
Three Sylvan Way
Parsippany, NJ 07054

Hugo Dunhill Mailing Lists, Inc.
630 Third Ave.
New York, NY 10017

Dunhill International List Co., Inc.
1100 Park Central Blvd., South
Pompano Beach, FL 33064

Karl Business Lists
135 Bedford Rd.
Armonk, NY 10504

Metromail Corporation
360 E. 22nd St.
Lombard, IL 60148

Names and Addresses, Inc.
4096 Commercial Ave.
Northbrook, IL 60062

PCS Mailing List Company
85 Constitution Ln.
Danvers, MA 01923

W. S. Ponton, Inc. of Pittsburgh
5149 Butler St.
Pittsburgh, PA 15201

Research Projects Corp.
Pomperaug Ave.
Woodbury, CT 06798

Edith Roman Associates, Inc.
253 West 35th St.
New York, NY 10001

Senior Citizens Unlimited, Inc.
711 Westchester Ave.
White Plains, NY 10604

The Specialists
1200 Harbor Blvd.
Weehawken, NJ 07087

TRW Target Marketing Services
901 International Pkwy.
Richardson, TX 75081

Fred Woolf List Col., Inc.
7 Corporate Park Dr.
White Plains, NY 10604

Alvin B. Zeller, Inc.
224 Fifth Ave.
New York, NY 10001

Zeller & Letica, Inc.
15 East 26th St.
New York, NY 10010

Mailing List Brokers: A Selected List

The following list brokerage firms offer services through *Direct Marketing List Source*, a publication of Standard Rate and Data Service.

The Abadi Group Inc.
1312 Allenhurst Ave.
Ocean, NJ 07712

A. B. Data, Ltd.
8050 N. Port Washington Rd.
Milwaukee, WI 53217

Aberdeen Marketing
2030 Powers Ferry Rd.
Atlanta, GA 30339

Accudata America
3723 Del Prado Blvd.
Cape Coral, FL 33904

Acculist
29169 W. Heathercliff Rd.
Malibu, CA 90265

Ace Mailing Service, Inc.
1961 South Cobb Industrial Blvd.
Smyrna, GA 30082

Action List Service
10 Mountainview Rd.
Upper Saddle River, NJ 07458

Action Media Services, Inc.
661 Palisade Ave.
Englewood Cliffs, NJ 07632

Addresses Unlimited
600 Essex Rd.
Neptune, NJ 07754

Addressing Unlimited, Inc.
14621 Titus St.
Van Nuys, CA 91402

Ad List Marketing
3140 Culver Rd.
Dearborn, MI 48124

Ad Postcards
26002 Marguerite Pkwy.
Mission Viejo, CA 26002

Advanced Automation
21 Alpha Rd.
Chelmsford, MA 01824

Advanced List Marketing Associates
12700 Fair Lakes Cir.
Fairfax, VA 22033

Advanced Mail Inc.
1825 Oxford Ave.
Eau Claire, WI 54701

Advance Printing & Mailing
1251 Bellevue Blvd.
Clearwater, FL 34616

Advantage Direct Marketing
  Group, Inc.
450 7th Ave.
New York, NY 10123

Advantage List Marketing, Inc.
385 Pleasant St.
Watertown, MA 02172

Ad-Vantage Marketing
305 Tesconi Circle
Santa Rosa, CA 95401

A. H. Direct Marketing, Inc.
7217 Gulf Blvd.
St. Petersburg, FL 33706

American International Marketing
P.O. Box 9055
Reno, NV 89507

Aldata
7000 W. 151st St.
Apple Valley, MN 55124

Alexander Marketing Services
215 Park Ave. South
New York, NY 10003

All American List Corp.
2841 Hartland Rd.
Falls Church, VA 22043

Fred. E. Allen, Inc.
P.O. Box 1595
Mt. Pleasant, TX 75456

Alliance International Marketing
3500 Oak Lawn Ave.
Dallas, TX 75219

Allied List Services, Ltd.
370 Seventh St.
Brooklyn, NY 11215

Allists, Inc.
9415 NE 26th St.
Bellevue, WA 98004

Allists Plus, Inc.
556 Keats Ave.
Erie, PA 16508

Allmedia, Inc.
4965 Preston Park Blvd.
Plano, TX 75093

Alpha List Marketing, Inc.
5300 Mainstream Circle
Norcross, GA 30092

America Direct, Inc.
1314 E. Pioneer Rd.
Draper, UT 84020

Americalist
8050 Freedom, N.W.
North Canton, OH 44720

American Advertising Distributors
57 W. Timonium Rd.
Timonium, MD 21093

American Data Consultants, Inc.
1010 Washington Blvd.
Stamford, CT 06901

America Direct, Inc.
P.O. Box 260
Burke, VA 22015

American Direct Marketing
  Services, Inc.
1120 Empire Central Pl.
Dallas, TX 75247

American Fundraising Lists, Inc.
600 Winter St.
Waltham, MA 02154·

American General Service Corp.
4945 Schaefer Rd.
Dearborn, MI 48126

American List Counsel, Inc.
88 Orchard Rd.
Princeton, NJ 08543

American Mailers
100 American Way
Detroit, MI 48209

American Mailing Lists Corp.
7777 Leesburg Pike
Falls Church, VA 22043

American Red Cross/Direct Lists
17th and D Sts., N.W.
Washington, DC 20006

American Target Marketing
770 Lake Shandelee Rd.
Livingston Manor, NY 12758

Amichetti, Lewis & Associates
724 Lancaster Ave.
Wayne, PA 19087

Am-Pro Mailing List Company, Inc.
435 Newbury St.
Danvers, MA 01923

AMS Response
16105 Gundry Ave.
Paramount, CA 90723

James P. Andersen & Co.
1036 N. Euclid Ave.
Oak Park, IL 60302

Andex Marketing Group, Inc.
1601 Palm Ave.
Pembroke Pines, FL 33026

Andrew Associates, Inc.
Ludlow Ind. Ctr.
Ludlow, MA 10156

Anne-Tisdale & Associates, Inc.
48 Tommy True Ct.
Baltimore, MD 21234

Answers Direct Mail, Ltd.
2909 Bankship Row
Atlanta, GA 30319

Antigone Associates, Ltd.
801 West Street Rd.
Feasterville, PA 19053

Applied List Mgmt., Inc.
3438 Maggie Blvd.
Orlando, FL 32811

ARS Strategic Mail Services
932 Main St.
Holyoke, MA 01040

Ash Business Lists
23801 Calabasas Rd.
Calabasas, CA 91302

Atlanta Direct Marketing, Inc.
3297 Northcrest Rd.
Atlanta, GA 30340

Atlantic List Company, Inc.
1525 Wilson Blvd.
Arlington, VA 22209

ATP Mailing List Center
1511 North Riverside
Medford, OR 97501

Austin List Services
12303-E Technology Blvd.
Austin, TX 78727

A. V. Mailing Lists Inc.
38345 30th St. East
Palmdale, CA 93550

Axon Lists
747 Dresher Rd.
Horsham, PA 19044

AZ Marketing Services, Inc.
31 River Rd.
Cos Cob, CT 06807

BD Communications, Inc.
518 North Ave.
Rock Hill, SC 29732

B. Direct Marketing
106 Canterbury Rd.
Circle Pines, MN 55014

Dave Benway & Associates
5555 Shorewood Ln.
Shorewood, MN 55331

Best Marketing of Central Florida
352 Melody Ln.
Casselberry, FL 32707

Bethesda List Center
6710 Fairfax Rd.
Bethesda, MD 20815

Better List Brokers
5030 Champion Blvd.
Boca Raton, FL 33496

B & K List Services
425 E. Sixth St.
Conway, AR 72032

Blackstone Lists
1275 SW 46th Ave.
Pompano Beach, FL 33069

R. T. Blass, Inc.
Box 74 Pitt Rd.
Old Chatham, NY 12136

Blue Ridge Marketing Group, Inc.
P.O. Box 646
Forest, VA 24551

Bocca Direct Marketing
P.O. Box 310
Manhattan Beach, CA 90266

The Boyle Group Inc.
18748 Birdseye Dr.
Germantown, MD 20874

Bridar, Inc.
25 Sand Creek Rd.
Albany, NY 12205

Arthur Brill Consultants
2 Halfax Ct.
Sterling, VA 22170

Brooks Mann, Inc.
1360 W. 9th St.
Cleveland, OH 44113

Matt Brown & Associates
2769 Orchard Run Rd.
Dayton, OH 45449

Bruckenthal Associates Inc.
47 Bryon Pl.
Scarsdale, NY 10583

The Bureau, Inc.
2555 S.E. Bonita St.
Sturar, FL 34997

Ron Burke & Associates
28916 Raab Dr.
Waterford, WI 53185

Ed Burnett Consultants
100 Paragon Dr.
Montvale, NJ 07645

Burnett Direct, Inc.
27692 Frankline Rd.
Southfield, MI 48034

Burnett Marketing, Inc.
800 Lee St.
Des Plaines, IL 60016

Bernice S. Bush Company
15052 Springdale St.
Huntington Beach, CA 92649

Business America Database
P.O. Box 608
Bedford, TX 76095

Business Extension Bureau of Texas
4802 Travis
Houston, TX 77002

A. Caldwell List Co., Inc.
4350 Georgetown Sq.
Atlanta, GA 30338

California Data Marketing
2818 E. Hamilton
Fresno, CA 93721

CAMA/Consumer's Advertising &
  Marketing Assoc.
20 Lake Dr.
Hightstown, NJ 08520

Cantrell Corporation
P.O. Box 3030
Oakton, VA 22124

Capitol List Company
316 Pennsylvania Ave., S.E.
Washington, DC 20003

Capstone Lists, Inc.
1315 Duke St.
Alexandria, VA 22314

John J. Caramanico Assoc.
2191 Defense Hwy.
Crofton, MD 21114

Carnegie Marketing Associates
3878 Carson St.
Torrance, CA 90503

CAS Marketing, Inc.
616 S. 75th St.
Omaha, NE 68114

Catalog Corp.
143 N. Cora
Fox Lake, IL 60020

Catalog Media Network
500 Davis Center
Evanston, IL 60201

Catalyst Direct Marketing
4640 Lankershim Blvd.
North Hollywood, CA 91602

Center Marketing
44 Commercial Wharf
Boston, MA 02110

Certified Mailing Lists Co.
4 Candlebush
Irvine, CA 92715

CFF Direct
6931 Arlington Rd.
Bethesda, MD 20614

Chesapeake Direct, Inc.
201 Balsam Dr.
Severna Park, MD 21146

Chilcutt Direct Marketing
9301 Cedar Lake Ave.
Oklahoma City, OK 73113

CI Communications
1229 23rd St.
Santa Monica, CA 90404

Cinamon Direct Response
  Consulting
121 Mt. Vernon St.
Boston, MA 02108

Civista Direct
101 N. Main St.
North Canton, OH 44720

Columbia Direct Marketing
60 West St.
Annapolis, MD 21401

Compilers Plus Inc.
466 Main St.
New Rochelle, NY 10801

Compuletter, Inc.
7545 N. Natchez
Niles, IL 60648

Computerized Data Systems Inc.
4301 N.W. 63rd
Oklahoma City, OK 73116

Computermail Florida
2012 4th St.
St. Petersburg, FL 33704

Computers Unlimited
P.O. Box 6008
Boca Raton, FL 33427

Concept One List Brokers
P.O. Box 399
Katonah, NY 10536

Conrad Direct, Inc.
80 West St.
Englewood, NJ 07631

Consortium List Services
165 Arlington Heights Rd.
Buffalo Grove, IL 60089

Consumer Direct Response
  Marketing
2111 Hwy. 377 E.
Granbury, TX 76048

Contempo Marketing Co.
4100 N. Powerline Rd.
Pompano Beach, FL 33073

Convenient Name Bank
P.O. Box 670
Spring House, PA 19477

The Coolidge Co.
25 W. 43rd St.
New York, NY 10036

The Cooperative Marketing Co.
5550 Meadowbrook
Rolling Meadows, IL 60008

COR Information
117 Landmark Sq.
Va. Beach, VA 23452

Cornerstone Mailing Lists
87 E. Green St.
Pasadena, CA 91105

Country Marketing Ltd.
178 E. Main St.
Ilion, NY 13357

Covedale Lists Company
P.O. Box 58201
Cincinnati, OH 45258

Coyne & Associates
111 Marsh Rd.
Pittsford, NY 14534

Charles Crane Associates
2050 Center Ave.
Fort Lee, NJ 07024

Creative List Services, Inc.
40 Daniel St.
Farmingdale, NY 11735

Creative Marketing Programs
1706 Wyandotte
Kansas City, MO 64108

Creative Professional Services, Inc.
20 Cabot Rd.
Woburn, MA 01801

Creative Response Concepts
113 S. West St.
Alexandria, VA 22314

Crosslists Company
11370 Manchester Rd.
Kirkwood, MO 61122

C2M Direct
2628 N. Knollwood Circle
Tucson, AZ 85715

Custom Mailing Services
145 Grove St.
Peterborough, NH 03458

Customized Mailing Lists, Inc.
1906 Field Rd.
Sarasota, FL 34276

Datachase, Inc.
500 Market St.
Portsmouth, NH 03801

Data Lists and Mailing, Inc.
2121 South Hudson St.
Denver, CO 80222

Data Specifics Ltd.
3335 Kettering Place
Greensboro, NC 27410

Datamarq
1683 Larkin Williams Rd.
Fenton, MO 63026

Valerie Davis & Associates
175 Canal St.
Manchester, NH 03101

Dependable Lists, Inc.
950 S. 25th Ave.
Bellwood, IL 60104

Devon Marketing Services
2816 Palos Verdes Dr., W.
Palos Verdes, CA 90274

D/E/Z Associates, Inc.
190 Weston Rd.
Weston, CT 06883

DFK Associates, Inc.
1270 N.W. 102nd Ave.
Portland, OR 97229

Dickinson Direct Mail
120 Campanelli Dr.
Braintree, MA 02184

Dillon, Agnew & Martin
535 Walnut St.
Norwood, NJ 07648

Dimac Direct
One Corporate Woods Dr.
Bridgeton, MO 63044

Dimarc Communications
1534 Contour Dr.
San Antonio, TX 78212

Dimark, Inc.
2050 Cabot Blvd. W.
Langhorne, PA 19047

Direct Chanel Inc.
875 Providence Hwy.
Dedham, MA 02026

Direct Communications Corp.
24 Wales St.
Rutland, VT 05701

Direct Contact Marketing Corp.
P.O. Box 10011
Arlington, VA 22210

Direct Effect
1049 Camino del Mar
Del Mar, CA 92014

Direct Hit Marketing, Inc.
2575 Stephens Rd.
Boulder, CO 80303

Direct Hits Mailing Lists
4529 Old Princess Anne Rd.
Virginia Beach, VA 23462

Directional Marketing
Two Grand Central Tower
New York, NY 10170

Direct List Technology
1590 N. Brian St.
Orange, CA 92667

Direct Mail Advertising
5870 Miami Lakes Dr.
Miami Lakes, FL 33014

Direct Mail Center Inc.
2952 N.W. 60th St.
Ft. Lauderdale, FL 33309

Direct Mail Coordinators
1558 Menlo Ave.
Clovis, CA 93612

Direct Mail of Texas
P.O. Box 12004
Lubbock, TX 79452

Direct Mail Source
7330 E. Earli Dr.
Scottsdale, AZ 85251

Direct Mail Systems
11801 28th St., N.
St. Petersburg, FL 33716

Direct Market Concepts, Inc.
11700 Central Pkwy.
Jacksonville, FL 32216

Direct Marketing Enterprises
374 Circle of Progress
Pottstown, PA 19464

Direct Marketing Mailing Lists
23 Drydock Ave.
Boston, MA 02210

Direct Marketing/QMC Inc.
4124 Fields Dr.
Lafayette Hill, PA 19444

Direct Marketing Resources, Inc.
1985 Corporate Sq. Dr.
Longwood, FL 32750

The Direct Media Group
200 Pemberwick Rd.
Greenwich, CT 06830

Direct Media Marketing, Inc.
8480 Carlton Way
Los Angeles, CA 90069

Direct Partners International
1217 Hilversum
Trompenbergerweg 16
The Netherlands

Direct Response Marketing Group
P.O. Box 516
Bethel, CT 06801

Dirmark Lists
9582 Tara Blvd.
Jonesboro, GA 30236

Discount List Brokerage
188 Broadway
Woodcliff Lake, NJ 07675

D-J Associates
77 Danbury Rd.
Ridgefield, CT 06877

DMR List Services
15481 110th St.
Lenexa, KS 66219

Dresden Direct, Inc.
1200 High Ridge Rd.
Stamford, CT 06905

Alan Drey Company, Inc.
333 N. Michigan Ave.
Chicago, IL 60601

DRK Inc. List Managers & Brokers
101 Summer St.
Boston, MA 02110

Dunhill of Washington Inc.
1990 M St., N.W.
Washington, DC 20036

Dunnings Diversified
1004 Scenic Way Dr.
Ventura, CA 93003

Eagle Direct
5105 E. 41st Ave.
Denver, CO 80216

Eastern Direct Marketing, Inc.
100 N. Washington St.
Falls Church, VA 22046

Edmaro's, Inc.
301 Wilcrest
Houston, TX 77042

Endata Direct
501 Great Circle Rd.
Nashville, TN 37228

Entrepreneur List Rental Inc.
2392 Mores Ave.
Irvine, CA 92714

ERS Media Services, Inc.
24009 Ventura Blvd.
Calabasas, CA 91302

ESA Direct Marketing
1890 E. 40th St.
Cleveland, OH 44103

Estee List Services
P.O. Box 1765
New Rochelle, NY 10802

The Evergreen Group
2755 Bristol St.
Costa Mesa, CA 92626

Evergreen List Company
2 Maple St.
Middlebury, VT 05753

Evergreen Marketing
RD 1 Box 812
Landisburg, PA 17040

Exclusive Marketing Group, Ltd.
36 Reichert Circle
Westport, CT 06880

Execulists, Inc.
3085 Center Green Dr.
Boulder, CO 80301

Vijay Faioa & Associates
20518 Toluca Ave.
Torrance, CA 90503

Fairfield Marketing Group
830 Sport Hill Rd.
Easton, CT 06612

The Fairmont Press
700 Indian Trail
Liburn, GA 30247

Fasano & Associates
3599 Cahuenga Blvd. W.
Los Angeles, CA 90068

FCB Direct
11601 Wilshore Blvd.
Los Angeles, CA 90025

Fiduciary Lists
850 S. Boulder Hwy.
Henderson, NV 89015

Fils Company
50 King Phillips Path
Duxbury, MA 02331

Financial Enterprises
P.O. Box 747
Walnut, CA 91789

Financial Marketing Plus Inc.
1019 W. Park Ave.
Libertyville, IL 60048

Financial Marketing Services Inc.
180 Cook St.
Denver, CO 80206

Finest Direct Marketing
7300 W. McNab Rd.
Tamarac, FL 33319

First-Class Mailing Service, Inc.
1409 E. Olive Ct.
Ft. Collins, CO 80524

First Financial Response
587 N. Ventu Park Rd.
Newbury Court, CA 91320

First National List Service
2265 W. Eastwood
Chicago, IL 60625

5M List Company
2525 Wilson Blvd.
Arlington, VA 22201

Flexmail Direct
413 Oak Place
Port Orange, FL 32127

Flynn Direct Response Inc.
62 Spring Hill Rd.
Trumbull, CT 06611

FMIS, Inc.
2012 E. Randol Mill Rd.
Arlington, TX 76011

440 Financial Group
440 Lincoln St.
Worcester, MA 01605

Franklin & Welker, Inc.
10800 Biscayne Blvd.
Miami, FL 33161

Freedom List Corp.
4501 Daly Dr.
Chantilly, VA 22021

Neal L. Friedman
P.O. Box 569
Canoga Park, CA 91305

Saul Gale Associates, Inc.
57-03 Kissena Blvd.
Flushing, NY 11355

Gancom
201 Senate Ave.
Camp Hill, PA 17011

Gannett Direct Marketing Services
3400 Robards Ct.
Louisville, KY 40218

Gayle Phillips Inc.
271 Madison Ave.
New York, NY 10016

Gelderman Group, Inc.
2 Old New Milford Rd.
Brookfield, CT 06804

GGC Associates, Inc.
3100 Airway
Costa Mesa, CA 92626

Gilbert Rogers & Graves
21 Underhill Rd.
Ossining, NY 10562

Gish, Sherwood & Friends, Inc.
4235 Hillsboro Rd.
Nashville, TN 37215

J. F. Glaser, Inc.
999 Main St.
Glen Ellyn, IL 60137

Global Direct Marketing
189 Knickerbocker Rd.
Closter, NJ 07624

Global Services Foundation
3936 S. Semoran Blvd.
Orlando, FL 32812

Gnames Enterprises
1431 Greenway Dr.
Irving, TX 75038

Good Fortune Marketing Inc.
210 Commerce Blvd.
Round Rock, TX 78664

M. Goodman & Company
4206 S. Terrace
Chattanooga, TN 37412

GPI, Ltd.
Five Ridge Rd.
Danbury, CT 06810

Mary Elizabeth Granger &
  Associates, Inc.
205 E. Joppa Rd.
Baltimore, MD 21286

Group Direct/Collier
2706 S. Horseshoe Dr.
Naples, FL 33942

GSP List Services
156 N. Jefferson St.
Chicago, IL 60606

The Guild Company
171 Terrace St.
Haworth, NJ 07641

Guru Systems, Inc.
2907 Ridge Rd.
Lansing, IL 60438

Harvard Professional Lists, Inc.
1430 Massachusetts Ave.
Cambridge, MA 02138

Healthcare Direct
P.O. Box 75056
Atlanta, GA 30374

Healthcare Lists USA
P.O. Box 16067
Irvine, CA 92713

Hemisphere Marketing, Inc.
100 Spear St.
San Francisco, CA 94105

Hemmings, Birkholm & Grizzard
1480 Colorado Blvd.
Los Angeles, CA 90041

Hendrix Associates, Inc.
10292 Jamaica Ln.
Manassas, VA 22110

Leon Henry, Inc.
455 Central Ave.
Scarsdale, NY 10583

Heron Lists
437 Madison Ave.
New York, NY 10022

Hippo Direct
4502 Groveland
University Heights, OH 44118

Hogan & Associates
6700 Antioch
Shawnee Mission, KS 66204

Holland Mark Martin
174 Middlesex Turnpike
Burlington, MA 01803

The Horah Group
274 Madison Ave.
New York, NY 10016

Horizon Mailing List & Marketing
160 Overlook Ave.
Hackensack, NJ 07601

Hotline List Corp.
535 Fifth Ave.
New York, NY 10077

HR Direct
508 N. Second St.
Fairfield, IA 52556

HVB List Promotions
P.O. Box 1832
Middleburg, VA 22117

IC Direct
2175 Francisco Blvd.
San Rafael, CA 94901

Idealists
1901 Research Blvd.
Rockville, MD 20850

IMPCO Direct Response
100 Rockwood St.
Rochester, NY 14610

Infocore, Inc.
135 S. Sierra Ave.
Solana Beach, CA 92075

Infocus Lists
341 Victory Dr.
Herndon, VA 22070

Infodirect
1638-B Monte Sano Blvd.
Huntsville, AL 35801

Infolists, Inc.
1730 Stickney Point Rd.
Sarasota, FL 34231

Infomat
1815 W. 213th St.
Torrance, CA 90501

Informationbanc Incorporated
5623 S. Ivy Court
Englewood, CO 80111

Information Marketing Services
8130 Boone Blvd.
Vienna, VA 22182

Initio List Marketing, Inc.
725 Dell Rd.
Carlstadt, NJ 07072

Innotrac Corporation
1828 Meca Way
Norcross, GA 30093

Insert Marketing
527 Third Ave.
New York, NY 10016

Inside Contacts USA
1630 S.W. Morrison
Portland, OR 97205

Integrated Management Solutions
4728 E. Michigan St.
Orlando, FL 32812

Intelligent Marketing Systems
7900 Xerxes Ave. So.
Minneapolis, MN 55431

Inter-Group Marketing, Inc.
4011 Shoreside Circle
Tampa, FL 33624

International Direct Response, Inc.
60 Chestnut Ave.
Devon, PA 19333

International Marketing Ventures
7211D Hanover Pkwy.
Greenbelt, MD 20770

J.S. Direct,
5-2362 Cornwell Ave.
Vancouver, BC
Canada

JAMI Marketing Services
2 Blue Hill Plaza
Pearl River, NY 10965

Jamron, Inc.
1310 N. Ritchie Ct.
Chicago, IL 60610

Jaybett Direct, Inc.
1387 King James Ct.
Agoura, CA 91301

J.B.W. Direct
1 Madison Ave.
Grand Junction, TN 38039

JC Lists Company
4301 Connecticut Ave., N.W.
Washington, DC 20008

JHL Mail Marketing
3100 Borham Ave.
Stevens Point, WI 54481

Jordan Direct
959 W. Partridge Dr.
Palatine, IL 60067

Joyce Letter Shop
647 Summer St.
Boston, MA 02210

J. R. Direct
4703 51 St.
Delta BC CN V4K 2W1
Canada

Just Lists Inc.
235 E. 95th St.
New York, NY 10128

The Kaplan Agency, Inc.
1200 High Ridge Rd.
Stamford, CT 06905

Walter Karl Inc.
135 Bedford Rd.
Armonk, NY 10504

Kelk & Associates
36 Ferndale Rd.
Deer Park, IL 60010

Key Contacts & Communications
911 First St.
Rockville, MD 20850

Kingswood Advertising
Cricket Terrace
Ardmore, PA 19003

Kistler Graphics, Inc.
4000 Dahlia St.
Denver, CO 80217

The Kleid Company
530 Fifth Ave.
New York, NY 10036

John Klein & Associates
20700 Miles Ave.
Cleveland, OH 44128

K. M. Lists Inc.
203 Centennial Ctr.
Berlin, NJ 08009

Kobs Gregory Pasavant
225 N. Michigan Ave.
Chicago, IL 60601

The Jerry Kraft Group, Inc.
3355 N. Arlington Heights Rd.
Arlington Hts., IL 60004

Kroll Direct Marketing Inc.
666 Plainsboro Rd.
Plainsboro, NJ 08536

KSA & Company
916 West Glade Rd.
Hurst, TX 76054

Ladd Associates, Inc.
2527 Fillmore St.
San Francisco, CA 94115

Larimar Creative Marketing
6500 Greenville Ave.
Dallas, TX 75206

Lawrence Direct Marketing
54 E. Lee St.
Watertown, VA 22186

LDMI/Lortz Direct Marketing
11316 P St.
Omaha, NE 68137

Lee Data Mail Services
1617 Terre Colony Ct.
Dallas, TX 75212

Lee Direct Marketing
P.O. Box 145
Vernon Hills, IL 60061

Letterworks International
18 Ashmont St.
Portland, ME 04103

Lewis Advertising Company
325 E. Oliver St.
Baltimore, MD 21202

Lifecycle Learning
1320 Centre St.
Newton, MA 02159

Link Direct Mail
22 S. Fairview
Santa Barbara, CA 93117

Linkage Direct, Inc.
110 Hartwell Ave.
Lexington, MA 02173

List Advisor, Inc.
20 Broadway
Massapequa, NY 11758

List America
1202 Potomac St., N.W.
Washington, DC 20007

The List Authority
192 Third Ave.
Westwood, NJ 07675

List Brokers International
1916 Brooks
Missoula, MT 59801

Listco Mailing Lists
620 Frelinghuysen Ave.
Newark, NJ 07114

The List Connection Inc.
540 W. Boston Post Rd.
Mamaroneck, NY 10543

List Counsellors, Inc.
3 South Main St.
Allentown, NJ 08501

List Directors, Inc.
P.O. Box 5129
Brookfield, CT 06804

The List Emporium, Inc.
2000 Shawnee Mission Pkwy.
Westwood, KS 66205

L.I.S.T. Inc.
320 Northern Blvd.
Great Neck, NY 11021

List Locators & Managers, Inc.
11020 King St.
Overland Park, KS 66210

List Management Inc.
1401 W. 76th St.
Minneapolis, MN 55423

List Marketing Ltd.
1037 E. Putnam Ave.
Riverside, CT 06878

The Listmaster
700 Fifth Ave.
San Rafael, CA 94901

The List Network, Inc.
2901 Blackbridge Rd.
York, PA 17402

List Options Inc.
P.O. Box 6634
Falls Church, VA 22040

List Process Company, Inc.
420 E. 79th St.
New York, NY 10021

List Pro of America
3089-C Clairemont Dr.
San Diego, CA 92117

Lists By Design
280 N.W. 12th Ave.
Deerfield Beach, FL 33442

List Search, Inc.
477 Madison Ave.
New York, NY 10022

Lists Media International
25-15 50th St.
Woodside, NY 11377

The List Source Inc.
1415 Route 70 E.
Cherry Hill, NJ 08034

List Strategies, Inc.
1290 Ave. of Americas
New York, NY 10104

List Technology Systems Group
1001 Ave. of Americas
New York, NY 10018

Listline
187 Ballardvale St.
Wilmington, MA 11887

The Listworks Corp.
One Campus Dr.
Pleasantville, NY 10570

List World
152 Deforest Rd.
Burlington, VT 05404

The Litchfield Group
115 Cat Swamp Rd.
Woodbury, CT 06798

LR Direct Ltd.
972 Post Rd.
Darien, CT 06820

T. Lynn Associates
109 Wallace St.
Tuckahoe, NY 10707

Macromark, Inc.
65 W. 96th St.
New York, NY 10025

Madison Direct Marketing
500 West Putnam Ave.
Greenwich, CT 06830

Madison Lists
1408 N. Fillmore St.
Arlington, VA 22201

Magazine Marketing, Inc.
191 Clarksville Rd.
Lawrenceville, NJ 08648

The Mailbox
521 Bedford Ave.
Bellmore, NY 11710

Mail Communications, Inc.
721 Olive St.
St. Louis, MO 63101

Mailgraphics, Inc.
5441 Western Ave.
Boulder, CO 80301

Mailing Concepts, Inc.
12625 Stowe Dr.
Poway, CA 92064

Mailing Corporation of America
300 C. Bedford St.
Manchester, NH 03101

Mailing Data Services, Inc.
6055 E. Washington Blvd.
Commerce, CA 90040

Mailings Lists & Marketing, Inc.
3094 Mercer Univ. Dr.
Atlanta, GA 30341

Mailing Lists Plus
1239 120th Ave. NE
Bellevue, WA 98005

Mailing Services Inc.
1319 N. Broad St.
Hillside, NJ 07205

Mailmasters
2777 152nd Ave. NE
Redmond, WA 98052

A Mail'n List Company 4 You
19634 Ventura Blvd.
Tarzana, CA 91356

Mail Order Direct Advertising
955 Hilltop Rd.
Plainfield, NJ 07060

Mailpro
502 North Quince St.
Escondido, CA 92025

Mailworks, Inc.
230 N. Michigan Ave.
Chicago, IL 60601

Mal Dunn Associates
Hardscrabble Rd.
Croton Falls, NY 10519

Manus Direct
1130 Ranier Ave. So.
Seattle, WA 98144

Mardev USA
245 W. 17th St.
New York, NY 10011

Marketaide, Inc.
P.O. Box 500
Salina, KS 67402

Market Direct, Inc.
P.O. Box 2539
Stuart, FL 34995

Market Finders Inc.
1705 14th St.
Boulder, CO 80302

The Marketing Advantage
3600 Cantrell Rd.
Little Rock, AR 72202

Marketing Bulletin Board
117 W. Michehorena
Santa Barbara, CA 93101

Marketing Communications, Inc.
10605 W. 84th Ter.
Lenexa, KS 66214

Marketing Economics, Inc.
1636 N. Wells
Chicago, IL 60614

Marketing Frontiers, Inc.
500 W. Cummings Park
Woburn, MA 01801

Marketing Intelligence
3256 Belvidere Ave., S.W.
Seattle, WA 98126

Marketing Investors Group
1120 Empire Central Place
Dallas, TX 75247

Marketing List Professionals
P.O. Box 1513
Madison, CT 06443

The Marketing Place
12455 Branford St.
Arieta, CA 91331

Marketing Services International
625 N. Michigan Ave.
Chicago, IL 60611

Marketing Solutions
800 Douglas Entrance
Coral Gables, FL 33134

Marketing Solutions Company
26 Lake St.
Ramsey, NJ 07446

Marketing Visions, Inc.
1928 N.E. 154th St.
North Miami Beach, FL 33162

Market Mapping Plus
3087 30th St.
Grandville, MI 49418

Marketry, Inc.
2020 116th Ave. NE
Bellevue, WA 98004

Market Share
5726 Cortez Rd. W.
Bradenton, FL 34210

Market Street Lists
91 Portsmouth Ave.
Stratham, NH 03885

Market Vision
470 S. Beverly Dr.
Beverly Hills, CA 90212

Hank Marshall Marketing Co.
P.O. Box 2729
Laguna Hills, CA 92654

Mastermailer, Inc.
3914 N. 29th Ave.
Hollywood, FL 33020

Master Response
729 Grapevine Hwy.
Hurst, TX 76054

Mavis & Moore
1706 Cambridge Rd.
Ann Arbor, MI 48104

Max Media, Inc.
415 Centerbury Rd.
Bay Village, OH 44140

J. May Marketing/Media
104 S. Main St.
Park Ridge, IL 60068

MBS Associates
312 Washington St.
Peekskill, NY 10566

P. J. McCarthy & Associates
1617 Royal Oak Rd.
Darien, IL 60561

McGuinness-Enterprises
2383 Akers Mill Rd.
Atlanta, GA 30339

McIntyre & Dodd Marketing Inc.
3049B Deacon Rd.
Dollard des Ormeaux, Quebec
Canada

The McNichols Group, Inc.
51 Sherwood Ter.
Lake Bluff, IL 60044

MEC List Management
Box 3727
Santa Monica, CA 90408

Media Horizons, Inc.
94 East Ave.
Norwalk, CT 06851

Media Marketplace, Inc.
6 Penns Trail
Newtown, PA 18940

Media Mart
1101 King St.
Alexandria, VA 22314

Medical Marketing Service
700 N. Wood Dale Rd.
Wood Dale, IL 60191

Mega Marketing Group
18368 Redmond Fall City Rd.
Redmond, WA 98052

Mega Media Associates
P.O. Box 4259
Newport Beach, CA 92661

Merrimack Inc.
2533 N. Carson St.
Carson City, NV 89706

Metro Direct Marketing
333 Seventh Ave.
New York, NY 10001

MGI Media Services
1613 Duke St.
Alexandria, VA 22314

M.G.M. Mailing Lists
32 Pinyon Way
East Falmouth, MA 02536

Mid-American Lists
315 3rd Ave.
Cedar Rapids, IA 52401

Midwest Lists & Media
9301 N. Milwaukee Ave.
Niles, IL 60648

Millard Group, Inc.
10 Vose Farm Rd.
Peterborough, NH 03458

Miller Communications, Inc.
8400 Westpark Dr.
McLean, VA 22102

Milwaukee Direct Marketing
240 Regency Ct.
Waukesha, WI 53186

Mission: A Consulting Group
19 Compo Rd., South
Westport, CT 06880

Mission Direct Marketing, Inc.
5845 Horton
Mission, KS 66202

Moe's Direct Marketing
3517 Marconi Ave.
Sacramento, CA 95821

Donald Moger Direct Marketing
750 N. Kings Rd.
Los Angeles, CA 90069

Mokrynski & Associates
401 Hackensack Ave.
Hackensack, NJ 07601

Moran-Cottier, Inc.
7101 Westcoat Dr.
Colleyville, TX 76034

Morris Direct Marketing, Inc.
300 W. 55th St.
New York, NY 10019

MPG List Company
115 S. Union St.
Alexandria, VA 22314

MPM Services Inc.
1206 Sterling Rd.
Dania, FL 33004

MSC Lists
450 Los Verdes
Santa Barbara, CA 93111

Muldoon List Center
300 Park Ave. So.
New York, NY 10010

Multimedia Marketing and
  Communications
7401 Carmel Executive Park
Charlotte, NC 28226

Multinational Concepts Ltd.
Box 5003
Cary, NC 27511

Tony Murray & Associates
9663C Main St.
Fairfax, VA 22032

Name Bank
824 E. Baltimore St.
Baltimore, MD 21202

Namebank of America
17 Battery Pl.
New York, NY 10004

Name Exchange, Inc.
7015 Old Keene Mill Rd.
Springfield, VA 22150

Name-Finders Lists
3180 18th St.
San Francisco, CA 94110

Names & Addresses, Inc.
160 E. Marquardt Dr.
Wheeling, IL 60090

Names in the Mail, Inc.
10710 Shiloh Rd.
Dallas, TX 75228

Names in the News California
1 Bush St.
San Francisco, CA 94104

Names in the News Inc.
411 Theodore Fremd Ave.
Rye, NY 10580

Names Unlimited
345 Park Ave. South
New York, NY 10010

NAM Mailing Lists
P.O. Box 970
Santa Cruz, NM 87567

National List Exchange
26750 US Hwy. 19 N.
Clearwater, FL 34621

National Mailing Services, Inc.
3580 ZIP Industrial Blvd.
Atlanta, GA 30354

Nationwide Mail Marketing
2231 Perimeter Park Dr.
Atlanta, GA 30341

New Customer Acquisition/Jon Jay
  Corp.
620 Franquette St.
Medford, OR 97501

New Lists Company
30-60 Whitestone Expwy.
Flushing, NY 11354

Newclients, Inc.
211 Ruthers Rd.
Richmond, VA 23235

New Start Direct Marketing Group
11505 Sunset Hills Rd.
Reston, VA 22090

Nice Lines Direct Mail
2564 Blvd. of the Generals
Norristown, PA 19403

North American List Associates
401 N. Broad St.
Philadelphia, PA 19108

North American List Marketing
20 Maple Ave.
Armonk, NY 10504

North Carolina Direct Marketing
P.O. Box 2478
Durham, NC 27715

Novus Marketing
601 Lakeshore Pkwy.
Minneapolis, MN 55305

NPO: Lists
1728 Abbot Kinney Blvd.
Venice, CA 90291

NRL Brokerage
100 Union Ave.
Cresskill, NJ 07626

Robert Nulf Associates
P.O. Box 36728
Charlotte, NC 28236

Nurre Direct Mail Consulting
2012 H St.
Sacramento, CA 95814

Old Dominion List Company
809 Brook Hill Circle
Richmond, VA 23227

Omega List Company
8245 Boone Blvd.
Vienna, VA 22182

Omni Mail
473 President St.
Brooklyn, NY 11215

Organizational Training Services
3224 Tanager St.
Raleigh, NC 27606

Orion Direct Marketing
10611 Allenwood Ln.
Great Falls, VA 22066

The Other List Co., Inc.
P.O. Box 286
Matawan, NJ 07747

Pacific Lists Inc.
131 Camino Alto
Mill Valley, CA 94941

Packaged Promotions, Inc.
136 Whitaker Rd.
Lutz, FL 33549

Page & Associates
743 Gantt Ave.
Sarasota, FL 34232

PA List Company
RD 2, Box P-17
Muncy, PA 17756

Paradysz Matera & Co.
19 W. 21st St.
New York, NY 10010

Paragon Printing & Mailing
706C Brentwood
Austin, TX 78752

Paramount Lists, Inc.
P.O. Box 3552
Erie, PA 16508

Partners Marketing, Inc.
555 Tollgate Rd.
Elgin, IL 60123

Paulmark, Inc.
6635 W. Commercial Blvd.
Tamarac, FL 33319

PCS Mailing List Company
85 Constitution Ln.
Danvers, MA 01923

Pennrich
8042 Oliver Rd.
Erie, PA 16509

Peterscore Mailing & Data Resources
31230 Cedarvalley Dr.
Westlake Village, CA 91362

Phillips Publishing, Inc.
7811 Montrose Rd.
Potomac, MD 20854

Pick Publications, Inc.
24151 Telegraph Rd.
Southfield, MI 48034

Pinnacle List Company
2800 Shirlington Rd.
Arlington, VA 22206

PMM Marketing Inc.
333 Route 25A
Rocky Point, NY 11778

Polaris Communications
6001 Chapel Hill Rd.
Raleigh, NC 27607

Political Resources Inc.
P.O. Box 4278
Burlington, VT 05406

W. S. Ponton, Inc.
5149 Butler St.
Pittsburgh, PA 15201

Preferred Lists
5201 Leesburg Pike
Falls Church, VA 22041

Primenet Datasystems
8711 Lyndale Ave. So.
Minneapolis, MN 55420

Priority Systems Inc.
1510 Skokie Blvd.
Northbrook, IL 60062

Prodirect List Brokerage
3308 W. Burbank Blvd.
Burbank, CA 91505

Progressive Resources
4230 Del Rey Ave.
Marina Del Rey, CA 90292

Promo Concepts
2 Charlesgate West
Boston, MA 02215

Promotion Management, Inc.
5561 W. 74th St.
Indianapolis, IN 46268

Pro/Phase Marketing, Inc.
700 S. Fifth St.
Hopkins, MN 55343

Publishers Mailing Lists
624 Patton Ave.
Asheville, NC 28806

Puget Sound Direct
P.O. Box 1965
Woodinville, WA 98072

Pullman List Management
507 N. New York Ave.
Winter Park, FL 32789

Quality Lists and Publications
62 Birch Dr.
Swoyersville, PA 18704

Quebecor List Services
121 Bloor St. E.
Toronto, Ontario, M4W 3M5, Canada

Rad Marketing Communications
220 E. 42nd St.
Davenport, IA 52801

Rapidmail, Inc.
315 W. 4th St.
Davenport, IA 52801

Rapp Collins Marcoa
1440 Corporate Dr.
Irving, TX 75038

Rein Associates, Inc.
837 Broad St.
Shrewsbury, NJ 07702

Reinking Enterprises
9060 Zachery Ln. N.
Maple Grove, MN 55369

The Reis Company
12911 Palomar Way
Santa Ana, CA 92705

Jay Reiss Mailing Lists
160-D N. Fairview Ave.
Goleta, CA 93117

Religious Lists
86 Maple Ave.
New City, NY 10956

Resource & Development Group
8416 Melrose Dr.
Lenexa, KS 66214

Response Concepts & Analysis
1123 S. University
Little Rock, AR 72204

Response Group Inc.
4291 Sicard Hollow Rd.
Birmingham, AL 35242

Response Mailing Lists
20200 NE 10th Pl.
Miami, FL 33179

Response Marketing Network
118 Rte. 9
Wappingers Falls, NY 12590

Response Marketing Resources
2600 Clark Ave.
St. Louis, MO 63103

Response Media Products, Inc.
2323 Perimeter Park Dr.
Atlanta, GA 30341

Response Media Services Inc.
820 N. Orleans
Chicago, IL 60610

Response Technologies, Inc.
376 Nash Rd.
New Bedford, MA 02746

Response Unlimited, 251
c/o The Old Plantation
Rt. 5
Waynesboro, VA 22980

The Rich List Co.
4 E. 81st St., Pnthse.
New York, NY 10028

Robert Rickard List Marketing
5512 Merrick Rd.
Massapequa, NY 11758

Rifkin Direct, Inc.
64 Appletree Ln.
Roslyn Heights, NY 11577

RMI Direct Marketing
4 Skyline Dr.
Hawthorne, NY 10532

Robertson Mailing List Co.
1467 Vance Ave.
Memphis, TN 38104

Edith Roman Associates
253 W. 35th St.
New York, NY 10001

Doug Ross Communications, Inc.
3225 South Hardy Dr.
Tempe, AZ 85282

Andrea Rubin Marketing, Inc.
441 Lexington Ave.
New York, NY 10017

Rubin Response Services, Inc.
1111 Plaza Dr.
Schaumburg, IL 60173

Saavoy Direct Response Group
P.O. Box 1765
Paramus, NJ 07652

Sanmar Associates
177 Main St.
Fort Lee, NJ 07024

Saugatuck Marketing Group
18 Kings Hwy.
North Westport, CT 06880

Saultech
16776 Bernardo Center Dr.
San Diego, CA 92128

Saxe Marketing, Inc.
42 E. 75th St.
New York, NY 10021

Scarborough List Services
3695 Wimbledon Dr.
Pensacola, FL 32504

S.C.I. Marketing
2901 W. Busch Blvd.
Tampa, FL 33618

Sci/Tech Marketing, Inc.
200 E. 27th St.
New York, NY 10016

J. Scott Direct
2011 Pennington Dr.
Arlington, TX 76014

SCS Direct Mail Marketing
P.O. Box 53706
Fayetteville, NC 28305

Seacoast Marketing
7 Winterbrook Ct.
York Village, ME 03909

Seco Financial Services
2201 State Route 38
Cherry Hill, NJ 08002

Select List Corp.
26 Garvies Pt. Rd.
Glen Cove, NY 11542

Select Mailing Lists
45 Legion Dr.
Cresskill, NJ 07626

Select Marketing
9020-11 Capital of Texas Highway
North Austin, TX 78759

Seminar List Management
P.O. Box 9297
Canoga Park, CA 91309

Seminars List Services
1402 E. Skyline Dr.
Madison, WI 53705

Send-It Corp.
210 Dowdle
Algonquin, IL 60102

S & G Business Associates
P.O. Box 302
Elkhart, IN 46515

Sheiner Direct, Inc.
13261 Moorpark St.
Sherman Oaks, CA 91423

The Shields Group
P.O. Box 5231
Fredericksburg, VA 22403

Silver List Marketing
7910 Woodmont Ave.
Bethesda, MD 20814

Simon Direct Inc.
F-4 Brier Hill Ct.
East Brunswick, NJ 08816

Elaine Sims Direct Marketing
P.O. Box 233
Pomona, NY 10970

Sims List Brokerage
470 Lake St.
Excelsior, MN 55331

Fred Singer Direct Marketing
1329A North Ave.
New Rochelle, NY 10804

S.L. Lists Unlimited
P.O. Box 276067
Boca Raton, FL 33427

Smart-Mail of Austin
2600 McHale Ct.
Austin, TX 78758

M. Lee Smith Publishers
162 4th Ave. N.
Nashville, TN 37219

Snow Business Lists
2360 Congress Ave.
Clearwater, FL 34623

Southwest Data Management
6240 Arc Way
Ft. Myers, FL 33912

Spaulder & Associates
600 East Las Colinas Blvd.
Irving, TX 75039

The Specialists
1200 Harbor Blvd.
Weehawken, NJ 07087

Specialized Marketing Inc.
Mill Pond Office Center
Somers, NY 10589

Specialized Media Services
P.O. Box 3308
Chicago, IL 60654

Speciality Mail Services
7300 N. Lehigh Ave.
Chicago, IL 60648

Spring Green
776 Rudolph Way
Greendale, IN 47025

Stafford Response Marketing
208 Pennsylvania Ave.
Pasadena, MD 21122

Starkoff Direct Marketing
P.O. Box 811045
Boca Raton, FL 33481

Statlistics
123 Elm St.
Old Saybrook, CT 06475

The Stenrich Group
4413 Cox Rd.
Glen Allen, VA 23060

George Stern Agency
254 E. Grand Ave.
Escondido, CA 92025

Stezzi Direct Inc.
501 Armour Circle NE
Atlanta, GA 30324

Strafford Direct
1201 Peachtree St. NE
Atlanta, GA 30361

Stratmark Corp.
7515 Greenville Ave.
Dallas, TX 75231

Wm. Stroh, Inc.
568 54th St.
West New York, NJ 07093

Thomas Stuart Media Management
44 Franklin St.
Nashua, NH 03061

Summit Mailing Lists
18 E. Canon Perdido
Santa Barbara, CA 93101

Syncom Inc.
799 Roosevelt Rd.
Glen Ellyn, IL 60137

Target Advertising
6 William St.
Lynbrook, NY 11563

Targeted Marketing Inc.
Box 5125
Ridgewood, NJ 07451

Target Information Services
4151 Ashford-Dunwoody Rd.
Atlanta, GA 30319

Target Mailing Lists
51 Madison Ave.
New York, NY 10010

Target Marketing
1901 N.W. 23rd Ave.
Portland, OR 97210

Target Marketteam Inc.
3350 Peachtree Rd.
Atlanta, GA 30326

Target Response
5810 W. 78th St.
Bloomington, MN 55435

Taybi Direct Inc.
10468 San Pablo Ave.
El Cerrito, CA 94530

Technical Publications Mailing Lists
1016 Ascot Dr.
Crystal Lake, IL 60014

Telecom Advertising
72 N. Taylor Ave.
Norwalk, CT 06854

Tele-Mail Inc.
850 Kennesaw Ave.
Marietta, GA 30060

Telemarketing Concepts
2013 Crompond Rd.
Yorktown Hts., NY 10598

Thor Information Services
P.O. Box 158
Great Neck, NY 11022

3 Gen Corporation
643 Montgomery St.
Brooklyn, NY 11225

Thulin Communications
5757 Wilshire
Los Angeles, CA 90036

Times Direct Marketing
435 Brannan St.
San Francisco, CA 94107

Top Response Marketing Inc.
3644 SW 3rd Ave.
Miami, FL 33145

Total Media Concepts Inc.
222 Cedar Ln.
Teaneck, NJ 07666

Town & Country List Co.
199 Jericho Tpke.
Floral Park, NY 11001

Trans American Marketing
277 N. Prospect St.
Orange, CA 92669

Ernest Tricomi and Daughter
304 E. Chapel Ave.
Cherry Hill, NJ 08034

Trumbull Marketing Group
105 Beacon St.
Black Rock, CT 06605

Trump Card Marketing
222 Cedar Ln.
Teaneck, NJ 07666

Larry Tucker Inc.
188 Broadway
Woodcliff Lake, NJ 07675

Turner Marketing Systems
34768 Hwy. 79 South
Warner Springs, CA 92086

21st Century Marketing
2 Dubon Ct.
Farmingdale, NY 11735

Uni-Mail List Corp.
352 Park Ave. South
New York, NY 10010

United Advertising
Box 1383
Minneapolis, MN 55440

United Marketing Agency
11300 Rockville Pike
Rockville, MD 20852

University Advertising
3149 Bailey Ave.
Buffalo, NY 14215

Urban Response Inc.
1459 S. Main St.
N. Canton, OH 44720

Vainisi Marketing Inc.
2590 E. Devon Ave.
Des Plaines, IL 60018

Varied Associates
11419-10 Cronridge Dr.
Owings Mills, MD 21117

Venture Communications
 International
60 Madison Ave.
New York, NY 10010

The Victory Company
1003 Woodbine Ave.
Toronto, Ontario, M4C 4C2
Canada

Vomack and Laban Advertising
1 Bennington Ave.
Freeport, NY 11520

Washburn Direct Marketing
1123 S. Church St.
Charlotte, NC 28203

Washington Lists
510 King St.
Alexandria, VA 22314

Watson Mailing Service
2401 Revere Beach Pkwy.
Everett, MA 02149

Watts List Brokerage
455 Horner Ave.
Toronto, Ontario, M8W 4W9
Canada

Webb Marketing Corp.
9304 Forest Ln.
Dallas, TX 75423

Weiss Publishing
2200 N. Florida Mango Rd.
West Palm Beach, FL 33409

Western Advertising Agency
4005 South Western Ave.
Sioux Falls, SD 57117

Western International Media Corp.
8544 Sunset Blvd.
Los Angeles, CA 90069

Western Mailing Lists
14621 Titus St.
Van Nuys, CA 91402

W. I. Mail Marketing
470 Main St.
Ridgefield, CT 06877

Winthill List Management
801 Wayne Ave.
Silver Spring, MD 20910

WOL Direct
Oak & Pawnee Sts.
Scranton, PA 18515

Fred Woolf List Co.
7 Corporate Park Dr.
White Plains, NY 10604

World Advertising Services
7138 N. Tripp Ave.
Lincolnwood, IL 60646

World Innovators Inc.
72 Park St.
New Canaan, CT 06840

Worldata
5200 Town Center Circle
Boca Raton, FL 33486

G. A. Wright
4010 Holly St.
Denver, CO 80216

Yankee List Marketing
1010 Palmer Rd.
Ft. Washington, MD 20744

Yeck Brothers
2222 Arbor Blvd.
Dayton, OH 45439

Yost List Company
3 Jordan East
Irvine, CA 92715

Zentek Corporation
3670-12 W. Oceanside Rd.
Oceanside, NY 11572

Mailing List Managers: A Selected List

The following list management firms offer their services through *Direct Marketing List Source,* a publication of Standard Rate and Data Service.

The Abadi Group Inc.
1312 Allenhurst Ave.
Ocean, NJ 07712

A. B. Data, Ltd.
8050 N. Port Washington Rd.
Milwaukee, WI 53217

Action List Service, Inc.
10 Mountainview Rd.
Upper Saddle River, NJ 07458

Adco List Management Services
333 N. Michigan Ave.
Chicago, IL 60601

Advanced List Marketing Associates
12700 Fair Lakes Circle
Fairfax, VA 22033

Advanced Technology
  Marketing, Inc.
6053 W. Century Blvd.
Los Angeles, CA 90045

Advantage Direct Marketing
  Group
450 7th Ave.
New York, NY 10123

Affinity Marketing Group, Inc.
P.O. Box 2409
Fairfax, VA 22032

Aggressive List Management, Inc.
18-2 East Dundee Rd.
Barrington, IL 60010

A. H. Direct Marketing, Inc.
7217 Gulf Blvd.
St. Petersburg, FL 33706

Fred E. Allen - List Management
P.O. Box 1595
Mt. Pleasant, TX 75456

Allmedia, Inc.
4965 Preston Park Blvd.
Plano, TX 75093

America Direct, Inc.
P.O. Box 260
Burke, VA 22015

American List Counsel, Inc.
88 Orchard Rd.
Princeton, NJ 08543

Barry Ancona
49 W. 16th St.
New York, NY 10011

Antigone Associates, Ltd.
801 West Street Rd.
Feasterville, PA 19053

Atlantic List Marketing
1525 Wilson Blvd.
Arlington, VA 22209

AZ List Managers
31 River Rd.
Cos Cob, CT 06807

Bethesda List Center
6710 Fairfax Rd.
Bethesda, MD 20815

Bocca Direct Marketing
P.O. Box 310
Manhattan Beach, CA 90266

Matt Brown & Associates
2769 Orchard Run Rd.
Dayton, OH 45449

Ron Burke & Associates
28916 Raab Dr.
Waterford, WI 53185

Ed Burnett Managed Lists
100 Paragon Dr.
Montvale, NJ 07645

Bernice S. Bush Company
15052 Springdale St.
Huntington Beach, CA 15052

Business Mailers, Inc.
2000 Clearwater Dr.
Oak Brook, IL 60521

Capstone Lists Inc.
1315 Duke St.
Alexandria, VA 22314

Carnegie Marketing Associates
3878 Carson St.
Torrance, CA 90503

Catalyst Direct Marketing
4640 Lankershim Blvd.
North Hollywood, CA 91602

CCS Direct, Inc.
3240 S. Dodge Blvd.
Tucson, AZ 85713

Certified Mailing Lists
4 Candlebush
Irvine, CA 92715

Chester Mailing List Consultants
3251 Old Lee Hwy.
Fairfax, VA 22030

Chilcutt Direct Marketing
1701 East 2nd
Edmond, OK 73083

Chilton Direct Marketing
Chilton Way
Radnor, PA 19089

CMS/West List Services
125 E. Sir Francis Drake Blvd.
Larkspur, CA 94939

Columbia Direct Marketing Corp.
60 West Street
Annapolis, MD 21401

Commonwealth Lists
4401 Fairlakes Court
Fairfax, VA 22033

Compuname, Inc.
411 Theodore Fremd Ave.
Rye, NY 10580

Computer Mailing Services Inc.
150 Danbury Rd.
Ridgefield, CT 06877

Conrad Direct, Inc.
80 West St.
Englewood, NJ 07631

Consumers Marketing Research
600 Huyler St.
South Hackensack, NJ 07606

Coolidge List Marketing
25 W. 43rd St.
New York, NY 10036

Cornerstone List Managers Inc.
2300 Yonge St.
Toronto, Ont., Canada

Country Marketing Ltd.
176 E. Main St.
Ilion, NY 13357

Charles Crane Associates
2050 Center Ave.
Fort Lee, NJ 07024

Crosslists Company
11370 Manchester Rd.
St. Louis, MO 63122

Custom Mailing Services
145 Grove St.
Peterborough, NH 03458

Database Management
304 Park Ave. So.
New York, NY 10010

Data Related Services
1004 Park Ave.
Utica, NY 13501

Dependable List Management
950 S. 25th Ave.
Bellwood, IL 60104

Dillon, Agnew & Marton
535 Walnut St.
Norwood, NJ 07648

Dimac Direct
One Corporate Woods Dr.
Bridgeton, MO 63044

Direct Communications Corp.
24 Wales St.
Rutland, VT 05701

Direct Effect
1040 Camino del Mar
Del Mar, CA 92014

Direct Marketing Enterprises
P.O. Box 721
Pottstown, PA 19464

Direct Media Consumer List
  Management
P.O. Box 4565
Greenwich, CT 06830

The Direct Media Group
P.O. Box 4565
Greenwich, CT 06830

Direct Media Insert
  Management Div.
200 Pemberwick Rd.
Greenwich, CT 06830

Direct Partners International
1217 BG Hilversum
Trompenbergerweg 16
The Netherlands

D-J Associates
77 Danbury Rd.
Ridgefield, CT 06877

Edmaro's, Inc.
301 Wilcrest
Houston, TX 77042

Enertex Marketing
99 Madison Ave.
New York, NY 10016

Evergreen Marketing
Rd #1, Box 812
Landisburg, PA 17040

Fairfield Marketing Group
830 Sport Hill Rd.
Easton, CT 06612

Fasano & Associates
3599 Cahuenga Blvd. West
Los Angeles, CA 90068

First Financial Response
587 N. Ventu Park Rd.
Newbury Park, CA 91230

Firstmark
34 Juniper Lane
Newton, MA 02159

5M List Company
2525 Wilson Blvd.
Arlington, VA 22201

Flynn Direct Response
62 Spring Hill Rd.
Trumbull, CT 06611

George-Mann Associates, Inc.
20 Lake Dr.
Hightstown, NJ 08520

Get-List
7500 Frankfort Rd.
Versailles, KY 40383

J. F. Glaser, Inc.
999 Main St.
Glen Ellyn, IL 60137

Gnames Enterprises
1431 Greenway Dr.
Irving, TX 75038

Good Fortune Marketing
210 Commerce Blvd.
Round Rock, TX 78664

Mary Elizabeth Granger
& Associates
205 E. Joppa Rd.
Baltimore, MD 21286

HR Direct
50 North Third St.
Fairfield, IA 52556

IBIS International Direct
152 Madison Ave.
New York, NY 10016

Idealists
1901 Research Blvd.
Rockville, MD 20850

Infocore, Inc.
135 S. Sierra Ave.
Solano Beach, CA 92075

Infocus Lists
341 Victory Dr.
Herndon, VA 22070

Infomat Inc.
1815 West 213th St.
Torrance, CA 90501

Information Marketing Services
8130 Boone Blvd.
Vienna, VA 22182

Initio List Marketing, Inc.
725 Dell Rd.
Carlstadt, NJ 07072

International Direct Response
60 Chestnut Ave.
Devon, PA 19333

Jami/Hotline List Div.
535 Fifth Ave.
New York, NY 10017

Jami Marketing Services
2 Blue Hill Plaza
Pearl River, NY 10965

JBW Direct
P.O. Box 449
Grand Junction, TN 38039

Johnson Direct Advertising
400 Seaport Ct.
Redwood City, CA 94063

J. R. Direct
4703 51 St.
Delta, BC, Canada

Just Lists Inc.
235 E. 95th St.
New York, NY 10128

The Kaplan Agency
1200 High Ridge Rd.
Stamford, CT 06905

Karl Business List Management
135 Bedford Rd.
Armonk, NY 10504

Kelk & Associates
36 Ferndale Rd.
Deer Park, IL 60010

The Kleid Company, Inc.
530 Fifth Ave.
New York, NY 10036

Lakewood Lists
50 S. Ninth St.
Minneapolis, MN 55402

LH Management Division
455 Central Ave.
Scarsdale, NY 10583

List Advisor Inc.
20 Broadway
Massapequa, NY 11758

List America
1202 Potomac St., N.W.
Washington, DC 20007

The List Authority
192 3rd Ave.
Westwood, NJ 07675

The List Bank
500 Davis Center
Evanston, IL 60201

Listco Mailing Lists
620 Frelinghuysen Ave.
Newark, NJ 07114

The List Connection
540 W. Boston Post Rd.
Mamaroneck, NY 10543

List Counsellors, Inc.
3 S. Main St.
Allentown, NJ 08501

The List Emporium Inc.
2000 Shawnee Mission Pkwy.
Westwood, KS 66205

L.I.S.T. Inc.
320 Northern Blvd.
Great Neck, NY 11021

Listline
176 Ballardvale St.
Wilmington, MA 01887

List Locators & Managers
11020 King St.
Overland Park, KS 66210

List Marketing, Ltd.
1037 E. Putname Ave.
Riverside, CT 06878

The Listmaster
700 Fifth Ave.
San Rafael, CA 94901

List Masters, Inc.
4124 Fields Dr.
Lafayette Hill, PA 19444

List Process Management
420 E. 79th St.
New York, NY 10021

List Services Corp.
6 Trowbridge Dr.
Bethel, CT 06801

List Strategies, Inc.
1290 Ave. of Americas
New York, NY 10104

List Technology Systems Gp.
1001 Ave. of Americas
New York, NY 10018

The Listworks Corp.
One Campus Dr.
Pleasantville, NY 10570

LR Direct Ltd.
972 Post Rd.
Darien, CT 06820

Mailing Lists (Asia) Ltd.
Lyndhurst Ter.
Nin Lee Com'l. Bldg.
45 Central, Hong Kong

Mail Marketing, Inc.
171 Terrace St.
Haworth, NJ 07641

Mal Dunn Associates
Hardscrabble Rd.
Croton Falls, NY 10519

Marketing Services International
625 N. Michigan Ave.
Chicago, IL 60611

Hank Marshall Marketing Co.
P.O. Box 2729
Laguna Hills, CA 92654

The McNichols Group
51 Sherwood Terr.
Lake Bluff, IL 60044

Media Horizons, Inc.
94 East Avenue
Norwalk, CT 06851

Media Management Group
666 Plainsboro Rd.
Plainsboro, NJ 08536

Media Marketplace, Inc.
6 Penns Trail
Newtown, PA 18940

Media Mart
1101 King St.
Alexandria, VA 22314

Media Masters, Inc.
51 Madison Ave.
New York, NY 10010

Medical Marketing Service, Inc.
700 N. Wood Dale Rd.
Wood Dale, IL 60191

Mega Media Associates, Inc.
P.O. Box 4259
Newport Beach, CA 92661

Meredith List Marketing
1716 Locust St.
Des Moines, IA 50309

Metro Direct Marketing, Inc.
333 Seventh Ave.
New York, NY 10001

MGI Media Services
1613 Duke St.
Alexandria, VA 22314

MGT Associates, Inc.
11111 Santa Monica Blvd.
Los Angeles, CA 90025

Millard Group Inc.
10 Vose Farm Rd.
Peterborough, NH 03458

Mokrynski & Associates, Inc.
401 Hackensack Ave.
Hackensack, NJ 07601

MPG List Company
115 S. Union St.
Alexandria, VA 22314

MSC Lists, Inc.
450 Los Verdes
Santa Barbara, CA 93111

Name Exchange, Inc.
7015 Old Keene Mill Rd.
Springfield, VA 22150

Name-Finders Lists, Inc.
3180 18th St.
San Francisco, CA 94110

NRL Direct
100 Union Ave.
Cresskill, NJ 07626

Old Dominion List Company
809 Brook Hill Circle
Richmond, VA 23227

Omega List Company
8245 Boone Blvd.
Vienna, VA 22182

The Other List Company, Inc.
Box 286
Matawan, NJ 07747

Pacific Lists Inc.
131 Camino Alto
Mill Valley, CA 94941

Pacific Media Concepts
2100 Main St.
Huntington Beach, CA 92648

PCS Mailing List Co.
85 Constitution Lane
Danvers, MA 01923

Phillips Publishing
7811 Montrose Road
Potomac, MD 20854

Pinnacle List Company
2800 Shirlington Rd.
Arlington, VA 22206

Pioneer Pacific List Marketing
3575 Cahuenga Blvd.
Los Angeles, CA 90068

Political Resources Inc.
P.O. Box 4278
Burlington, VT 05406

Preferred Lists
5201 Leesburg Pike
Falls Church, VA 22041

Qualified Lists Corp.
135 Bedford Rd.
Armonk, NY 10504

R. C. Direct, Inc.
200 S. Water St.
Milwaukee, WI 53204

Research Projects Corp.
Pomperaug Ave.
Woodbury, CT 06798

Research & Response Int'l.
250 W. 57th St.
New York, NY 10107

Response Mailing Lists
20200 NE 10th Pl.
Miami, FL 33179

Response Media Products, Inc.
2323 Perimeter Park Dr.
Atlanta, GA 30341

Response Unlimited, 251
c/o The Old Plantation, Rt. 5
Waynesboro, VA 22980

Robert Rickard List Marketing
5512 Merrick Rd.
Massapequa, NY 11758

Rifkin Direct, Inc.
64 Appletree Ln.
Roslyn Heights, NY 11577

RMI Direct Marketing
4 Skyline Dr.
Hawthorne, NY 10532

Robertson Mailing List Company
1467 Vance Ave.
Memphis, TN 38104

Edith Roman Associates, Inc.
253 W. 35th St.
New York, NY 10001

Doug Ross Communications
3225 South Hardy Dr.
Tempe, AZ 85282

Andrea Rubin Management, Inc.
441 Lexington Ave.
New York, NY 10017

Rubin Response Management
  Services
1111 Plaza Dr.
Schaumburg, IL 60173

Saavoy List Management
Box 9765
Paramus, NJ 07652

Sanmar Associates, Inc.
177 Main St.
Fort Lee, NJ 07024

Saultech,
16776 Bernardo Center Dr.
San Diego, CA 92128

SBA Lists, Inc.
420 Madison Ave.
New York, NY 10017

Select List Corp.
26 Garvies Point Rd.
Glen Cove, NY 11542

The Shields Group
P.O. Box 5231
Fredericksburg, VA 22403

The Specialists
1200 Harbor Blvd.
Weehawken, NJ 07087

Springdale Lists
15052 Springdale St.
Huntington Beach, CA 92649

Eleanor L. Stark Company
515 Madison Ave.
New York, NY 10022

Statlistics Management Group
123 Elm St.
Old Saybrook, CT 06475

Stevens-Know List Management
304 Park Ave. South
New York, NY 10010

Taybi Direct East, Inc.
13321 New Hampshire Ave.
Silver Spring, MD 20904

Technical Publications Mailing Lists
1016 Ascot Dr.
Crystal Lake, IL 60014

Thulin Communications
5757 Wilshire Blvd.
Los Angeles, CA 90036

Total Media Concepts, Inc.
222 Cedar Lane
Teaneck, NJ 07666

21st Century Marketing
2 Dubon Court
Farmingdale, NY 11735

Uni-Mail Business List Management
1701 E. Lake
Glenview, IL 60025

Venture Communications List
  Marketing
60 Madison Ave.
New York, NY 10010

Walsh America/MPSI
105 Terry Dr.
Newtown, PA 18940

H. A. Watts Ltd.
455 Horner Ave.
Toronto, Ontario, M8W 4W9
Canada

Weiss Publishing & Marketing
2200 N. Florida Mango Rd.
West Palm Beach, FL 33409

Wilson Marketing Group, Inc.
11924 W. Washington Blvd.
Los Angeles, CA 90066

Worldata
5200 Town Center Circle
Boca Raton, FL 33486

World Innovators
72 Park St.
New Canaan, CT 06840

World Wide Mailing, Inc.
1216 Eleventh Ave.
Altoona, PA 16601

Catherine Yost List Management
3 Jordon East
Irving, CA 92715

General Consumer List Sources

ABC Advanced Business
  Compilation
2101 Corporate Blvd.
Boca Raton, FL 33431

A. B. Data Ltd.
8050 North Pt. Washington Rd.
Milwaukee, WI 53217

Acton Direct
4900 Highway 77 North
Lincoln, NE 68507

Adco List Management
333 North Michigan Ave.
Chicago, IL 60601

American Data Resources, Inc.
24551 Raymond Way
Lake Forest, CA 92630

Baker Advertising & Mailing
3923 West Sixth St.
Los Angeles, CA 90020

Career Track Managed Lists
3085 Center Green Dr.
Boulder, CO 80301

CAS Marketing, Inc.
616 South 75th St.
Omaha, NE 68114

Catalyst Direct Marketing
4640 Lankershim Blvd. N.
Hollywood, CA 91602

Consumers Marketing Research, Inc.
600 S. Huyler St.
South Hackensack, NJ 07606

Coolidge List Marketing
25 West 43rd St.
New York, NY 10036

Crosslists Company
11370 Manchester Rd.
Kirkwood, MO 63122

Database America
99 West Sheffield Ave.
Englewood, NJ 07631

Dataquick List Services
1633 Bayshore Hwy.
Burlingame, CA 94010

Direct Marketing Technology, Inc.
955 American Ln.
Schaumburg, IL 60173

George-Mann Associates, Inc.
20 Lake Drive
Hightstown, NJ 08520

Mary Elizabeth Granger & Associates
205 E. Joppa Rd.
Baltimore, MD 21286

Hachette Magazines, Inc.
1633 Broadway
New York, NY 10019

InfoDirect
1638B Monte Sano Blvd.
Huntsville, AL 35801

Wayne C. Johnson Associates, Inc.
980 Ninth St.
Sacramento, CA 95814

Jefferson Mailing Lists
13222 Whitewater Dr.
Poway, CA 92064

Just Lists, Inc.
235 East 95th St.
New York, NY 10128

The Kleid Company
530 Fifth Ave.
New York, NY 10036

Lifestyle Change Communications, Inc.
5885 Glenridge Dr.
Atlanta, GA 30328

List America
1202 Potomac N.W.
Washington, DC 20007

The Listmaster
700 Fifth Ave.
San Rafael, CA 94901

List Services Corporation
6 Trowbridge Dr.
Bethel, CT 06801

The Listworks Corporation
One Campus Dr.
Pleasantville, NY 10570

LSA Databank
45 Legion Dr.
Cresskill, NJ 07626

Mailing Lists of America
P.O. Box 401
Money, PA 17756

Mal Dunn Associates
Hardscrabble Rd.
Croton Falls, NY 10519

Market Street Lists
91 Portsmouth Ave.
Stratham, NH 03885

The Media Organization
53 Holiday Dr.
Woodbury, NY 11797

Merril Associates
1250 North East Tenth Pl.
Bellevue, WA 98005

Metromail Corporation
529 Fifth Ave.
New York, NY 10017

MGT Associates, Inc.
11111 Santa Monica Blvd.
Los Angeles, CA 90025

National List Exchange, Inc.
26750 U.S. Hwy. 19 North
Clearwater, FL 34621

NCRI List Management
45 Legion Dr.
Cresskill, NJ 07626

NDL/The Lifestyle Selector
1621 18th St.
Denver, CO 80202

PCS Mailing List Company
85 Constitution Ln.
Danvers, MA 01923

Phillips Publishing, Inc.
7811 Montrose Rd.
Potomac, MD 20854

Pinnacle List Company
2800 Shirlington Rd.
Arlington, VA 22206

Pioneer Pacific List Marketing
3575 Cahuenga Blvd. W.
Los Angeles, CA 90068

Polk Direct
6400 Monroe Blvd.
Taylor, MI 48180

W. S. Ponton of Pittsburgh
5149 Butler St.
Pittsburgh, PA 15201

Priority List Company
P.O. Box 1650
Mannford, OK 74044

Qualified Lists Corporation
135 Bedford Rd.
Armonk, NY 10504

Research Projects Corporation
Pomperaug Ave.
Woodbury, CT 06798

Response Dynamics, Inc.
2070 Chain Bridge Rd.
Vienna, VA 22182

Response Media Products, Inc.
2323 Perimeter Park Dr.
Atlanta, GA 30341

Response Unlimited
Rt. 5, Box 251
Waynesboro, VA 22980

RMI Direct Marketing, Inc.
4 Skyline Dr.
Hawthorne, NY 10532

Andrea Rubin Management, Inc.
441 Lexington Ave.
New York, NY 10017

Stevens-Knox List Management
304 Park Ave. So.
New York, NY 10010

Total Media Concepts, Inc.
222 Cedar Ln.
Teaneck, NJ 07666

TRW Target Marketing Services
901 International Pkwy.
Richardson, TX 75081

Venture Communications List
 Marketing
60 Madison Ave.
New York, NY 10010

Western Mailing Lists
14621 Titus St.
Van Nuys, CA 91402

Fred Woolff List Company, Inc.
7 Corporate Park Dr.
White Plains, NY 10604

Business List Sources

ABC Advanced Business
  Compilation
2101 Corporate Blvd.
Boca Raton, FL 33431

Affinity Marketing Group, Inc.
P.O. Box 2409
Fairfax, VA 22032

Americalist
8050 Freedom Ave. N.W.
North Canton, OH 44720

America List Counsel, Inc.
88 Orchard Rd.
Princeton, NJ 08543

Matt Brown & Associates, Inc.
2769 Orchard Run Rd.
Dayton, OH 45449

Cahners Direct Mail Services
1350 Touhy Ave.
Des Plaines, IL 60018

CMP Publications
600 Community Dr.
Manhasset, NY 11030

Communications Channels, Inc.
6551 Powers Ferry Rd. N.W.
Atlanta, GA 30339

Consumers Marketing Research Inc.
600 Huyler St.
S. Hackensack, NJ 07606

Creative Access
415 W. Superior
Chicago, IL 60610

Customized Mailing Lists Inc.
1906 Field Rd.
Sarasota, FL 34276

Crosslists Company
11370 Manchester Rd.
Kirkwood, MO 63112

Database America
100 Paragon Dr.
Montvale, NJ 07645

Direct Media Group
P.O. Box 4565
Greenwich, CT 06830

The Dun & Bradstreet Information
  Services
3 Sylvan Way
Parsippany, NJ 07054

Hugo Dunhill Mailing Lists, Inc.
630 Third Ave.
New York, NY 10017

Dunhill International List Company
1100 Park Central Blvd. So.
Pompano Beach, FL 33064

Dunhill of Washington
1990 M St., N.W.
Washington, DC 20036

Mal Dunn Associates, Inc.
Hardscrabble Rd.
Croton Falls, NY 10519

George-Mann Associates, Inc.
20 Lake Dr.
Hightstown, NJ 08520

Mary Elizabeth Granger Associates
205 E. Joppa Rd.
Baltimore, MD 21286

Grey House Publishing, Inc.
Pocket Knife Sq.
Lakeville, CT 06039

The Harris Mail House, USA
2450 Fourth Ave.
Yuma, AZ 85364

InfoDirect
1638B Monte Sano Blvd.
Huntsville, AL 35801

Integrated Management Solutions,
  Inc.
4728 E. Michigan St.
Orlando, FL 32812

International Business Lists
162 N. Franklin
Chicago, IL 60606

JAMI Marketing Services, Inc.
2 Blue Hill Pl.
Pearl River, NY 10965

Karl Business Lists
135 Bedford Rd.
Armonk, NY 10504

L. H. Management Division
455 Central Ave.
Scarsdale, NY 10583

Lifestyle Change Communications,
  Inc.
5885 Glenridge Dr.
Atlanta, GA 30328

The Listworks Corporation
One Campus Dr.
Pleasantville, NY 10570

Marketry, Inc.
2020 116th Ave. N.E.
Bellevue, WA 94004

Marketing Services International
625 N. Michigan
Chicago, IL 60611

Market Street Lists
91 Portsmouth Ave.
Stratham, NH 03885

Media Management Group
666 Plainsboro Rd.
Plainsboro, NJ 08536

New Residata Marketing
101 West St.
Hillsdale, NJ 07642

PCS Mailing List Company
85 Constitution Ave.
Danvers, MA 01923

W. S. Ponton of Pittsburgh
5149 Butler St.
Pittsburgh, PA 15201

Qualified Lists Corporation
135 Bedford Rd.
Armonk, NY 10504

Research Projects Corporation
Pomperaug Ave.
Woodbury, CT 06798

Response Media Products, Inc.
2323 Perimeter Park Dr.
Atlanta, GA 30341

M. Lee Smith, Publishers
162 Fourth Ave. N.
Nashville, TN 37219

The Specialists
1200 Harbor Blvd.
Weehawken, NJ 07087

Standard & Poor's Corporation
25 Broadway
New York, NY 10004

Stephens-Knox List Management
304 Park Ave. So.
New York, NY 10010

Taybi Direct East, Inc.
13321 New Hampshire Ave.
Silver Spring, MD 20904

Thulin Communications, Inc.
5757 Wilshire
Los Angeles, CA 90036

TRW Business Credit Services
901 International Pkwy.
Richardson, TX 75081

Uni-Mail Business List Management
1701 E. Lake
Glenview, IL 60025

Wilson Marketing Group, Inc.
11924 W. Washington Blvd.
Los Angeles, CA 90066

Fred Woolff List Company, Inc.
7 Corporate Park Dr.
White Plains, NY 10604

Worldata, Inc.
5200 Town Center Circle
Boca Raton, FL 33486

Alvin B. Zeller, Inc.
224 Fifth Ave.
New York, NY 10001

Zeller & Letica, Inc.
15 East 26th St.
New York, NY 10010

Contributor List Sources

ABC Advanced Business
  Compilation
2101 Corporate Blvd.
Boca Raton, FL 33431

Advanced List Marketing Associates
12700 Fair Lakes Cir.
Fairfax, VA 22033

Affinity Marketing Group, Inc.
P.O. Box 2409
Fairfax, VA 22032

Allmedia, Inc.
4965 Preston Park Blvd.
Plano, TX 75093

American Fund Raising Lists
600 Winter St.
Waltham, MA 02154

American List Counsel, Inc.
88 Orchard Rd.
Princeton, NJ 08543

Antigone Associates
801 West St.
Feasterville, PA 19053

Atlantic List Company
1525 Wilson Blvd.
Arlington, VA 22209

Ed Burnett Managed Lists
100 Paragon Dr.
Montvale, NJ 07645

Catalyst Direct Marketing
4640 Lankershim Blvd.
North Hollywood, CA 91602

Charles Crane Associates Corp.
2050 Center Ave.
Fort Lee, NJ 07024

Chilcutt Direct Marketing
1701 East Second
Edmond, OK 73083

Columbia Direct Mail Corp.
60 West St.
Annapolis, MD 21401

Commonwealth Lists
4401 Fairbanks Ct.
Fairfax, VA 22033

Consumers Marketing Research
600 Huyler St.
South Hackensack, NJ 07606

Coolidge List Marketing
25 West 43rd St.
New York, NY 10036

CMS/West List Services
125 East Sir Francis Drake Blvd.
Larkspur, CA 94939

Dependable Lists, Inc.
950 South 25th Ave.
Bellwood, IL 60104

Direct Communications Corp.
24 Wales St.
Rutland, VT 05701

Direct Media
200 Pemberwick Rd.
Greenwich, CT 06830

Doubleday Mailing Lists
401 Franklin Ave.
Garden City, NY 11530

Estee List Services, Inc.
P.O. Box 1765
New Rochelle, NY 10802

George-Mann Associates, Inc.
20 Lake Dr.
Hightstown, NJ 08520

Mary Elizabeth Granger & Assoc.
205 E. Joppa Rd.
Baltimore, MD 21286

Hatchette Magazines, Inc.
1633 Broadway
New York, NY 10019

Idealists
1901 Research Blvd.
Rockville, MD 20850

Infocus Lists
341 Victory Dr.
Hearndon, VA 22070

Just Lists, Inc.
235 East 85th St.
New York, NY 10128

The Kleid Company
530 Fifth Ave.
New York, NY 10036

Lifestyle Change Communications,
  Inc.
5885 Glenridge Dr.
Atlanta, GA 30328

List America
1202 Potomac, N.W.
Washington, DC 20007

Listco Mailing Lists
620 Frelinghuysen Ave.
Newark, NJ 07114

List Strategies, Inc.
1290 Ave. of the Americas
New York, NY 10104

The List Works Corp.
One Campus Dr.
Pleasantville, NY 10570

P. J. McCarthy & Associates
1617 Royal Oak Rd.
Darien, IL 60561

Metro Direct Marketing
333 Seventh Ave.
New York, NY 10001

Metromail Corp.
529 Fifth Ave.
New York, NY 10017

Name-Finders Lists, Inc.
3180 18th St.
San Francisco, CA 94110

Names in the News/California
One Bush St.
San Francisco, CA 94104

NAM Lists
P.O. Box 970
Santa Cruz, NM 87567

National Fundraising Lists
1682 Village Green
Crofton, MD 21114

NDL/The Lifestyle Selector
1621 18th St.
Denver, CO 80202

NRL Direct
100 Union Ave.
Cresskill, NJ 07626

Old Dominion List Co.
809 Brook Hill Circle
Richmond, VA 23227

Omega List Company
8245 Boone Blvd.
Vienna, VA 22182

PCS Mailing List Company
85 Constitution Ave.
Danvers, MA 01923

Phillips Publishing, Inc.
7811 Montrose Rd.
Potomac, MD 20854

Praxis List Company
1609 Shoal Creek
Austin, TX 78701

Preferred Lists
5201 Leesburg Pike
Falls Church, VA 22041

Qualified Lists Corp.
135 Bedford Rd.
Armonk, NY 10504

R.C. Direct, Inc.
200 So. Water St.
Milwaukee, WI 53204

Response Dynamics, Inc.
2070 Chain Bridge Rd.
Vienna, VA 22182

Response Media Products, Inc.
2323 Perimeter Park Dr.
Atlanta, GA 30341

Response Unlimited
Rt. 5, Box 251
Waynesboro, VA 22980

The Rich List Company
4 East 81st St.
New York, NY 10028

RMI Direct Marketing, Inc.
4 Skyline Dr.
Hawthorne, NY 10532

Rubin Response Management
  Services, Inc.
1111 Plaza Dr.
Schaumburg, IL 60173

Sanmar Associates, Inc.
177 Main St.
Fort Lee, NJ 07024

Select List Corporation
26 Garvies Point Rd.
Glen Cove, NY 11542

Senior Citizens Unlimited, Inc.
711 Westchester Ave.
White Plains, NY 10604

Strub Media Group, Inc.
P.O. Box 1274
New York, NY 10113

Transmark Lists
555 West Adams St.
Chicago, IL 60661

Willow-Haynes Publishing Company
P.O. Box 43-1710
Miami, FL 33243

Zeller & Letica, Inc.
15 East 26th St.
New York, NY 10010

Fred Woolff List Company, Inc.
7 Corporate Park Dr.
White Plains, NY 10604

Appendix **G**

Medical
List Sources

ABC Advanced Business
  Compilation
2101 Corporate Blvd.
Boca Raton, FL 33431

Action Direct
4900 Hwy. 77 North
Lincoln, NE 68507

American Academy of Family
  Physicians
8880 Ward Pkwy.
Kansas City, MO 64114

American Ass'n. of Clinical Chemists
2021 L St., N.W.
Washington, DC 20037

American List Counsel, Inc.
88 Orchard Rd.
Princeton, NJ 08543

Buckley Dement, Direct
612 S. Clinton St.
Chicago, IL 60607

Business Mailers, Inc.
2000 Clearwater Dr.
Oak Brook, IL 60521

Cahners Direct Marketing Svces.
1350 Touhy Ave.
Des Plaines, IL 60018

Clark-O'Neill, Inc.
One Broad Ave.
Fairview, NJ 07022

CMG Information Services
187 Ballardvale St.
Wilmington, MA 01887

Coolidge List Marketing
25 West 43rd St.
New York, NY 10036

Customized Mailing Lists, Inc.
1906 Field Rd.
Sarasota, FL 34276

Direct Media Group
P.O. Box 4565
Greenwich, CT 06830

Hugo Dunhill Mailing Lists, Inc.
630 Third Ave.
New York, NY 10017

Dunhill International List Company
1100 Park Central Blvd. So.
Pompano Beach, FL 33064

Mal Dunn Associates
Hardscrabble Rd.
Croton Falls, NY 10519

Firstmark
34 Juniper Ln.
Newton, MA 02159

InFocus Lists
341 Victory Dr.
Herndon, VA 22070

JAMI Marketing Services, Inc.
2 Blue Hill Plaza
Pearl River, NY 10965

Karl Business Lists
135 Bedford Rd.
Armonk, NY 10504

The Kleid Company
530 Fifth Ave.
New York, NY 10036

Listline
187 Ballardvale St.
Wilmington, MA 01887

Little Brown & Company
34 Beacon St.
Boston, MA 02108

Mailings Clearinghouse,
601 E. Marshall St.
Sweet Springs, MO 65351

Medical Marketing Service, Inc.
700 N. Wood Dale Rd.
Wood Dale, IL 60191

PCS Mailing List Company
85 Constitution Ave.
Danvers, MA 01923

Research Projects Corp.
Pomperaug Ave.
Woodbury, CT 06798

Edith Roman Associates
235 West 35th St.
New York, NY 10001

SK&A Research, Inc.
2151 Michelson Dr.
Irvine, CA 92715

The Specialists
1200 Harbor Blvd.
Weehawken, NJ 07057

Stevens-Knox List Management
304 Park Ave. So.
New York, NY 10010

Taybi Direct East, Inc.
13321 New Hampshire Ave.
Silver Spring, MD 20904

Trans American Marketing
277 North Prospect St.
Orange, CA 92669

Uni-Mail Business List
   Management
1701 E. Lake
Glenview, IL 60025

Venture Communications List
   Marketing
60 Madison Ave.
New York, NY 10010

Wals America/PMSI
105 Terry Dr.
Newtown, PA 18940

Williams & Wilkins
428 East Preston St.
Baltimore, MD 21202

Fred Woolff List Company
7 Corporate Park Dr.
White Plains, NY 10604

World Innovators
72 Park St.
New Canaan, CT 06890

Zeller & Letica, Inc.
15 East 26th St.
New York, NY 10010

Nursing and Health List Sources

ABC Advanced Business
  Compilation
2101 Corporate Blvd.
Boca Raton, FL 33431

Buckley Dement Direct
612 S. Clinton St.
Chicago, IL 60607

Business Mailers, Inc.
2000 Clearwater Dr.
Oak Brook, IL 60521

Compuname, Inc.
411 Theodore Fremd Ave.
Rye, NY 10580

Direct Media Group
P.O. Box 4565
Greenwich, CT 06830

Elsevier Business Lists
P.O. Box 650
Morris Plains, NJ 07950

Listline
187 Ballardvale St.
Wilmington, MA 01887

Medical Marketing Service, Inc.
700 N. Wood Dale Rd.
Wood Dale, IL 60191

Name-Finders Lists, Inc.
3180 18th St.
San Francisco, CA 94110

Oryx Press
4041 N. Central
Phoenix, AZ 85012

PCS Mailing List Company
85 Constitution Ave.
Danvers, MA 01923

Edith Roman Associates
235 West 35th St.
New York, NY 10001

S-N Publications
103 No. Second St.
West Dundee, IL 60118

Springhouse List Management
1111 Bethlehem Pike
Springhouse, PA 19477

Stevens-Knox List Management
304 Park Ave. So.
New York, NY 10010

Wilson Marketing Group, Inc.
11924 West Washington Blvd.
Los Angeles, CA 90066

Fred Woolff List Company
7 Corporate Park Dr.
White Plains, NY 10604

Appendix I

College and University List Sources

Affinity Marketing Group, Inc.
P.O. Box 2409
Fairfax, VA 22032

American List Counsel, Inc.
88 Orchard St.
Princeton, NJ 08543

American Medical Student Ass'n.
1890 Preston White Dr.
Reston, VA 22091

R. R. Bowker/Cahners Direct
 Marketing
1350 E. Touhy
Des Plaines, IL 60018

CMG Information Services
187 Ballardvale St.
Wilmington, MA 01887

Customized Mailing Lists, Inc.
1906 Field Rd.
Sarasota, FL 34276

E-Z Addressing Service Corporation
80 Washington St.
New York, NY 10006

J. F. Glaser, Inc.
999 Main St.
Glen Ellyn, IL 60137

JAMI Marketing Services, Inc.
2 Blue Hill Plaza
Pearl River, NY 10965

Karl Business List Management
135 Bedford St.
Armonk, NY 10504

Katzen List Company
Chestnut Hill Rd.
Pottstown, PA 19464

Mail Marketing, Inc.
171 Terrace St.
Haworth, NJ 07641

Mailing Lists of America
P.O. Box 401
Money, PA 17756

Mailings Clearing House
601 E. Marshall St.
Sweet Springs, MO 65351

Mal Dunn Associates
Hardscrabble Rd.
Croton Falls, NY 10519

Market Data Retrieval, Inc.
16 Progress Dr.
Shelton, CT 06484

MGI Media Services
1613 Duke St.
Alexandria, VA 22314

Names in the News/California, Inc.
One Bush St.
San Francisco, CA 94104

PCS Mailing List Company
85 Constitution Ave.
Danvers, MA 01923

Edith Roman Associates, Inc.
253 West 35th St.
New York, NY 10001

Doug Ross Communications, Inc.
2225 South Hardy Dr.
Tempe, AZ 85282

Appendix J
The Direct Marketing Association

The Direct Marketing Association, Inc., or DMA, is the oldest and largest international trade association within the direct marketing community. Its headquarters are at 11 West 42d Street in New York City.

To serve the varying interests of its membership, the DMA operates numerous special-interest groups called *councils*, where specialists from within the direct marketing community meet to discuss issues of common interest, problems, and opportunities. These DMA special-interest groups include the following:

- Alternate Response Media Council
- Business-to-Business Council
- Catalog Council
- Circulation Council
- Computer/Information Technology Council
- Customer Relations Council
- Direct Marketing Insurance Council
- Directo-Council for Hispanic Marketing
- Financial Services Council
- International Council
- List Council
- Marketing Council

- Non-Profit Council
- Telephone Marketing Council

The DMA holds a major annual conference and a spring conference at which the direct marketing industry's most respected thinkers share their views on current trends and their visions for the future.

In addition, there are numerous conferences throughout the year dedicated to special segments within the industry including: Annual Catalog Conference and Exhibition, Business-to-Business Days, Business-to-Business Direct Marketing Conference, Catalog Management Issues Weekend, Circulation Day, Direct Marketing Insurance Council Seminar and Exhibition, DM West Conference and Exhibition, Government Affairs Conference, List Day, Non-Profit Conference, Non-Profit Day, and Telephone Marketing Conference.

DMA also holds a variety of small, informal seminars, led by respected authorities of long experience. Most of these seminars are for one or two days.

DMA members are also able to obtain answers to their direct marketing questions through the DMA Library and Resource Center and through the DMA DIRECT LINK database. DIRECT LINK, which is the largest direct marketing database in existence, is constantly updated.

For DMA membership information call the membership department at (212) 768-7277, extension 155; or write to the Direct Marketing Association, 11 West 42d Street, New York, NY 10036-8096.

DMA Guidelines for Ethical Business Practice

The Direct Marketing Association Guidelines for Ethical Business Practices (July 1993), reprinted here with DMA permission, are intended to provide individuals and organizations involved in direct mail and direct marketing with principles of conduct that are generally accepted nationally and internationally. These Guidelines reflect DMA's long-standing policy of promoting high levels of ethics among direct marketers and its responsibility to maintain consumer and community relationships that are based on fair and ethical principles.

The Terms of the Offer

Article 1: Honesty

All offers should be clear, honest, and complete so that the consumer may know the exact nature of what is being offered, the price, the terms of payment (including all extra charges), and the commitment involved in the placing of an order. Before publication of an offer, direct marketers should be prepared to substantiate any claims or offers made. Advertisements or specific claims which are untrue, misleading, deceptive, fraudulent, or unjustly disparaging of competitors should not be used.·

Article 2: Clarity

A simple statement of all the essential points of the offer should be clearly displayed in the promotional material. When an offer illustrates goods that are not included or that cost extra, these facts should be made clear.

Article 3: Print Size

Print which by its small size, placement, or other visual characteristics is likely to substantially affect the legibility of the offer or exceptions to it should not be used.

Article 4: Actual Conditions

All descriptions and promises should be in accordance with actual conditions, situations, and circumstances existing at the time of the promotion. Claims regarding any limitations (such as time or quantity) should be legitimate.

Article 5: Disparagement

Disparagement of any person or group on grounds of race, color, religion, national origin, sex, marital status, or age is unacceptable.

Article 6: Standards

Solicitations should not contain vulgar, immoral, profane, or offensive matter nor promote the sale of pornographic material or other matter not acceptable for advertising on moral grounds.

Article 7: Advertising to Children

Offers suitable for adults only should not be made to children.

Article 8: Photographs and Art Work

Photographs, illustrations, artwork, and the situations they represent should be accurate portrayals and current reproductions of the products, services, or other subjects in all particulars.

Article 9: Sponsor and Intent

All direct marketing contacts should disclose the name of the sponsor and each purpose of the contact. No one should make offers or solicitations in the guise of research or a survey when the real intent is to sell products or services or to raise funds.

Article 10: Identity of Seller

Every offer and shipment should sufficiently identify the name and street address of the direct marketer so that the consumer may contact the individual or company by mail or phone.

Article 11: Solicitations in the Guise of an Invoice

Offers that are likely to be mistaken for bills or invoices should not be used.

Article 12: Postage and Handling Charges

Postage or shipping charges, or handling charges, if any, should reflect as accurately as practicable actual costs incurred.

Special Offers

Article 13: Use of the Word "Free" and Other Similar Representations

A product or service which is offered without cost or obligation to the recipient may be unqualifiedly described as "free."

If a product or service is offered as "free," for a nominal cost, or at a greatly reduced price, and/or if the offer requires the recipient to purchase some other product or service, all terms and conditions should be clearly and conspicuously disclosed, in close conjunction with the use of the term "free" or other similar phrase.

When the term "free" is used or other similar representations are made (for example, 2-for-1, half-price or 1-cent offers), the product or service required to be purchased should not have been increased in price or decreased in quality or quantity.

Article 14: Negative Option Selling

All direct marketers should comply with the FTC regulation governing Negative Option Plans. Some of the major requirements of this regulation are as follows:

1. Offers which require the consumer to return a notice sent by the seller before each periodic shipment to avoid receiving merchandise should contain all important conditions of the plan including:

   a. A full description of the obligation to purchase a minimum number of items and all the charges involved, and
   b. the procedures by which the consumer will receive the announcements of selections, and a statement of their frequency, as well as how to reject unwanted items, and how to cancel after completing the obligation.

2. The consumer should be given advance notice of the periodic selection so that the consumer may have a minimum of ten days to exercise a timely choice.
3. Because of the nature of this kind of offer, special attention should be given to the clarity, completeness, and prominent placement of the terms of the initial offering.

Sweepstakes

Article 15: Use of the Term "Sweepstakes"

Sweepstakes, as defined here, are promotional devices by which items of value (prizes) are awarded to participants by chance without the promoter's requiring them to render something of value to be eligible to participate (consideration). The co-existence of all three elements—prize, chance, and consideration—in the same promotion constitutes a lottery. It is illegal for any private enterprise to run a lottery.

Only those promotional devices which satisfy the definition stated above should be called or held out to be a sweepstakes.

Article 16: No-Purchase Option

The no-purchase option as well as the method for entering without ordering should be clearly disclosed. Response devices used only for entering the sweepstakes should be as visible as those utilized for ordering the product or service.

Article 17: Prizes

Sweepstakes prizes should be advertised in a manner that is clear, honest, and complete so that the consumer may know the exact nature of what is being offered.

Photographs, illustrations, artwork, and the situations they represent should be accurate portrayals of the prizes listed in the promotion.

No award should be held forth directly or by implication as having substantial monetary value if it is of nominal worth. The value of a prize given should be stated at regular retail value, whether actual cost to the sponsor is greater or less.

Prizes should be delivered without cost to the participant. If there are certain conditions under which a prize or prizes will not be awarded, this fact should be disclosed in a manner that is easy to find and understand.

Article 18: Premium

If a premium, gift, or item of value is offered by virtue of a participant's merely entering a sweepstakes, without any selection process taking place, it should be clear that everyone will receive it.

Article 19: Chances of Winning

No sweepstakes promotion, or any of its parts, should state or imply that a recipient has won a prize when this is not the case.

Article 20: Disclosure of Rules

All terms and conditions of the sweepstakes, including entry procedures and rules, should be easy to find, read, and understand.

The following should be set forth clearly in the rules:

- No purchase of the advertised product or service is required in order to win a prize.
- Procedures for entry.
- If applicable, disclosure that a facsimile of the entry blank or promotional device may be used to enter the sweepstakes.
- The termination date for eligibility in the sweepstakes. The termination date should specify whether it is a date of mailing or receipt of entry deadline.

- The number, retail value, and complete description of all prizes offered, and whether cash may be awarded instead of merchandise. If a cash prize is to be awarded by installment payments, that fact should be clearly disclosed, along with the nature and timing of the payments.
- The approximate odds of winning a prize or a statement that such odds depend on number of entrants.
- The method by which winners will be selected.
- The geographic area covered by the sweepstakes and those areas in which the offer is void.
- All eligibility requirements, if any.
- Approximate dates when winners will be selected and notified.
- Publicity rights re the use of winner's name.
- Taxes are the responsibility of the winner.
- Provision of a mailing address to allow consumers to submit a self-addressed, stamped envelope to receive a list of winners of prizes over $25.00 in value.

Special Claims

Article 21: Price Comparisons

Price comparisons may be made two ways: (*a*) between one's price and a former, future, or suggested price, (*b*) between one's price and the price of a competitor's comparable product.

In all price comparisons, the compared price against which the comparison is made should be fair and accurate.

In each case of comparison to a former, suggested, or competitor's comparable product price, substantial sales should have been made at that price in the recent past.

For comparisons with a future price, there should be a reasonable expectation that the new price will be charged in the foreseeable future.

Article 22: Guarantees

If a product or service is offered with a "guarantee," or a "warranty," either the terms and conditions should be set forth in the promotion, or the promotion should state how the consumer may obtain a copy. The guarantee should clearly state the name and address of the guarantor and the duration of the guarantee.

Any requests for repair, replacement, or refund under the terms of a "guarantee" or "warranty" should be honored promptly. In an unqualified offer of refund, repair, or replacement, the customer's preference shall prevail.

Article 23: Use of Test or Survey Data

All test or survey data referred to in advertising should be competent and reliable as to source and methodology, and should support the specific claim for which it is cited. Advertising claims should not distort the test or survey results nor take them out of context.

Article 24: Testimonials and Endorsements

Testimonials and endorsements should be used only if they are: (*a*) authorized by the person quoted, (*b*) genuine and related to the experience of the person giving them, and (*c*) not taken out of context so as to distort the endorser's opinion or experience with the product.

The Product

Article 25: Product Safety

Products should be safe in normal use and free of defects likely to cause injury. To that end, they should meet or exceed the current, recognized health and safety norms, and should be adequately tested, when applicable. Information provided with the product should include proper directions for its use and full instructions covering assembly and safety warnings, whenever necessary.

Article 26: Product Distribution Safety

Products should be distributed only in a manner that will provide reasonable safeguards against possibilities of injury.

Article 27: Product Availability

Direct marketers should offer merchandise only when it is on hand or when there is a reasonable expectation of its receipt.

Direct marketers should not engage in dry testing, unless that special nature of the offer is disclosed in the promotion.

Fulfillment

Article 28: Unordered Merchandise

Merchandise should not be shipped without having first received the customer's permission. The exceptions are samples of gifts clearly marked as such, and merchandise mailed by a charitable organization soliciting contributions, as long as all items are sent with a clear and conspicuous statement informing the recipient of an unqualified right to treat the product as a gift and to do with it as the recipient sees fit, at no cost or obligation to the recipient.

Article 29: Shipments

Direct marketers are reminded that they should abide by the FTC regulation regarding the prompt shipment of prepaid merchandise, the Mail Order Merchandise (Thirty-Day) Rule.

Beyond this regulation, direct marketers are urged to ship all orders as soon as possible.

Credit and Debt Collection

Article 30: Equal Credit Opportunity

A creditor should not discriminate on the basis of race, color, religion, national origin, sex, marital status, or age. If an individual is rejected for credit, the creditor should be prepared to give reasons why.

Article 31: Debt Collection

Unfair, misleading, deceptive or abusive methods should not be used for collecting money. The direct marketer should take reasonable steps to assure that those collecting on the direct marketer's behalf comply with this guideline.

Use of Mailing Lists

Article 32: List Rental Practices

Consumers who provide data that may be rented, sold, or exchanged for direct marketing purposes periodically should be informed of the potential for the rental, sale, or exchange of such data. Marketers should offer an opportunity to have a consumer's name deleted or suppressed upon request.

List compilers should suppress names from lists when requested by the individual.

For each list that is to be rented, sold, or exchanged, the DMA Mail Preference Service name-removal list and, when applicable, the DMA Telephone Preference Service name-removal list should be used. Names found on such suppression lists should not be rented, sold, or exchanged, except for suppression purposes.

All persons involved in the rental, sale, or exchange of lists and data should take reasonable steps to ensure that industry members follow these guidelines.

Article 33: Personal Information

Direct marketers should be sensitive to the issue of consumer privacy and should limit the combination, collection, rental, sale, exchange and use of consumer data to only those data which are appropriate for direct marketing purposes.

Information and selection criteria that may be considered to be personal and intimate in nature by all reasonable standards should not provide the basis for lists made available for rental, sale, or exchange when there is a reasonable expectation by the consumer that the information will be kept confidential.

Any advertising or promotion for lists being offered for rental, sale, or exchange should reflect the fact that a list is an aggregate collection of marketing data. Such promotions should also reflect a sensitivity for the consumers on those lists.

Article 34: List Usage Agreements

List owners, brokers, compilers, and users should make every attempt to establish the exact nature of the list's intended usage prior to the sale or rental of the list. Owners, brokers, and compilers should not permit the sale or rental of their lists for an offer that is in violation of any of the Ethical Guidelines of DMA. Promotions should be directed to those segments of the public most likely to be interested in their causes or to have a use for their products or services.

Article 35: List Abuse

No list or list data should be used in violation of the lawful rights of the list owner nor the agreement between the parties; any such misuse should be brought to the attention of the lawful owner.

Telephone Marketing

Articles 36 through 40 covered in Appendix M

Fund-Raising

Article 41: Commission Prohibition/Authenticity of Organization

Fund-raisers should make no percentage or commission arrangements whereby any person or firm assisting or participating in a fund-raising activity is paid a fee proportionate to the funds raised, nor should they solicit for nonfunctioning organizations.

Laws, Codes, and Regulations

Article 42

Direct marketers should operate in accordance with the Better Business Bureau's Code of Advertising and be cognizant of and adhere to laws and regulations of the United States Postal Service, the Federal Trade Commission, the Federal Reserve Board, and other applicable federal, state and local laws governing advertising, marketing practices, and the transaction of business by mail, telephone, and the print and broadcast media.

Federal Trade Commission Guides for the Advertising of Warranties and Guarantees

These Guides are intended to help advertisers avoid unfair or deceptive practices in the advertising of warranties or guarantees. The Guides do not purport to anticipate all possible unfair or deceptive acts or practices in the advertising of warranties or guarantees and should not be interpreted to limit the Commission's authority to proceed against such acts or practices....The Commission may bring an action under section 5 against any advertiser who misrepresents the terms or conditions of the warranty offered, or who employs other deceptive or unfair means.

239.2: Disclosures in warranty or guarantee advertising

(*a*) If an advertisement mentions a warranty or guarantee that is offered on the advertised product, the advertisement should disclose, with such clarity and prominence as will be noticed and understood by prospective purchasers, that prior to sale, at the place where the product is sold, prospective purchasers can see the written warranty or guarantee for complete details.

(*b*) If an advertisement in any catalogue, or in any other solicitation for mail order sales or for telephone order sales mentions a warranty or guarantee that is offered on the advertised product, the advertisement should disclose, with such clarity and prominence as will be noticed and understood by prospective purchasers, that prospective purchasers can obtain complete details of the written warranty or guarantee free from the seller upon specific written request or from the catalogue or other solicitation (whichever is applicable).

A. "ABC quality cutlery is backed by our 10-year warranty. Write to us for a free copy at: (address)."

B. "ABC power tools are guaranteed. Read about our limited 90-day warranty in this catalogue."

C. "Write to us for a free copy of our full warranty. You'll be impressed how we stand behind our product."

239.3: "Satisfaction Guarantees" and similar representations in advertising; disclosure in advertising that mentions "satisfaction guarantees" or similar representations

(*a*) A seller or manufacturer should use the terms "Satisfaction Guarantee," "Money Back Guarantee," "Free Trial Offer," or similar representations in advertising only if the seller or manufacturer, as the case may be, refunds the full purchase price of the advertised product at the purchaser's request.

(*b*) An advertisement that mentions a "Satisfaction Guarantee" or a similar representation should disclose, with such clarity and prominence as will be noticed and understood by prospective purchasers, any material limitations or conditions that apply to the "Satisfaction Guarantee" or similar representation.

Illustrative examples for print and broadcast advertising:

Example A: (In an advertisement mentioning a satisfaction guarantee that is conditioned upon return of the unused portion within 30 days) "We guarantee your satisfaction. If not completely satisfied with Acme Spot Remover, return the unused portion within 30 days for a full refund."

Example B: (In an advertisement mentioning a money back guarantee that is conditioned upon return of the product in its original packaging) "Money Back Guarantee! Just return the ABC watch in its original package and ABC will fully refund your money."

239.4: "Lifetime" and similar representations

If an advertisement uses "lifetime," "life," or similar representations to describe the duration of a warranty or guarantee, then the advertisement should disclose with such clarity and prominence as will be noticed and understood by prospective purchasers, the life to which the representation refers.

239.5: Performance of warranties or guarantees

A seller or manufacturer should advertise that a product is warranted or guaranteed only if the seller or manufacturer, as the case may be, promptly and fully performs its obligations under the warranty or guarantee.

DMA Guidelines for Marketing by Telephone

The Direct Marketing Association Guidelines for Marketing by Telephone (July 1993), reprinted here with DMA permission, are intended to provide individuals and organizations involved in direct telephone marketing with accepted principles of conduct that are consistent with the ethical guidelines recommended for other marketing media.

Article 1: Prompt Disclosure/Identity of Seller

When speaking with a customer, telephone marketers should promptly disclose the name of the sponsor, the name of the individual caller, and the primary purposes of the contact.

Article 2: Honesty

All offers should be clear, honest, and complete so that the customer will know the exact nature of what is being offered and the commitment involved in the placing of an order. Before making an offer, telephone marketers should be prepared to substantiate any claims or offers made. Advertisements or specific claims which are untrue, misleading, deceptive, fraudulent, or unjustly disparaging of competitors should not be used.

Article 3: Terms of the Offer

Prior to commitments by customers, telephone marketers should disclose the cost of the merchandise or service and all terms and conditions, including payments plans, refund policies, and the amount or existence of any extra charges such as shipping and handling and insurance.

Article 4: Reasonable Hours

Telephone marketers should avoid making contacts during hours which are unreasonable to the recipients of the calls.

Article 5: Use of Automatic Equipment

When using automatic dialing equipment, telephone marketers should only use equipment which allows the telephone immediately to release the line when the called party disconnects.

ADRMPS (Automatic Recorded Message Players) and pre-recorded messages should be used only in accordance with tariffs, state and local laws, and these Guidelines. When a telephone marketer places a call to a customer for solicitation purposes, and desires to deliver a recorded message, permission should be obtained from the customer by a live "operator" before the recorded message is delivered.

Article 6: Taping of Conversations

Taping of telephone conversations made for telephone marketing purposes should not be conducted without legal notice to or consent of all parties or the use of a beeping device.

Article 7: Name Removal

Telephone marketers should remove the name of any individual from their telephone lists when requested directly to do so by the customer, by use of the DMA Telephone Preference Service name-removal list and, when applicable, the DMA Mail Preference Service name-removal list.

Article 8: Minors

Because minors are generally less experienced in their rights as consumers, telephone marketers should be especially sensitive to the obligations and responsibilities involved when dealing with them. Offers suitable only for adults should not be made to children.

Article 9: Monitoring

Monitoring of telephone marketing and customer relations conversations should be conducted only after employees have been informed of the practice.

Article 10: Prompt Delivery

Telephone marketers should abide by the FTC's Mail-Order Merchandise (Thirty-Day) Rule when shipping prepaid merchandise. As a normal business procedure, telephone marketers are urged to ship all orders as soon as practical.

Article 11: Cooling-Off Period

Telephone marketers should honor cancellation requests that originate within three days of sales agreement.

Article 12: Restricted Contacts

Telephone marketers should remove the name of any customer from their telephone lists when requested by the individual. Marketers should use the DMA Telephone Preference Service name-removal list and, when applicable, the DMA Mail Preference Service name-removal list. Names found on such suppression lists should not be rented, sold, or exchanged except for suppression purposes.

A telephone marketer should not knowingly call anyone who has an unlisted or unpublished telephone number except in instances when the number was provided by the customer to the marketer.

Random dialing techniques, whether manual or automated, in which identification of those parties to be called is left to chance should not be used in sales and marketing solicitations.

Sequential dialing techniques, whether a manual or automatic process, in which selection of those parties to be called is based on the location of their telephone numbers in a sequence of telephone numbers should not be used.

Article 13: Transfer of Data

Telephone marketers who receive or collect customer data as a result of a telephone marketing contact, and who intend to rent, sell, or exchange those data for direct marketing purposes should inform the customer. Customer requests regarding restrictions on the collection, rental, sale, or exchange of data relating to them should be honored.

Names on the DMA Telephone Preference Service name-removal list should not be transferred except for suppression purposes.

Article 14: Law, Codes, and Regulations

Telephone marketers should operate in accordance with the laws and regulations of the United States Postal Service, the Federal Communications Commission, the Federal Trade Commission, the Federal Reserve Board and other applicable Federal, state, and local laws governing advertising, marketing practices, and the transaction of business by mail, telephone, and the print and broadcast media.

USPS Standard Endorsements for Third-Class Bulk Mail

When you mail to rental lists, as a rule, a percentage of your mailing will not be delivered. By adding a USPS-approved endorsement to your mailing piece, you can indicate exactly how you want the carrier to handle your mail if not deliverable. Your local postmaster will advise you on fees for using any of these United States Postal Service endorsements:

Mailer Endorsement	Post Office Action
No Endorsement *or* Do Not Forward	No forwarding or return service is provided.
Address Correction Requested	No forwarding service is provided. Address correction is provided with a Notice to Mailer of Correction to Address form or Undeliverable Third-Class Matter form.
Forwarding and Return Postage Guaranteed	Mail is forwarded at no charge. If mail is not forwardable, return the entire mail piece with reason for nondelivery; charge is appropriate third-class weighted fee.

Forwarding and Return Postage Guaranteed; Address Correction Requested

Mail is forwarded at no charge. If separate address correction notice is provided, the address correction fee is charged. If mail is not forwardable, the entire piece is returned with reason for nondelivery; the appropriate third-class weighted fee is charged.

Do Not Forward; Address Correction Requested; Return Postage Guaranteed

Mail is not forwarded. Entire mail piece is returned with the new address or reason for nondelivery; charge is the appropriate single-piece third-class rate; no address correction fee is charged.

Appendix O

USPS Standard Abbreviations for Postal Addressing

Two-Letter State and Possession Abbreviations

Alabama	AL	Iowa	IA
Alaska	AK	Kansas	KS
Arizona	AZ	Kentucky	KY
Arkansas	AR	Louisiana	LA
American Samoa	AS	Maine	ME
California	CA	Marshall Islands	MH
Colorado	CO	Maryland	MD
Connecticut	CT	Massachusetts	MA
Delaware	DE	Michigan	MI
District of Columbia	DC	Minnesota	MN
Federated States of Micronesia	FM	Mississippi	MS
Florida	FL	Missouri	MO
Georgia	GA	Montana	MT
Guam	GU	Nebraska	NE
Hawaii	HI	Nevada	NV
Idaho	ID	New Hampshire	NH
Illinois	IL	New Jersey	NJ
Indiana	IN	New Mexico	NM

New York	NY	South Dakota	SD
North Carolina	NC	Tennessee	TN
North Dakota	ND	Texas	TX
Northern Mariana Islands	MP	Utah	UT
Ohio	OH	Vermont	VT
Oklahoma	OK	Virginia	VA
Oregon	OR	Virgin Islands	VI
Palau	PW	Washington	WA
Pennsylvania	PA	West Virginia	WV
Puerto Rico	PR	Wisconsin	WI
Rhode Island	RI	Wyoming	WY
South Carolina	SC		

Directional Abbreviations

North	N	Northeast	NE
East	E	Southeast	SE
South	S	Southwest	SW
West	W	Northwest	NW

Abbreviations for Street Designators (Street Suffixes)

Alley	ALY	Bypass	BYP
Annex	ANX	Camp	CP
Arcade	ARC	Canyon	CYN
Avenue	AVE	Cape	CPE
Bayou	BYU	Causeway	CSWY
Beach	BCH	Center	CTR
Bend	BND	Circle	CIR
Bluff	BLF	Cliffs	CLFS
Bottom	BTM	Club	CLB
Boulevard	BLVD	Corner	COR
Branch	BR	Corners	CORS
Bridge	BRG	Course	CRSE
Brook	BRK	Court	CT
Burg	BG	Courts	CTS

Cove	CV	Island	IS
Creek	CRK	Islands	ISS
Crescent	CRES	Isle	ISLE
Crossing	XING	Junction	JCT
Dale	DL	Key	KY
Dam	DM	Knolls	KNLS
Divide	DV	Lake	LK
Drive	DR	Lakes	LKS
Estates	EST	Landing	LNDG
Expressway	EXPY	Lane	LN
Extension	EXT	Light	LGT
Fall	FALL	Loaf	LF
Falls	FLS	Locks	LCKS
Ferry	FRY	Lodge	LDG
Field	FLD	Loop	LOOP
Fields	FLDS	Mall	MALL
Flats	FLT	Manor	MNR
Ford	FRD	Meadows	MDWS
Forest	FRST	Mill	ML
Forge	FRG	Mills	MLS
Fork	FRK	Mission	MSN
Forks	FRKS	Mount	MT
Fort	FT	Mountain	MTN
Freeway	FWY	Neck	NCK
Gardens	GDNS	Orchard	ORCH
Gateway	GTWY	Oval	OVAL
Glen	GLN	Park	PARK
Green	GRN	Parkway	PKY
Grove	GRV	Pass	PASS
Harbor	HBR	Path	PATH
Haven	HVN	Pike	PIKE
Heights	HTS	Pines	PNES
Highway	HWY	Place	PL
Hill	HL	Plain	PLN
Hills	HLS	Plains	PLNS
Hollow	HOLW	Plaza	PLZ
Inlet	INLT	Point	PT

Port	PRT		Stream	STRM
Prairie	PR		Street	ST
Radial	RADL		Summit	SMT
Ranch	RNCH		Terrace	TER
Rapids	RPDS		Trace	TRCE
Rest	RST		Track	TRAK
Ridge	RDG		Trail	TRL
River	RIV		Trailer	TRLR
Road	RD		Tunnel	TUNL
Row	ROW		Turnpike	TPKE
Run	RUN		Union	UN
Shoal	SHL		Valley	VLY
Shoals	SHLS		Viaduct	VIA
Shore	SHR		View	VW
Shores	SHRS		Village	VLG
Spring	SPG		Ville	VL
Springs	SPGS		Vista	VIS
Spur	SPUR		Walk	WALK
Square	SQ		Way	WAY
Station	STA		Wells	WLS
Stravenue	STRA			

Domestic Postal Rates, Size Standards, and Standard Envelope Sizes

First-Class Mail

Weight not exceeding (ounces)	Postage
1	$0.32
2	0.55
3	0.78
4	1.01
5	1.24
6	1.47
7	1.70
8	1.93
9	2.16
10	2.39
11	2.62

Over 11 ounces, see Priority Mail rates. *Note:* Priority Mail up to but not exceeding two pounds goes at $3.00 rate to all postal zones.

Third-Class Mail (Single-Piece Rates)

Weight not exceeding (ounces)	Postage
1	$0.32
2	0.55
3	0.78
4	1.01
5	1.24
6	1.47
7	1.70
8	1.93
9	2.16
10	2.39
11	2.62
Over 11 but less than 13	2.90
Over 13 but less than 16	2.95

Regular and special bulk rates available only to authorized mailers.

Envelope Sizes

Commercial and Window Envelopes

No. $6\frac{1}{4}$	$3\frac{1}{2}'' \times 6''$
No. $6\frac{3}{4}$	$3\frac{5}{8}'' \times 6\frac{1}{2}''$
No. 7	$3\frac{3}{4}'' \times 6\frac{3}{4}''$
No. 8 (Monarch)	$3\frac{7}{8}'' \times 7\frac{1}{2}''$
No. 9	$3\frac{7}{8}'' \times 8\frac{7}{8}''$
No. 10 (Official)	$4\frac{1}{8}'' \times 9\frac{1}{2}''$
No. 11	$4\frac{1}{2}'' \times 10\frac{3}{8}''$
No. 12	$4\frac{3}{4}'' \times 11''$
No. 14	$5'' \times 11\frac{1}{2}''$

All rates in this appendix are effective as of January 1, 1995.

Booklet Envelopes

No. 3	$4\frac{3}{4}'' \times 6\frac{1}{2}''$
No. 5	$5\frac{1}{2}'' \times 8\frac{1}{8}''$
No. 6	$5\frac{3}{4}'' \times 8\frac{7}{8}''$
No. 6½	$6'' \times 9''$
No. 7	$6\frac{1}{4}'' \times 9\frac{5}{8}''$
No. 9	$8\frac{3}{4}'' \times 11\frac{1}{2}''$
No. 9½	$9'' \times 12''$
No. 10	$9\frac{1}{2}'' \times 12\frac{5}{8}''$
No. 13	$10'' \times 13''$

Size Standards for Domestic Mail

Minimum Size

Pieces must meet the following requirements to be mailable:

a. All pieces must be at least .007 inch thick.
b. Pieces (except keys and identification devices) that are ¼ inch or less thick must be:

    (1) Rectangular in shape,
    (2) At least $3\frac{1}{2}$ inches high, and
    (3) At least 5 inches long.

c. Pieces greater than ¼ inch thick can be mailed even if they measure less than $3\frac{1}{2}$ by 5 inches.

Nonstandard Mail and Surcharges

First-Class Mail (except Presort First-Class and carrier route First-Class weighing one ounce or less) and all single-piece rate third-class mail weighing one ounce or less are nonstandard (and subject to a $0.10 surcharge in addition to the applicable postage and fees) if:

a. Any of the following dimensions are exceeded:

    (1) Length—$11\frac{1}{2}$ inches,
    (2) Height—$6\frac{1}{8}$ inches,
    (3) Thickness—¼ inch, or

b. The length divided by the height (aspect ratio) is less than 1.3 or more than 2.5.

For nonstandard Presort First-Class and carrier route First-Class, the surcharge is $0.05 in addition to applicable postage.

The above information is from *U.S. Postal Service Notice 59* (July 1991).

Appendix 9

International Direct Marketing Associations

Argentina

Asociacion De Marketing Directo
De Argentina
Tucaman 1455 5to Pico "F" 1050,
Buenos Aires, Argentina
Contact: Alejandro di Paola

Australia

Australian Direct Marketing
Association
G.P.O. Box 3982 / 10F, 52-58 Clarance
Street, 10th Floor
Sidney, N.S.W. 1000, Australia
Contact: Greg Baker, National
Director

Belgium

Groupement De La Vente
Par Correspondance
Rue de la Science, 3/1040,
Brussels, Belgium
Contact: Guy Olivier

Flemish Direct Marketing Association
Bierbeekstraat #14/3030
Heverlee, Belgium
Contact: Ad Van Poppel, President

Association Du Marketing Direct
Rue de Stalle 142/1180,
Brussels, Belgium
Contact: Yves Poll, Chairman

Brazil

Associacao Brasileirade De
Marketing Direto
Alemeda Compinas 433, 8 Andar
Sao Paulo, SP 01404-901, Brazil
Contact: Pio Borges, President

Canada

Canadian Direct Marketing
Association
1 Concorde Gate,
Don Mills, Ontario M3C 3N6,
Canada
Contact: Terence Belgue, President

Mid-Western Direct Marketers
Association
1340 Church Avenue,
Winnipeg, Manitoba R2X 1G4,
Canada
Contact: H. Douglas McLaughlin,
President

Denmark

The Danish Direct Marketing Club
Dansk Markedsforing Forbund
Vesterbrogade #24
DK-1620, Copenhagen, Denmark
Contact: Kresten Bager, Chairman

Finland

Finnish Direct Markting Association
Fredrikinkatu 58 A4/SF-00100
Helsinki, Finland
Contact: Martti Immonen, Chairman

France

Union Francaise De La Publicite
  Directe
60 rue La Boetie/75008,
Paris, France
Contact: Bernard Siouffi, Delegue
  General

Germany

DDV-Deutscher Direktmarketing
  Verband e.v.
Schiersteiner Strasse 20/D-6200
Wiesbaden, Germany
Contact: Dr. Hasso Herbst

Bundesverband Des Deutschen
  Versandhandels E.V.
Johann-Klotz Strasse 12/D-6000
Frankfurt/Main 71, Germany
Contact: Peter Fritsche,
Hauptgeschaftsfuhrer

Hong Kong

Hong Kong Direct Mail & Marketing
  Association
G.P.O. Box 7416, Hong Kong
Contact: Godfrey Rooke, Chairman

Ireland

Irish Direct Marketing Association
1/2 Upper O'Connell Street,
Dublin 1, Ireland
Contact: John P. Keane, Chairman

Italy

Associazione Nationale Fra Aziende
  Di Vendita Per Corrispondenza
Via Melchiore Giola 70/20125
Milan, Italy
Contact: Granziano Fiorelli,
  President

AIDIM (Associazione Italiana Per Il
  Direct Marketing)
Corso Venezia 16/20121,
Milan, Italy
Contact: Dr. Pietro Sanfelice de
  Monteforte, President

Japan

Japan Direct Mail Association (JDMA)
Dai Hachi Kojimachi Building,
  3F/4-5
Kojimachi, Chiyoda-ku,
Tokyo 102, Japan
Contact: Hideo Furuoka, Chairman

Japan Direct Marketing Association
  (JADMA)
32, Mori Building, 3-4-30 Shiba-Koen
Minato-ku, Tokyo, Mail 105, Japan
Contact: Kaoru Nomiyama,
  Managing Director

Nihon Direct Marketing Association
  (NDMA)
2-2-15 Minami Aoyama, Wion
  Aoyama 337
Minato-ku, Tokyo 107, Japan
Contact: Buichi Kurozumi, Chairman

Mexico

Asociacion Mexicana
  Demercadotecnia Directa
Sta. Maria de la Rabida 62,
Col. Echegaray 53300
Naucalpan, Edo de Mexico, Mexico
Contact: Martha E. Zozueta, Director

The Netherlands

Direct Marketing Instituut Nederland
Weerdestein 96/1083GG
Amsterdam, The Netherlands
Contact: F. H. Van Dorst, Managing
  Director

Nederlandspostorderbond
Lange Voorhout 86/2514 EJ
Den Haag,
The Netherlands
Contact: Aad Weening, Secretary

New Zealand

New Zealand Direct Marketing
  Association
P.O. Box 937, Auckland, New
Zealand
Contact: Keith W. Norris, President

Singapore

Direct Marketing Association of
  Singapore
450 Alexandria Road,
#10-00 Inchcape Hov,
Singapore, 0511
Contact: Charlie In, Chairman

South Africa

The South African Direct Marketing
  Association
P.O. Box 85370, Emmerentia 2029
Republic of South Africa
Contact: Gillian Williams, Executive
  Director

Spain

Asociacion Espanola De Marketing
  Directo
Provenza, 238,
Barcelona 08008, Spain
Contact: Juan Menal, President

Sweden

Swedish Direct Marketing Association
P.O. Box 14038/104-40
Stockholm, Sweden
Contact: Sture Sandberg

United Kingdom

Association of Mail Order
  Publishers
1 New Burlington Street
London W1X 1FD, United Kingdom
Contact: Leonard Critchley,
  Director

The British Direct Marketing
  Association
Grosvenor Gardens House, 35
Grosvenor Gardens
London SW1W OBX,
United Kingdom
Contact: Colin Fricker, Director
  General

Direct Mail Producers Association
34 Grand Avenue,
London, N10 3BP,
United Kingdom
Contact: Mark Elwes

Uruguay

Asociacion De Dirigentes De
  Marketing Del Uruguay
Itvzaingo 1324, Escritorio 304
Montevideo, Uruguay
Contact: Jose Luis Simone, Director

Venezuela

Asociacion Venezolana De Mercadeo
  Directo
Av. Fco Miranda c/c Av. Diego
  Cisneros,
Ctro Emp. Miranda,
Piso 5, Of. EF
Los Ruices, Caracas 1071, Venezuela
Contact: Eduardo Alvarez, Presidente

Pan-European

Europan Direct Marketing
  Association
4, Rue de las Scie/CH-1207,
Geneva, Switzerland
Contact: Ernst Siegenthaler, Secretary
  General

Directory of Card Pack Printing Sources

Collated Industries Corporation
716 Pulaski Hwy.
Bear, DE 19701
Telephone: 302-324-9450

MGA Marketing Ltd.
Metropolitan Graphic Arts
930 Turret Court
Mundelein, IL 60060
Telephone: 708-566-9502;
1-800-755-5936

Schmidt Printing
1815 14th St. N.W.
Rochester, MN 55901
Telephone: 507-252-2419

Scoville Press
14505 27th St. North
Plymouth, MN 55441
Telephone: 612-553-1400

Solar Press, Inc.
1120 Frontenac Rd.
Naperville, IL 60563
Telephone: 708-983-1400;
1-800-323-2751

Solar Press-Europe
3e Industriezone
9320 Aalst-Erembodegem
Belgium
Telephone: 053-83-90-10;
053-83-95-00 (Fax)

Seven Key Steps in Planning and Producing a Catalog

This appendix is condensed and adapted with permission from "Maxwell Sroge's Catalog Planning" in *The Vest Pocket Marketer* by Alexander Hiam, Prentice-Hall, Englewood Cliffs, NJ, 1991. Original material appeared in *How to Create Successful Catalogs* by Maxwell Sroge, NTC Publishing Group, Lincolnwood, IL, 1985, pp. 5–7.

1. Dummying the Catalog (The Placement and Grouping of Products to Maximize Sales)

The format you choose for your catalog and the technique you use (the physical design of the grouping, such as symmetrical or asymmetrical) dictate how soon and how deeply the graphic designer and product artist become involved with the dummying process.

If you have chosen to have a symmetrical layout with a product or theme/function format, it is fairly easy to proceed with the dummying. Art and copy sizes are balanced proportionately and may be predetermined by the merchandiser because of a limited number of common sizes.

Keeping the products in categories such as stationery, kitchen, office forms, desks, and twine is pretty cut and dried. But when an asymmetrical layout is chosen requiring different sizes per individual product, the knowledge, talent, and guidance of a graphic designer and artist become critical to the outcome.

All of these factors must be considered when you're making up a schedule: a symmetrical layout will take less time and most likely involve fewer people. The asymmetrical layout will take longer to dummy and will involve a number of people and perhaps several meetings.

2. Product Review

The selling message to the customer begins with a product review by the copywriters, the artists, and the merchandiser and other product buyers. New products are introduced to the creative staff, and the catalog art and copy are planned in product work sessions.

These sessions are vitally important and productive. A minimum of 15 minutes should be devoted to each new product, to bring out why it was selected, why the customer will purchase it, which competitors sell it, how the art might be approached, and what needs to be included in the copy.

If you have only a few new products (nine or ten) you might be able to get by with one long review session. But if you have 100 new products you may have to schedule many sessions. Do not expect the artist to work on layout or design or the copywriter to produce copy without the benefit of these meetings.

3. Design Layout

The design will take considerable time. Even though the products have been assigned to pages and the basic idea as to how they should be presented has been formulated, ample time should be allowed for the artists to create a visual presentation that must catch the customer's eye.

4. Copy

The copywriters must assemble the facts, emphasize the benefits, and sell the customer. Extra time should be allowed for any legal releases from the manufacturer for copy claim protection. Rewrite time must be considered, too, as the duty of revising copy for seasonal changes usually falls on the shoulders of the copywriter. Don't shortchange this time.

5. Photography

You should not think that photographing catalog products is easy because the photographer is provided with detailed, to-size layout sketches of how the shot should look. The right props have to be found, the models arranged for, the background readied, and lighting planned. The layout provided for the photographer may not work well once the real products are positioned and viewed through the photographic lens. Time for reshooting needs to be allowed.

6. Press Preparation

Much is included in this task. Typesetting, mechanical pasteups, transparency assembly, and color separation all take a good share of time. The better prepared the work is, the fewer problems will occur at press. If the camera-ready art is smooth, no headlines, type, inserts, or photos are missing, and everything is in line, then the printer won't have to piece things together and there will be minimal chance of error. So the time spent at this stage will save time and trouble at press.

7. Printing/Lettershop

Time at this stage is pretty standard. Four-color printing generally takes six weeks from the time the job is received by the printer to the time the first catalog drops in the mail.

Appendix T

FCC Regulations on Telephone Solicitation

As a result of the "Telephone Consumer Protection Act of 1991" (Public Law 102-243), the following regulations were issued by the Federal Communications Commission on February 7, 1992. These regulations are designed to protect the privacy rights of residential telephone subscribers and to provide them with a way of stopping unwanted calls.

Restrictions on Telephone Solicitation

No person or entity shall initiate any telephone solicitation to a residential telephone subscriber:

(1) Before the hour of 8 a.m. or after 9 p.m. (local time at the called party's location), and

(2) Unless such person or entity has instituted procedures for maintaining a list of persons who do not wish to receive telephone solicitations made by or on behalf of that person or entity. The procedures instituted must meet the following minimum standards:

    (i) Written policy.

    Persons or entities making telephone solicitations must have a written policy, available on demand, for maintaining a do-not-call list.

(ii) Training of personnel engaged in telephone solicitation.

Personnel engaged in any aspect of telephone solicitation must be informed and trained in the existence and use of the do-not-call list.

(iii) Recording, disclosure of do-not-call requests.

If a person or entity making a telephone solicitation...receives a request from a residential telephone subscriber not to receive calls from that person or entity, the person or entity must record the request and place the subscriber's name and telephone number on a do-not-call list at the time the request is made.

If such requests are maintained by a party other than the person or entity on whose behalf the solicitation is made, the person or entity on whose behalf the solicitation is made will be liable for any failures to honor the do-not-call request. In order to protect the consumer's privacy, persons or entities must obtain a customer's prior express consent to share or forward the consumer's request not to be called to a party other than the person or entity on whose behalf a solicitation is made or an affiliated entity.

(iv) Identification of telephone solicitor.

A person or entity making a telephone solicitation must provide the called party with the name of the individual caller, the name of the person or entity on whose behalf the call is being made, and a telephone number or address at which the person or entity may be contacted. If a person or entity makes a solicitation using an artificial or prerecorded voice message, transmitted by an autodialer, the person or entity must provide a telephone number other than that of the autodialer or prerecorded message player which placed the call.

(v) Affiliated persons or entities.

In the absence of a specific request by the subscriber to the contrary, a residential subscriber's do-not-call request shall apply to the particular business entity making the call (or on whose behalf a call is made), and will not apply to affiliated entities unless the consumer reasonably would expect them to be included given the identification of the caller and the product being advertised.

(vi) Maintenance of do-not-call lists.

A person or entity making telephone solicitations must maintain a do-not-call list for the purpose of any future telephone solicitations.

As used in the above section (47CFR 64.1200):

The terms automatic *telephone dialing system* and *autodialer* mean equipment which has the capacity to store or produce telephone numbers to be called using a random or sequential number generator and to dial such numbers.

The term *telephone solicitation* means the initiation of a telephone call or message for the purpose of encouraging the purchase or rental of, or investment in, property, goods, or services, which is transmitted to any person, but such term does not include a call or message:

  (i) To any person with that person's prior express invitation or permission.
  (ii) To any person with whom the caller has an established business relationship; or
  (iii) By a tax-exempt nonprofit organization.

The term *established business relationship* means a prior or existing relationship formed by a voluntary two-way communication between a person or entity and a residential subscriber with or without an exchange of consideration, on the basis of an inquiry, application, purchase or transaction by the residential subscriber regarding products or services offered by such a person or entity, which relationship has not been previously terminated by either party.

Appendix U
Writing Words That Sell: Guidelines From the Experts

This appendix is adapted with permission from *Words That Sell: The Thesaurus to Help You Promote Your Products, Services, and Ideas* by Richard Bryan, Caddylak Systems, 1984.

1. Don't Lose Sight of Your Primary Goal: To Sell Your Product or Service

Your writing should be more than a flat presentation of the facts. (Remember that a copywriter must persuade and motivate.) On the other hand, don't let runaway creativity bury the message. The most brilliant efforts will be wasted if your audience can't remember your company's name. Write to sell.

2. Don't Fill Your Copy With Empty Overstatements

Too many words like *fabulous* and *extraordinary* within a brief space will destroy your credibility. You don't want your audience to dismiss you as a propagandist. Instead, try to *convince* the audience that your product is fabulous. Make *them* say, "That's really extraordinary!"

3. Be Accurate

Be sure you get the facts straight. Don't leave yourself open to claims of false advertising by making statements that can't be substantiated. Above all, be *truthful*. Resist the temptation to distort the facts for an easy sale. (Your sins will find you out, anyway.)

4. Be Specific

Don't use vaporous abstractions or vague approximations when you have a chance to create vivid images with simple observable details. Would you rather eat a "frozen dessert" or a "raspberry ice"? And try to avoid the notorious "than what?" comparisons: for example, "lasts longer" (than what?) or "gets the job done faster" (than what?).

5. Be Organized

Your message should progress logically and inexorably from the headline to the clincher. Don't bury essential information in the darkest recesses of your copy or lead off with trivia that stops the reader cold. Like an old-fashioned short story, your copy should have a beginning, a middle, and an end.

6. Write for Easy Reading

Your style should suit the audience you're addressing, but certain rules apply to *all* copy. Cultivate a style that flows smoothly and rapidly, a style that's clear, uncluttered, involving, and persuasive. Avoid long, convoluted sentence constructions. Affect a crisp but friendly and extroverted tone. *Communicate*. You want to do everything possible to ensure that your message gets read.

7. Don't Offend

Humor is a controversial issue among advertising insiders. A good many experts preach against it, but there's no denying that humor can be an effective tool—if it suits the subject or situation. (You don't want to joke about insurance or funerals.) Sarcasm, cynicism, and other extreme forms of individuality are not likely to meet with mass approval. Don't criticize your audience's taste in clothes, music, pets, or anything else. Don't preach. Be of sunny disposition, and aim to please.

8. **Revise and Edit Your Work**

Cut out all dead wood; every word should pull its weight. (Copywriting is like poetry in this respect.) Be your own critic. Check your facts, your syntax, your spelling. Make sure you haven't left anything out.

Glossary of Mail-Order, Mailing List, and Related Terms

Advertising Contract: An agreement between an advertiser and the entity controlling the medium in which the advertiser intends to place an advertisement. The contract specifies such matters as the amount of advertising space that will be taken, the rate at which the advertiser will pay for the ad or ads, and the applicable discounts and terms of payment.

Advertising Negative: A format favored by many publications for submission of advertising. The most popular is "right-reading, emulsion side down."

Advertising Rate Card: A printed card issued by the publisher of a print advertising medium providing full details of advertising costs, sizes, mechanical requirements, and other information useful to potential advertisers and advertising agencies.

Advertising Side: The side of a direct response card in a card pack carrying the advertising. *See also* Business Reply Side.

Advertising Target Market: The specific audience to which an advertising message is aimed.

Agate Line: A unit of measurement used to sell advertising space, particularly in newspapers. The cost per agate line is usually for space occupying the depth of one agate line ($5\frac{1}{2}$ points) by the width of one column. There are 14 agate lines to the column inch.

Agency Discount: Most publishers of co-op card packs give a 15 percent discount to recognized advertising agencies (and often list brokers, as well) when payment is made within 30 days of date of invoice.

Art: Any part of an advertisement that is not typeset.

Audit Bureau of Circulation (A.B.C.): An organization whose purpose is to determine correct circulation figures for periodicals of publisher members and to distribute these for the benefit of the membership as a whole.

Back of Book: The section of a magazine following the main editorial section.

Booklet: A series of printed pages usually bound together by saddle stitching, but sometimes glued. Sizes usually vary from 6 by 9 inches to $8\frac{1}{2}$ by 11 inches, and may be either vertical or horizontal. *See also:* Covered Booklet, Self-Cover Booklet.

Bounceback/Bounce Back: Ad advertising piece sent to a customer as an enclosure with an outgoing shipment, or with an invoice or statement. On the premise that the best customer is one who has already bought, the bounceback is a highly effective selling vehicle.

Broadside: A large single sheet of advertising, printed on one or both sides and folded for mailing. It is generally designed to be read longways. When designed so that the printed page is longer than it is wide, it is known as a *Portrait Format*.

Brochure: A pamphlet, folder, or booklet containing advertising matter usually including headline, text, and graphics. Brochures vary widely in size and format and may be either folded or stitched.

Business Reply Side: The side of a direct response card in a card pack containing the return address. *See also* Advertising Side.

Card Pack: A collection of business reply cards, usually in loose format, each containing an advertisement that the recipient can complete and mail back (usually with postage paid) to an advertiser and receive a product, service, or additional information.

Card Pack Envelope Formats (Packaging Materials): Card packs are wrapped in a variety of packaging materials including: metalized polypropylene, demetalized polypropylene, poly, pearlized poly, paper, and recycled paper.

Card Pack Exchange: The insertion of a direct response card by an advertiser in the pack of a competitor in exchange for placing the competitor's card in an advertiser-sponsored pack.

Card Pack Postal Requirements: All cards must be at least .007 of an inch thick and measure at least 3 by 5 inches.

Card Rate: The standard rate charged for a specified quantity of advertising space by a communications medium without regard to any discounts; the charges listed on the advertising rate card.

Card Size: The width and length of a card in a card pack, most usually $5\frac{1}{2}$ by $3\frac{1}{2}$ inches. Some variations include: $5\frac{5}{8}$ by $3\frac{1}{2}$ inches; $5\frac{1}{8}$ by $3\frac{1}{2}$ inches; and $5\frac{3}{8}$ by $3\frac{1}{2}$ inches.

Catalog: A bound book or booklet giving descriptions and prices of merchandise. *See also:* Mail-Order Catalog.

Catalog Card Pack: A type of proprietary card pack sponsored by a mail-order catalog company and containing only the sponsor's inserts. Catalog card packs are usually used by mail-order catalogers between catalog mailings, for testing, and for special promotions.

Checking Copy: (1) A copy of a specific issue of a publication in which an advertisement has been inserted. (2) A duplicate copy of a rented mailing list, used to check response.

Circular: A small, inexpensively produced advertising piece, usually on a single sheet of paper which may be distributed flat or folded for mailing in an envelope. *See also* Flyer/Flier.

Circulation: The number of copies of a publication that are distributed. *See also* Audit Bureau of Circulation (A.B.C.).

Classified Advertising: Newspaper and magazine advertising subdivided according to the types of things being offered or sought.

Closing Date: The last date on which a publication will accept an advertisement for a specific issue.

Cold Calling: Telephone calls to a list of people who have not shown any prior interest in the product or service that is being promoted.

Column: An area of print running down a page of a periodical, composed of lines of equal width.

Column Inch: Advertising space equal to a publication's column width by one inch of depth. Sometimes the smallest unit of advertising space sold by a publication.

Computer Letter: A computer-printed message containing personalized, fill-in information from a source file, in prespecified positions.

Consumer Card Pack: A card pack targeted toward a specific group of general consumers, such as outdoors enthusiasts (hunters and fishermen) or seniors over the age of 60.

Contract Rate: A special discounted rate given an advertiser for advertising placed within a specified period, usually a year. *See also* Contract Year.

Contract Year (Advertising): A 12-month period that starts on the date of the first advertising insertion, and guarantees the special contract advertising rate for all insertions during that period.

Controlled Circulation: A business publication containing at least 25 percent editorial matter, issued on a regular basis, and circulated free or mainly free to individuals within a particular profession, business, or industry.

Co-Op Pack/Cooperative Card Pack: A card pack in which individual cards represent different advertisers. The publisher of the card pack sells the cards to advertisers and handles all details of printing, mailing, and distribution.

Corporate Card Pack: A proprietary card pack published by a corporation and containing only offers for the sponsor's products and services. *See also* Proprietary Card Pack.

Cost Per Card: Although the participation cost in a co-op card pack is usually a fixed price for each card purchased, many card pack advertisers view card cost in terms of cost per name reached.

Cost Per Name: Cost per name reached for a co-op card pack participation will vary widely from one co-op pack to another. As the quality of the audience reached increases, the cost per name increases accordingly.

Covered Booklet: A booklet with heavier paper used for the outside covers. *See also* Booklet.

Daily Rate: The advertising space rate charged by a daily newspaper for all editions published Monday through Friday, or Monday through Saturday.

Direct Mail Package: (1) Typically the mailing piece as placed in the mail. (2) All of the elements involved in any particular direct mail effort. *See also:* Direct Mail Package, Classic.

Direct Mail Package, Classic: The classic direct mail package consists of these elements: Outer or mailing envelope, letter, reply form, and return card or envelope.

Display Advertising: *See* Space Advertising.

Double-Page Spread/Double Spread: *See* Spread (Advertising).

Echo Effect of Card Packs: The *echo effect* is a term used to describe sales made as a result of a card pack mailing but without the postcard being returned to the advertiser (e.g., the mailing recipient who takes a co-op book promotion card to a local bookstore and purchases the book there).

800 Number/800 Service: Inbound long-distance telephone service in which the owner of the 800 number pays for the call. Also referred to as *toll-free calling* or *toll-free telephone service. See also* Telemarketing, Inbound.

Envelope Stuffer: Advertising inserted into invoices, statements, or outgoing correspondence. *See also:* Package Insert, Statement Stuffer.

Facing Text Matter: A position request used by periodical advertisers who wish to have advertising placed opposite editorial matter.

Federal Communications Commission (FCC): The federal agency that oversees and regulates all wire and radio communications.

Firm Order: An advertiser's positive order that cannot be canceled.

Firm Order Date: A date after which an order for advertising space cannot be canceled.

Five-Up Configuration: A printing format used by some card pack printers in which each direct response card is duplicated five times down the sheet.

Five-Way Split Tests: A random testing method possible to card pack participants when card pack printers use the five-up configuration (see above). This unique approach permits an advertiser to test five different elements very inexpensively.

Fixed Location: A space in a periodical occupied by an advertiser for two or more consecutive issues; also a space in a periodical specified by an advertiser.

Flyer/Flier: A small, inexpensively produced advertising piece usually on a single sheet of paper which may be folded for mailing in an envelope, or distributed flat. Also called *Circular*. In the United Kingdom, it is called a *Leaflet*.

Format: The size, shape, style, and general appearance of a promotional effort.

Frequency Discount: A discounted advertising rate given by a publication to an advertiser for a given number of insertions stipulated by the publisher within a contract year. *See also* Contract Rate.

Horizontal Card: One in which the printing runs the long way on a card. This is the way most people read cards and most card packs are printed this way. Horizontal cards generally pull better than vertical cards. *See also* Vertical Card.

House Cards: Cards inserted into a co-op card pack by the card pack sponsor and promoting the company's own products or services (i.e., a subscription offer from a magazine publisher sponsoring a co-op pack).

In-House Telemarketing: Telemarketing performed by employees with a company or organization as a primary or supplementary means of marketing and selling its products or services.

Insertion Order (Advertising): A set of instructions issued to a periodical or print medium authorizing publication of an advertisement on a particular date or in a particular issue in accordance with the specifications stated on the order.

Issue Date for Co-Op Packs: Virtually all co-op packs have a month or seasonal issue date, like January, April, and September; or if seasonal, spring and fall (for seasonal packs, month of issue varies with each pack).

Journal: (1) Usually a periodical that publishes original research papers and other research material that has not been previously published. By contrast, magazines do not carry original research papers. (2) A periodical for practitioners in a specific field or profession. *See also* Magazine.

Letter Format: A sales message usually printed or written on the mailer's letterhead and enclosed in an envelope for mailing. In some promotional letters, a headline will be substituted for the letterhead. *See also:* Computer Letter; Direct Mail Package, Classic; Lift Letter.

Lift Letter: A supplementary message insert accompanying a mailing package; a second letter providing some additional message related to the mail offer. Sometimes called a *publisher's letter* because it is widely used in selling magazine subscriptions.

Line Rate: A charge per line for newspaper advertising space.

List Buyer: Term for an individual who rents lists from others for one-time use for a specific payment or cost per thousand names.

List Broker: A mailing list specialist who recommends suitable lists for a particular mailing program and makes arrangements for ensuring that the lists arrive on a timely basis. The broker works for the mailer, but is paid a commission by the list owner whose list is being rented.

List Format: The physical makeup in which the list is furnished. Some formats are magnetic tape, Cheshire labels, pressure-sensitive labels, typed or printed sheets, 3- by 5-inch cards, and floppy disks.

List Compiler: One who develops lists of names, often from directories, public records, or other available printed sources. Lists compiled from directories should be from directories of recent origin, since directory-compiled lists become undeliverable at the rate of about 20 percent a year from date of compilation.

List Count: Total number of names on a mailing list. Be sure to verify the count before planning a mailing, and again when names are received for the actual mailing. Before printing any promotion, be sure to base the print quantity on the delivered name count, and not on the listed count.

List-Order Cancellations: Usually a list-order cancellation will be accepted if no work has been done on the order. If any work has been done, you are obligated to pay for it or part of it; for example, a *run charge.* Some list owners expect payment in full if the list is canceled after a mail date.

List-Order Confirmation: A form issued by the list broker or manager to the list renter spelling out the details of an oral list order. The list renter must sign and return a copy and, unless corrected or amended, it is considered a contractual agreement between the renter and the list owner.

List Protection: List owners use several methods for protection of their rented lists. One is inserting "seeds" or names of persons known to them so that a renter's use of the list can be monitored. Another method is getting a written guarantee from the renter that the renter will use the list one time only. Yet another method is for the owner to have the list renter's mailing addressed and mailed on his premises, or through his mailing service.

List Rental: Arrangement where list owner makes a mailing list available to a mailer for one-time use for specific payment or cost per thousand names.

List-Rental Payments: Normal terms are usually 30 days after the mail date. Prepayment is usually required with the initial order.

List Sequence: The order in which names appear on a mailing list. Most lists are supplied in ZIP Code sequence. Other arrangements include alphabetically by state, and by city within state.

Lookup Service: An organization that locates and appends telephone numbers to a list of names and addresses for a fee.

Magazine: A paper-covered periodical containing a collection of articles, stories, pictures, or other features, and usually advertising. Some business or professional magazines use "Journal" in their titles, but are classified as magazines.

Magazine Insert: An insert enclosed with a periodical. Typically, most are in card form, either blown in during the process or bound in.

Mailing Card: A self-mailer printed on card stock with a minimum thickness of .007 inch to conform with U.S. Postal Service regulations. *See also:* Self-Mailer.

Mail-Order Advertising: Advertising soliciting an order for purchase, primarily using the U.S. Postal Service as a means of returning the order to the person or organization making the offer. With 800 telephone service, many mail-order advertisements produce a high volume of telephone orders as well.

Mail-Order Catalog: A book or booklet showing merchandise with descriptive details and prices, designed to elicit orders by mail or phone.

Media Rep: A sales representative of an advertising medium—either newspaper or magazine. Sometimes called *space rep* or *space salesperson*.

Minimum Depth Requirement: A requirement of newspapers that advertisements have a certain proportion of depth to width, usually one inch per column.

National Advertising Rate: A periodical rate charged for advertising placed by national or regional advertisers; usually higher than the rate for local advertising.

Newsletter Format: A publication dominated by short news items of special interest to its intended recipients. Usually contains 12 or fewer pages, unbound, and is mailable in a No. 10 envelope.

One-Time Rate: The rate charged for a single, unrepeated advertisement. *See also* Open Rate.

Open Rate: The highest rate charged by a medium for advertising. Also called *Card Rate*.

Package: *See* Direct Mail Package; Direct Mail Package, Classic.

Package Insert: A promotional insert included in a package shipment. *See also:* Bounceback, Statement Stuffer, Stuffer.

Packaging Materials: *See* Card Pack Envelope Formats.

Per-Inquiry Advertising: Advertising for which the publication is paid according to the number of inquiries or completed sales that result.

Plate Charge: A separate charge applied for making printing plates for a card pack sponsor. Card pack printers usually specify a first-time cost for the plates used in printing package wraps. These plates are then stored and reused.

Precall Planning: Preparation of telephone sales representatives before the start of a calling session. (A detailed and very useful precall planning checklist may be found in *In-House Telemarketing* by Thomas A. McCafferty, Probus Publishing, Chicago, 1994.)

Preferred Position: The location for an advertisement in a periodical that an advertiser demands and for which he pays a higher-than-usual rate, or a specific premium over the usual rate.

Premium: An extra charge or higher total cost for a preferred advertising position or for special treatment of an advertisement.

Position Charge: Many co-op card packs charge an additional premium for particular card positions within the deck. Premium charges may be applied to such positions as: First card or last card in the pack; second to fifth card; second to tenth card; second to twentieth card; top five cards, top ten, or top twenty.

Proprietary Card Pack: A general term for any card pack that contains only the sponsoring organization's cards.

Publisher's Letter: *See* Lift Letter.

Regional Card Pack: Card packs mailed only to specific geographic parts of the country.

Regional Edition: An edition of a nationally distributed periodical that is distributed within one geographic area. Advertising space for the edition can be purchased separately.

Regional Split: The option of having a card in a card pack mailing included only in a selected geographic region or regions.

Run-of-Paper: Periodical advertising positioned at the publisher's discretion, with or without regard to position requests made by the advertisers. While some publishers treat all advertisements as run-of-paper, others will endeavor to honor preferred-position requests.

Self-Cover Booklet: One that is covered with the same paper as the inside pages. *See also* Booklet.

Self-Mailer: Any direct mail piece that can be mailed without an envelope or separate wrapping. It is the cheapest of all direct mail formats.

Seven-Point Matte Stock: A matte finished paper manufactured to the minimum postal mailing requirement of seven points thickness (.007″) on a micrometer reading.

70# High Bulk Vellum: An uncoated, vellum finish, text-weight paper stock that is specifically manufactured to "bulk" to the minimum postal mailing requirements of seven points thickness (.007″) on a micrometer reading. The great majority of card packs are produced on this stock.

Shooter Labels: The card pack industry saw the introduction of "shooter" labels in the 1980s when each pack included a card-size sheet bearing six peel-off labels, each containing the name and address of the pack recipient, to enable easier response. By 1994, the technology had been improved by Solar Press of Naperville, IL, to permit shooter labels in configurations of 3, 9, 12, or 22 pre-addressed labels.

Side-by-Side Pack: A card pack arrangement, introduced in 1991 by Solar Press of Naperville, IL, in which card packs of between 41 and 64 cards are split in even halves and placed side by side for packaging, allowing the pack to be mailed at a lower postage rate (letter category).

Space Discount: A discount for purchase of a certain quantity of advertising space.

Space Schedule: A schedule of advertising space to be bought, specifying the publications, dates of appearance, size of advertisements, and the cost, submitted to a client by an advertising agency.

Split Testing: A method of varying the elements in a direct response card and randomly distributing the cards with the varying elements throughout the mailing.

Spread (Advertising): (1) Two facing pages in a periodical. (2) An advertisement printed across two such pages.

Stamp Format: Promotions in which postage-stamp-like printed sheets are used as order vehicles. Printed stamp sheets may contain anywhere from 1 to 120 stamps. Stamps may accompany an independent direct mail effort or be used as envelope or shipment enclosures. Each stamp illustrates or identifies a single product (usually a book), and the recipient need only remove and moisten the stamp and affix it to an order vehicle or on a letterhead to place an order.

Statement Stuffer: A term generally applied to advertising enclosed with an invoice or statement. *See also* Package Insert.

Stuffer: Usually refers to advertising matter enclosed with outgoing merchandise, statements, invoices, or mailings for other products. *See also:* Package Insert, Statement Stuffer.

Sweepstakes: An advertising or promotion effort in which prizes are awarded by chance, such as a lottery, to those who respond to the promotion.

Tear Sheet: A page torn from a specific issue of a publication containing an advertisement and sent to an advertiser or advertising agency as proof of insertion.

Telemarketing/Telephone Marketing: Use of the telephone in conjunction with the generation of sales or services.

Telemarketing, Inbound: Receiving calls generated by a customer or prospect. *See also* 800 Number/800 Service; Telemarketing, Outbound.

Telemarketing, Outbound: Telemarketing originating from a business or telemarketing service calling center in conjunction with the generation of sales or sales leads. *See also* Telemarketing, Inbound.

Telemarketing Test: A test usually conducted through an independent telemarketing service agency. Test may be of an offer, a mailing list, a price, or a script. Payment to the agency may be at a fixed rate per hour for an agreed-upon number of hours.

Telemarketing Service Agency: A service agency that handles either inbound or outbound calls or sometimes both for clients on a prearranged fee basis. Inbound service usually involves the use of 800 toll-free numbers. Calls received at the telemarketing agency calling center are transmitted to the client company. Outbound telemarketing may involve preparation of sales scripts and sales campaigns on specific projects, using the sponsoring company's customer list or other appropriate lists.

Telephone Consumer Protection Act: This Act, which went into effect on December 20, 1992, instructs the Federal Communications Commission (FCC) to develop regulations to protect the privacy rights of residential telephone subscribers and to provide them with a way of stopping unwanted calls.

Telephone List: This term may be used to refer to a list of customers acquired through a telemarketing effort, or to a mailing list with telephone numbers appended.

Telephone Sales (FCC Definition): The initiation of a telephone call or message for the purpose of encouraging the purchase or rental of, or investment in, property, goods, or services, as is transmitted to any person.

Third Cover: The inside back cover of a periodical, catalog, or booklet. Sometimes referred to as *Cover 3*.

Till Forbid: An advertisement placed with the instruction that it be run in every issue until the advertiser orders it to stop, or until forbidden to run. Such ads are called *t.f. ads*.

Vertical Card: A direct response card in which the advertising matter runs the short way. Vertical cards are generally believed to be at a disadvantage over horizontal cards in that readers quickly scanning a pack of cards may not want to go out of their way to try to read a message they can't grasp instantly. *See also* Horizontal Card.

Vertical Half-Page: An advertisement occupying half the entire width of the full height of a periodical page.

Visuals: Photographs or illustrations on the offer side of a response card insert, used to attract the reader's attention or enhance the printed matter.

Glossary of Envelope Terms

Announcement Envelope: A square-flapped envelope, generally used for formal announcements and invitations.

Bind-In Envelope: An envelope stapled into a catalog or mailing piece that can be removed and used as a response vehicle.

Bankers Flap Envelope: A heavy-duty envelope with a pointed flap, used for bulky correspondence or enclosure material.

Bond Envelope: One made of bond paper; a type that is relatively strong and firm.

Booklet Envelope: An open-sided envelope used for booklets and direct mail pieces. Its unseamed back is appropriate as a printing surface.

Clasp Envelope: A strong envelope with a metal clasp that fits through a hole in the flap.

Closed-Face Envelope: A regular envelope with no window.

Commercial Envelope: A pointed, flapped envelope in standard sizes used for business correspondence and mail promotions; also called a regular envelope.

Cover Envelope: One that can be made of the cover paper used for booklets. Most cover papers are manufactured in light weights, which allow the fabrication and use of envelopes in harmony with the enclosed booklet cover.

Envelope: (1) A Container, usually made of paper and used to mail written or printed matter. Basic parts of an envelope are the seal flap, the seal gum on the flap, the shoulders (the flaps to which the envelope back is pasted), the throat (the open area under the flap which provides clearance for inserting), the front or face, the side flaps, and the bottom flap. (2) One of the basic components of a direct mail package.

Envelope Clearance: For mass mailings that will be machine inserted, the inserts should be at least one-half inch narrower than envelope length and at least one-quarter inch shorter than the envelope height.

Envelope Corner Card: The name and address imprint of a mailer in the upper left-hand corner of an envelope. The mailer's name and address must be presented with postal requirements.

Envelope Ordering Requirements: (1) When the envelopes will be needed, (2) the size or bulk of the contents, (3) how the contents will be inserted, (4) the type of postage used, (5) whether a window envelope will help, (6) what type of closure—regular gum or pressure sensitive, (7) color of paper stock.

Envelope Package: A mailing with the contents encased in an envelope.

Envelope Requirements for International Mailings: (1) All forms of international mailings must be enclosed in a sealed envelope before being mailed (self-mailers are illegal in most countries). (2) Envelopes bearing a window must have a cellophane covering over the window.

Manila Envelope: A light brown envelope made of manila paper, a strong, durable paper suitable for mailing large items.

Open-End (Catalog) Envelope: An oversized envelope on which the opening is on the short end.

Open-Side (Booklet) Envelope: An oversized envelope on which the opening is on the long side.

Open-Window Envelope: A window envelope in which the opening is not covered.

Regular Envelope: Another term for commercial envelope.

Tyvek Envelope: A strong, lightweight envelope produced by the DuPont Company and favored by international mailers because of the savings in postage due to its light weight.

Wallet-Flap Envelope: An envelope with a large flap, which can be removed and returned in the envelope either as an order form or response vehicle. The printing is usually on the inside of the flap.

Window Envelope: An envelope with a die-cut opening, usually glassine covered, through which the mailing address shows.

Window Envelope, Open-Face: An envelope with a plain die-cut opening.

Wove Envelope: A wove envelope is made of a smooth white paper that is somewhat softer, bulkier, and not so strong as bond. It is widely used in direct mail promotion.

Glossary of Paper Terms

Antique Paper: Paper with a surface of relatively rough texture.

Basis Size/Basic Size: Specific standard sheet size from which weight of a given grade of paper is determined.

Basis Weight/Basic Weight: Weight of a ream (500 sheets) of paper in the standard (basic) size for that class of paper; also called substance.

Bible Paper: A thin, opaque printing paper for use when low bulk is important.

Bond Paper: A grade of writing or printing paper for which strength, durability, and permanence are essential requirements.

Book Paper: Any kind of paper suitable for printing, except for newsprint. Book paper is used for books, periodicals, leaflets, and folders. Available in a variety of finishes and in a wide range of thicknesses.

Brightness (paper): A characteristic of paper that affects the contrast or sparkle of the printed subject. Artificial brighteners are sometimes added, such as fluorescent additives.

Bristol Board: Any of a variety of stiff, moderately heavy papers used for booklets, postcards, index cards, display cards, etc. Various types include: plain bristol, index bristol, coated bristol, cardboard.

Bulk: The thickness of printing paper. It is expressed in pages per inch.

Caliper: The thickness of a sheet of paper. It is expressed in thousandths of an inch.

Cheshire Paper/Stock: The paper used for Cheshire labels. The most commonly used is the plain label paper in 20-pound white offset stock, which requires a vegetable-adhesive base. There is also gummed paper which adheres when moistened.

Chipboard: A low-density board, used as a stiffener and protective covering; a type of bristol paper.

Cover Paper: A classification of paper that is characterized by its weight and durability. Cover paper is heavier than book or text papers and lighter than bristol.

Enamel Paper: Paper coated to give it a glossy surface. It can be glossy (shiny) or matte (dull).

English Finish: A paper finished with a very smooth surface.

Gloss-Coated Paper: A paper finished to have a glossy surface.

Grain (paper): The direction in which the fibers in paper lie. Grain is an important factor in paper folding; paper folds more easily and tears more cleanly with the grain than against the grain.

Grammage: The metric equivalent of basis weight or substance for paper, expressed as grams per square meter.

High-Opacity Paper: Paper with little show-through of printing from the opposite side of the sheet.

Label Paper, Gum-Perforated: Labels on perforated sheets with gum backing that adherers when moistened.

Label Paper, Heat Transfer/Heat Activated: Label paper that becomes adhesive when heat is applied.

Label Paper, Plain: Usually 16- to 20-pound white offset stock.

Label Paper, Pressure-Sensitive: Label paper that adheres when pressed on to an envelope or mailing piece.

Laid Paper: Paper that when held up to light reveals fine parallel lines (wire marks) and cross lines (chain marks). It is commonly used for letterheads.

Linen Finish: A bond paper with a woven or linenlike texture.

Machine Coated: Coating applied while paper is still on the paper machine.

Machine Finish: A paper finish that is smooth, but not as smooth as English finish.

Manila Paper: A smooth sturdy light brown paper commonly used for manila envelopes or for mailing large items.

Matte Finish: Papers with little or no gloss that are suitable for all types of lithographic reproduction.

Opacity: The amount of show-through on the opposite side of a printed sheet or the adjoining sheet.

Pressure Sensitive Label: An adhesive-backed label that will adhere to a mailing piece when applied with pressure.

Pressure Sensitive Paper: Paper stock with an adhesive coating that is protected by a backing sheet until used. When the backing is removed, the paper will stick without moistening with just the application of pressure.

Rag Bond: A bond paper made either entirely or mainly with rag fibers.

Sheet: A piece of paper with two sides, of which each side is a page.

Short Grain: Grain running with the short dimension of a sheet of paper.

Skid Paper: Paper a printer uses frequently and buys in bulk—by the skid, and has on hand at all times.

Stock: A commonly used term for paper of any kind.

Supercalendered Paper: A paper that has been given extra gloss and smoothness during manufacture.

Text Paper: An uncoated book paper characterized by a relatively rough surface, opacity, and strength. Used for books, promotion pieces, and envelopes. Standard size: 25 by 38 inches.

Textured Coated Paper: Another term for gloss-coated paper.

Uncoated Paper: Paper without an enamel coating.

Weight: The basis on which paper is sold; 60-pound (or 60 substance) paper means a ream of paper in a certain size (usually 25" × 38") that weighs 60 pounds. *See also* Basis Weight.

Glossary of Postal Terms

Advance Deposit Account: A mailer account maintained by the U.S. Postal Service from which postage is deducted at the time of mailing.

Bulk Business Mail: A class of mail that includes third-class and parcels weighing less than 16 ounces. Material sent by bulk business mail includes, but is not limited to, catalogs and circulars (also called *advertising mail*).

Business Reply Mail: Specially printed cards and envelopes that may be mailed without prepayment of postage. The postage and fees are collected when the mail is delivered to the addressee.

Carrier Route Presort Third-Class Mail: A category of third-class mail. Mailers who sort bulk third-class mail by individual carrier routes may earn a discount off the basic bulk third-class rate.

Faced: Mail arranged with all addresses and stamps or indicia facing the same way.

First-Class Mail: Letters, postcards, and postal cards, and all matter wholly or partially in writing, computer printed, or typewritten, and all matter sealed or otherwise closed against inspection.

Metered Mail: Any class of mail with postage printed by a USPS approved meter. In general, the privileges and conditions that apply to material mailed with stamps also apply to material mailed with a meter imprint. Metered mail must be deposited within the jurisdiction of the post office shown in the meter stamp.

Precanceled Stamps: Stamps canceled by printing across the face before they are sold to mailers.

Third-Class Mail: Usually circulars, printed matter, pamphlets, and merchandise weighing less than 16 ounces. *See also* Bulk Business Mail.

ZIP + 4 Code: The nine-digit code, established in 1981, composed of: (1) *ZIP Code*. The first five digits identify the individual post office or metropolitan area delivery station associated with the address.

(2) *Expanded code.* The additional four digits identify: (*a*) Sector: The first two additional digits designate a geographic portion of a zone. It can also indicate a portion of a rural route, part of a box section, or official designation. (*b*) Segment: The last two additional digits designate a specific block face, apartment house, bank of boxes, firm, building, or other specific delivery location.

Bibliography

Andrews, Les (Editor). *The Post Office Direct Mail Handbook.* Watford, England: Exley Publications, Ltd., 1984.

Baier, Martin. *Elements of Direct Marketing.* New York: McGraw-Hill, 1983.

Barton, Roger (Editor). *Handbook of Advertising Management.* New York: McGraw-Hill, 1970.

Bauer, Larry. *How to Publish a Card Pack.* Naperville, IL: Solar Press, 1988.

Bell, Harry A. *Getting the Right Start in Direct Advertising.* New York: Graphic Books, 1946.

Bencin, Richard L., and Donald J. Jonovic. *Encyclopedia of Telemarketing.* Englewood Cliffs, NJ: Prentice-Hall, 1989.

Bird, Drayton. *Commonsense Direct Marketing.* 2d Ed. Lincolnwood, IL: NTC Business Books, 1990.

Bly, Robert W. *Business to Business Direct Marketing.* Lincolnwood, IL: NTC Business Books, 1991.

Bodian, Nat G., and Robert Luedtke. *Beyond Lead Generation: Merchandising through Card Packs.* Naperville, IL: Solar Press, 1986.

Bodian, Nat G. *Book Marketing Handbook, Volume One: Tips and Techniques for the Sale and Promotion of Scientific, Technical, Professional and Scholarly Books and Journals.* New York: Bowker, 1980.

———*Book Marketing Handbook, Volume Two: Over 1,000 More Tips and Techniques.* New York: Bowker, 1983.

———*The Copywriter's Handbook: A Practical Guide.* Philadelphia: ISI Press, 1984.

———*NTC's Dictionary of Direct Mail and Mailing List Terminology and Techniques.* Lincolnwood, IL: NTC Business Books, 1990.

———*The Publisher's Direct Mail Handbook.* Philadelphia: ISI Press, 1987.

Brann, Christian. *Cost-Effective Direct Marketing.* Gloucestershire, England: Collectors' Books Ltd., 1984.

Burns, Karen L. (Editor). *Mailing Lists: A Practical Guide.* New York: DMA, 1984.

Burstiner, Irving. *Mail Order Selling.* New York: Fireside, 1993.

Caples, John. *How to Make Your Advertising Make Money.* Englewood Cliffs, NJ: Prentice-Hall, 1983.

Card Pack Media Directory. Naperville, IL: Solar Press. Published annually.

Catalog Age (magazine). Cowles Business Media, 911 Hope St., Stamford, CT 06907. Published monthly.

Cohen, William A. *Building a Mail Order Business,* 3d Ed. New York: Wiley, 1991.

Direct Marketing Association. *DMA Fact Book on Direct Marketing.* New York: DMA, 1983.

———*Mailing Lists: A Practical Guide.* New York: DMA, 1984.

———*Statistical Fact Book: Current Information About Direct Marketing.* New York: DMA. Published annually in October.

Direct Marketing International (magazine). Peterborough, England: Detailextra Ltd. Published monthly. (Available in the United States from Mercury Airfreight International Ltd., 2323 Randolph Ave., Avenel, NJ 07001).

Direct Marketing Market Place. New Providence, NJ: National Register Publishing Co. Updated annually in March. Available from Reed Reference Publishing, 121 Chanlon Road, New Providence, NJ 07974.

Direct Marketing (magazine). Hoke Communications, 224 Seventh Street, Garden City, NY 11530. Published monthly.

Direct: The Magazine of Direct Marketing Management. Cowles Business Media, Skokie, IL 60077. Published monthly.

DM News: The Newspaper of Direct Marketing. Mill Hollow Corp., 19 West 21st Street, New York, NY 10010. Published every Monday.

Dunhill, Hugo. *How to Write an Effective Money-Making Direct Mail Letter.* New York: Hugo Dunhill Mailing Lists, 1989.

Encyclopedia of Associations. Detroit: Gale Research Company. Revised annually.

Flesch, Rudolph. *The Art of Plain Talk.* New York: Harper 1946; Macmillan (paper) 1985.

Fidel, Stanley Leo. *Start-Up Telemarketing: How to Launch a Profitable Sales Operation.* New York: Wiley, 1987.

Good, Bill. *Prospecting Your Way to Sales Success: How to Find New Business by Phone.* New York: Scribner, 1986.

Goodman, Gary S. *Reach Out and Sell Someone.* Englewood Cliffs, NJ: Prentice-Hall, 1983.

Goldberg, Vernie, and Tracy Emerick. *Business-to-Business Marketing Resource Guide.* Yardley, PA: Direct Marketing Publishing, 1991.

Gosden, Freeman F., Jr. *Direct Marketing Success: What Works and Why.* New York: Wiley, 1985.

Graham, Irvin (Editor). *Encyclopedia of Advertising.* New York: Fairchild, 1952.

Gray, Bill. *Tips on Type.* New York: Van Nostrand Reinhold, 1983.

Greene, Ron, and Jim Perry. *Marketing Masters: Secrets of America's Best Companies.* New York: HarperCollins, 1993.

Hahn, Fred E. *Do-It-Yourself Advertising.* New York: Wiley, 1993.

Hiam, Alexander, and Charles Schewe. *The Portable MBA in Marketing.* New York: Wiley, 1992.

Harper, Rose. *Mailing List Strategies: A Guide to Direct Mail Success.* New York: McGraw-Hill, 1986.

Hodgson, Richard S. *Direct Mail and Mail Order Handbook,* 3d Ed. Chicago: Dartnell, 1980.

———*The Greatest Direct Mail Sales Letters of All Time.* Chicago: Dartnell, 1986.

Holtz, Herman. *The Direct Marketer's Workbook.* New York: Wiley, 1986.

———*Starting and Building Your Catalog Sales Business.* New York: Wiley, 1990.

How to Plan Printing. Boston: S. D. Warren Company, 1982.

Jones, Susan K. *Creative Strategy in Direct Marketing*. Lincolnwood, IL: NTC Business Books, 1991.

Kleid, Lewis. *Mail-Order Strategies*. New York: Reporter of Direct Mail Advertising, 1956.

Kobs, Jim. *Profitable Direct Marketing*, 2d Ed. Lincolnwood, IL: NTC Business Books, 1992.

Kremer, John. *The Complete Direct Marketing Sourcebook*. New York: Wiley, 1992.

————*Mail Order Worksheet Kit*. Fairfield, IA: Open Horizons, 1991.

Levinson, Jay Conrad. *Guerrilla Marketing for the Nineties*. Boston: Houghton Mifflin, 1993.

Lewis, Herschell Gordon. *Direct Mail Copy That Sells*. Englewood Cliffs, NJ: Prentice-Hall, 1984.

————*How to Write Powerful Catalog Copy*. Chicago: Bonus Books, 1990.

————*More Than You Ever Wanted to Know About Mail Order Advertising*. Englewood Cliffs, NJ: Prentice-Hall, 1983.

————*Power Copywriting*. Chicago: Dartnell, 1992.

Linchitz, Joel. *The Complete Guide to Telemarketing Management*. New York: Amacom Books, 1990.

Lumley, James. *Sell It by Mail*. New York: Wiley, 1986.

Magazine Week: The Newsweekly of Magazine Publishing. Lighthouse Communications, 223 West Central Street, Natick, MA 01760.

Mahfood, Phillip E. *Teleselling*. Chicago: Probus Publishing, 1993.

Mailing List Systems. The Merge/Purge Fact Book, 2d Ed. Arlington, TX: Mailing List Systems Corp., 1988.

McLean, Ed. *The Basics of Copy*. Yonkers, NY: Ryan Gilmore Publishing, 1977.

————*The Basics of Testing*. New York: Ryan Gilmore Publishing, 1978.

Metzger, George P. *Copy*. New York: Doubleday, 1926.

Morgan, Carol, and Doran Levy. *Segmenting the Mature Market*. Chicago: Probus, 1993.

Nash, Edward L. (Editor). *The Direct Marketing Handbook*. New York: McGraw-Hill, 1984.

Nash, Edward L. *Direct Marketing: Strategy, Planning, Execution*, 2d Ed. New York: McGraw-Hill, 1986.

————*Database Marketing: The Ultimate Marketing Tool*. New York: McGraw-Hill, 1993.

Nicholas, Ted. *The Golden Mailbox*. Chicago: Dearborn Financial, 1992.

Norcutt, Bill. *Secrets of Successful Response Deck Advertising*. Arlington, TX: Thinkbank Publishers, 1984.

Ogilvy, David. *Confessions of an Advertising Man*. Lincolnwood, IL: NTC Business Books, 1963.

————*Ogilvy on Advertising*. New York: Wiley, 1987.

Pickens, Judy. *Copy to Press*. New York: Wiley, 1985.

Pinson, Linda, and Jerry Jinett. *Target Marketing for the Small Business*. Dover, NH: Upstart Publishing, 1993.

PMS Color Specifier. New York: Pantone, Incorporated. Updated periodically.

Pocket Pal: A Graphic Arts Production Handbook. New York: International Paper Co. Updated periodically.

Posch, Robert J. *The Direct Marketer's Legal Adviser.* New York: McGraw-Hill, 1983.

Preston, Harold P. *Successful Mail Selling.* New York: Ronald Press, 1941.

Richardson, Linda. *Selling by Phone: How to Reach and Sell Customers in the Nineties.* New York: McGraw-Hill, 1992.

Roman, Kenneth, and Jane Mass, 2d Ed. *The New How To Advertise.* New York: St. Martin. 1992.

Romano, Frank J. *The TypEncyclopedia.* New York: Bowker, 1984.

Sales and Marketing Strategies & News (magazine). Hughes Communications, 211 West State Street, Rockford, IL 61101. Published bimonthly.

Schwab, Victor O. *How to Write a Good Advertisement.* New York: Harper, 1962.

Schwartz, Eugene. *Mail Order! How to Get Your Share of the Hidden Profits that Exist in Your Business.* New York: Boardroom Books, 1982.

Simon, Julian L. *How to Start and Operate a Mail Order Business,* 5th Ed. New York: McGraw-Hill, 1993.

Slutsky, Jeff, and Marc Slutsky. *Streetsmart Selling.* Englewood Cliffs, NJ: Prentice-Hall, 1990.

Solar Reflections (semiannual newsletter). Naperville, IL: Solar Press.

Standard Rate and Data Service. *Card Deck Advertising Source.* (Renamed in 1994; previously *Card Deck Rates and Data.*) Wilmette, IL: SRDS. Published semiannually: Spring and Fall.

———*Direct Marketing List Source.* (Prior to 1994 was *Direct Mail List Rates and Data.*) Oak Brook, IL: SRDS. Published bimonthly: Even-numbered months.

———*Lifestyle Market Analyst,* published jointly with National Demographics & Lifestyles. Oak Brook, IL: SRDS. Published annually.

Stone, Bob. *Successful Direct Marketing Methods,* 5th Ed. Lincolnwood, IL: NTC Business Books, 1994.

Stone, Bob, and John Wyman. *Successful Telemarketing,* 2d Ed. Lincolnwood, IL: NTC Business Books 1992.

Strunk, William, Jr., and E. B. White. *The Elements of Style,* 3d Ed. New York: Collier Macmillan, 1979.

Shafiroff, Martin D. *Successful Telephone Selling in the Nineties.* New York: Harper Perennial, 1990.

Target Marketing: The Magazine of Direct Response Media. North American Publishing Co., 401 N. Broad St., Philadelphia, PA 19108. Published monthly.

Tepper, Ron. *Secrets of a Mail Order Guru.* New York: Wiley, 1988.

Waldrop, Judith. *The Seasons of Business: The Marketer's Guide to Consumer Behavior.* Ithaca, NY: American Demographics, 1992.

Weintz, Walter. *The Solid Gold Mailbox.* New York: Wiley, 1987.

Who's Mailing What! (newsletter). 401 N. Broad St., Philadelphia, PA 19108. Published monthly.

Wilbur, L. Perry. *Money in Your Mailbox,* 2d Ed. New York: Wiley, 1993.

Winston, Arthur. *Direct Marketing and the Law.* New York: Wiley, 1993.

Yeck, John D., and John T. Maguire. *Planning and Creating Better Direct Mail.* New York: McGraw-Hill, 1961.

Index